# No Holiday

**80 PLACES YOU DON'T WANT TO VISIT...**

a **disinformation**® travel guide

**Martin Cohen**

Photos are either in the public domain or from Wikimedia Commons unless otherwise credited (see photo credits page). Permission is granted to copy, distribute and/or modify those items under the terms of the GNU Free Documentation License, Version 1.2 or any later version published by the Free Software Foundation.

Published by The Disinformation Company Ltd.
163 Third Avenue, Suite 108, New York, NY 10003 / Tel.: +1.212.691.1605 / Fax: +1.212.691.1606
**www.disinfo.com**

Design & Layout: Rebecca Meek

Library of Congress Control Number: 2006925221
ISBN-13: 978-1-932857-29-0
ISBN-10: 1-932857-29-X

Printed and bound in Great Britain by William Clowes Ltd, Beccles, Suffolk

10 9 8 7 6 5 4 3 2 1

Distributed in the USA and Canada by: Consortium Book Sales and Distribution
1045 Westgate Drive, Suite 90, St Paul, MN 55114 / Toll Free: +1.800.283.3572 / Local: +1.651.221.9035 / Fax: +1.651.221.0124 / www.cbsd.com

Distributed in the United Kingdom and Eire by: Virgin Books
Thames Wharf Studios, Rainville Road, London W6 9HA / Tel.: +44.(0)20.7386.3300 / Fax: +44.(0)20.7386.3360 / E-Mail: sales@virgin-books.co.uk

Distributed in Australia by: Tower Books
Unit 2/17 Rodborough Road, Frenchs Forest NSW 2086 / Tel.: +61.2.9975.5566 / Fax: +61.2.9975.5599 / Email: towerbks@zip.com.au_

**For Wod!**

"Glorious, stirring sight!" murmured Toad, never offering to move. "The poetry of motion! The *real* way to travel! The *only* way to travel! Here today—in next week tomorrow! Villages skipped, towns and cities jumped—always somebody else's horizon! O bliss! O poop-poop! O my! O my!"

*The Wind in the Willows,* by Kenneth Grahame (1908)

# Contents

## USA

## Central America

## South America

## Oceania

## Australasia

## Africa

# The Middle East

# Europe

# No Holiday: Travel Advice

"The travel industry has almost fully rebounded from 9/11. Family tourism is up, and people seem more than willing to hop on planes and cross the globe. There are 'fun' holidays and 'adventure' holidays, honeymoons and Spring Break trips." Or so my travel advisor tells me. But there are few political holidays, for politics and vacations are thought not to mix. Yet holidays are also about discovering unknown aspects of the world. And so it might behoove us to visit not only the great "sights" but also the great "sores": from the cursed massacre sites of Africa and Central America to the poisoned shores of the Aral Sea and Scotland's "Anthrax Island."

In this book, we will line up—not at museums and art galleries—but at more sinister political monuments, like the CIA-funded "Academy of Terror." We will tread the no-man's lands of the various demilitarized zones, between North and South Korea, between Syria and Israel—even between Catholic and Protestant turf in Northern Ireland. We will go big game hunting like old-world imperialists in Tora Bora, Afghanistan. Then we will become prey in the streets of Belfast and Baghdad. If time permits (for the world is large and there is much to see), we will visit the "killing fields" of Cambodia, or Australia—or even Madagascar? On this tour, the traveler must be forgiven for losing track of their location. For in truth, the post-colonial landscape is similar the world over, and the difference is just a matter of time zone.

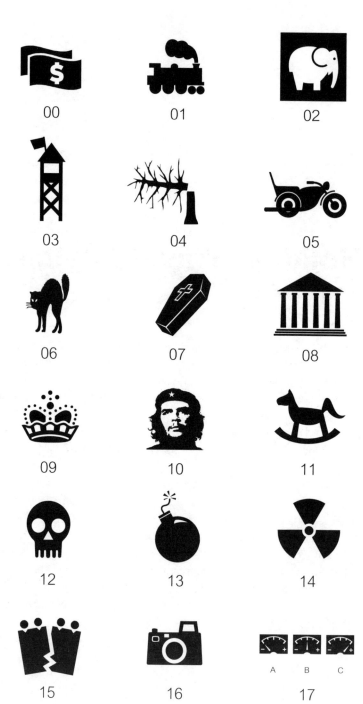

00

01

02

03

04

05

06

07

08

09

10

11

12

13

14

15

16

17

A    B    C

# No Holiday: Symbols

# Central Eurasia

## 1 No Holiday: **Chernobyl, Ukraine**

*Travel back in time to a concrete memorial to the heroic dreams of the USSR*

### How to get there

According to the London *Daily Telegraph*, Chernobyl has become "an unlikely tourist destination." But why so unlikely? After all, as the home of the world's worst nuclear disaster, surely it deserves a visit.

And these days, visitors have ready access. Scheduled flights to the capital of the Ukraine can be combined with competitively priced $190 packages specially tailored to visiting the infamous reactor.

### What to see

Travel companies in Kiev line up to take day-trippers on guided tours around the Chernobyl power plant and its poisonous environs.

One typical tour offers to let you "Experience the peace and quiet of the ghost-town Prypyat" (where "all 47,500 inhabitants had to abandon their homes the day after the accident"!) "Explore the deserted apartment blocks, schools, hotels, kinder gardens [sic]."

This is followed by lunch. We are reassured that "the quality of food is guaranteed" though its radioactivity levels are not. In the afternoon, a briefing is conducted by a specialist of a governmental agency to provide you with "answers to your questions about the current ecological situation and the future of the exclusion zone."

Lucky tourists, armed with Geiger counters, can even find their way into the radiation zone, where they will be shown family homes, abandoned "Pompeii-style" (the unfortunate Roman City buried in poisonous ash after the eruption of Vesuvius) and unchanged since they were evacuated at a few minutes' notice.

The zone is also a strange time capsule of the vanished Soviet era. A bust of Soviet founder Vladimir Lenin still greets the travelers at the plant's en-trance. Prypyat, once the area's largest city, is now a ghost town whose melancholy concrete apartment blocks, still bedecked with uplifting communist slogans, offer pitiful reminders of the desperate evacuation. In an abandoned playground, a motionless Ferris wheel waits forever for the children to return. Family photographs, upturned furniture, shoes, clothes and other belongings lie where they fell as the shroud of plutonium settled over the city.

Clutching their radiation badges ever more earnestly, tourists can also see a graveyard of vehicles used in the heroic attempts to seal the broken reactor—hundreds of trucks, helicopters and armored personnel vehicles which, boast the brochures, are "so soaked with radiation that it is dangerous to approach too close."

For naturalists, there are also some interesting botanical effects, in the inaccurately named "dead zone" or exclusion area around the ruined power station. In fact, wildlife has flourished since the local population fled. Nowadays the forests are rich in berries, mushrooms and animals, including some exotic varieties like the special Przhevalsky horses, brought in to eat the lush (and highly radioactive) grass. [📷] But the high point of the trip is the specially constructed viewing platform overlooking the concrete sarcophagus that encloses the remains of Chernobyl's Reactor Four...

Ominously, debris stacked against the inside of the existing shell's southern wall is slowly shifting and fissures are spreading across its surface.

## Useful information
The Chernobyl disaster occurred on April 26, 1986 when a powerful explosion destroyed the reactor, expelling a huge plume of radioactive dust that drifted across Europe.

Firefighters who fought the blaze were quickly killed by massive doses of radiation, and thousands of civilians are thought to have since died from radiation-induced cancers. About 200 tons of concrete and other debris mixed with nuclear fuel are still trapped under the hastily constructed concrete shell. In a comical attempt at security, areas of high radioactivity are marked off with triangular yellow signs.

Tour guides say that there is no health risk from taking the trips. Indeed, about 600 people have returned to live inside the dead zone, including Maria Dika, a security guard at Reactor Four on the night of the disaster, who had to have three months of treatment for acute radiation sickness. Now she reassures visitors that there are "no health problems. The radiation has got used to us."

Even if eighty-five percent of the children in Belarus are born unhealthy, as governments know very well, links between radiation and illness are hard to prove, as few studies are conclusive. Illnesses induced by radiation exposure have a long latency period.

### Risk factor
By Eastern European standards, the site is safe. By Western standards, the trip is probably more suitable for senior citizens who can benefit from the typically long latency period for after-effects of radiation.

# 2 No Holiday: **The Aral Sea, Uzbekistan**

*Sunbathe on the extensive shores of the world's fastest shrinking sea*

### How to get there
Fly to Tashkent and catch a daily train to Nukus. Moynaq itself is 130 miles (210 kilometers) north of Nukus; occasionally buses run between the two, otherwise it's a taxi ride. Don't try walking as the temperature can reach 140 degrees Fahrenheit (54 degrees Celsius).

### What to see
Moynaq is one of the two major fishing ports of the Aral Sea, which was the world's fourth largest lake up until the 1970s. Today though, the waters are much further away, about 25 miles (40 kilometers) distant. Although, to be more positive, that means there's plenty of beach. The rusted hulks of its fishing boats—once floating at anchor there—now lie on their sides, stranded in a sandy graveyard far from the shoreline. For tourists, they serve as monuments to one of the worst man-made environmental disasters.

Only some 2,000 or so people remain in the once thriving port, faces wrinkled up against the sand, salt and dust storms (all bearing toxic residues) that are another of its legacies.

Uzbekistan is mostly comprised of steppe and desert. The exception is the river delta where the Amu Darya, Central Asia's greatest waterway, empties into what remains of the Aral Sea. The richest farmland is to the east. It is nestled in the valleys of the mountains from which descend the life-giving waters, and in the alluvial flood plains at their base.

However, the United Nations predicts that the Aral Sea will disappear completely by about 2020. The only good thing (for No Holidaymakers) is that while the sea shrinks, it is leaving behind a toxic desert and—at its center, like the jewel in the crown—lies Vozrozhdeniye, site of a former Soviet germ warfare center and waste dump. [ 📷 ] Now this formerly isolated island is reconnected to the world by a land bridge…

The Soviets used Vozrozhdeniye Island as an open-air test site for biological weapons, including anthrax, plague, tularemia and smallpox. Additionally, large quantities of spores, partially decontaminated with bleach, were buried in pits on the island in 1988.

You can still see the facility today, covered in telephone poles spaced one kilometer apart. Sensors used to measure agent concentration were placed on the poles, which were also used to tether test animals including monkeys, horses, sheep and donkeys. The animals were then incinerated and their ashes are buried in the Voz Island cemetery. No memorial.

One intriguing scenario envisions the island's rats becoming infected with a strain of plague

bacteria and, now that the waters have receded, scampering towards the mainland. Mysteriously, in 1988, almost 500,000 antelope died on the nearby Turgay steppes in a matter of hours.

## Useful information

The Aral Sea became geologically separated from the Caspian Sea sometime after the last Ice Age. Arabic geographers refer to it as early as the 10th century as the Khwarazm Sea. In the 17th century Russian travelers reached it and called it the Blue Sea.

Funnily enough, the Aral Sea's dissipation can be traced back to the US. This is because prior to the American Civil War, the US exported much of its cotton production to Russia; but the war stopped all shipments, forcing the Czar to look elsewhere. His solution was to divert the rivers of Uzbekistan for cotton production. The Soviets went even further, ensuring that today no water at all gets to the Aral Sea and since the early 1960s the Syr Darya and Amu Darya rivers have been used for large-scale irrigation, causing a drop in the flow of freshwater into the sea. Programs put in place in the Soviet era are still wreaking havoc on the country. As a result, the sea has dwindled to a quarter of its original area, the fishing industry has been destroyed, there are four times as many rainless days as there were in the 1950s and the salination of soil and water as well as chemical residues from cotton farming have caused widespread health problems in the population. An estimated 75 million tons of salts and toxic dusts have been spread across Central Asia, according to France-based medical aid group Doctors Without Borders.

In 1997, the local government in the town of Aralsk took matters into its own hands. It deployed residents and earth-moving equipment to scoop sand from the seabed and build a dike 12 miles (20 km) long and 85 feet (25 m) wide between the two lakes.

Protected from the larger, contaminated body, the smaller lake's shoreline began to stretch again toward the ships' cemetery. Birds reappeared, including gulls, swans, and pheasants. Danish scientists analyzed fresh fish from its waters and declared them clean enough to eat.

### Risk factor

Some risk of airborne particles poisoning you. Little risk of drowning.

# 3 No Holiday: **Semipalatinsk, Kazakhstan**

*Deep in the Central Asian Steppe, perhaps the most heavily bombed spot on earth*

### How to get there

After seeing what's left of the Aral Sea, in the West of Kazakhstan, the No Holidaymaker will be eager to continue by taxi or rental car to the remote town of Kurchatov, once so secret it was not even on the maps. The explanation for that is nearby: the Semipalatinsk Test Site, where Stalin tested his first nuclear bomb.

### What to see

And he liked it so much that he tried out another four hundred or so more on that same spot, making the Semipalatinsk test range one of the most radioactive spots on earth. Even so, there are no fences or warning signs announcing that you have arrived. The windswept grasses of the steppe look much the same, if amongst them are ruined concrete bunkers and twisted remains of observation towers. It is only at closer inspection that the melted rock can be seen to have been splashed here and there onto the steel and concrete, where it cooled, forming a dark lacquer. [ 📷 ] And don't miss the unusual rock collection: marble-sized balls of soil turned into glass, which crunch underfoot.

### Useful information

As part of the experiments, tanks, aircraft and artillery pieces were bombed. The highly radioactive remnants were never cleaned up. Yet now they have disappeared, adopting a new life innocuously (but lethally) as scrap metal. Likewise, cattle and sheep are free to roam the radioactive plains, and the meat and milk find their way to the local markets.

### Risk factor

The land itself is "still hot" and even reckless visitors should take a Geiger counter and avoid touching any rocks.

# 4 No Holiday: **Tora Bora, Afghanistan**

*Travel by mule train to hideouts high in the mountains of Tora Bora*

## How to get there
Fly to Kabul and charter a horse and cart to take you into the mountains. (Clear the better part of a year for this endeavor.) Tora Bora, or "land of black dust," is one of many hideouts tucked away between jagged peaks perennially covered in snow and ice. Strategically located between two mountain ridges in the White Mountains of eastern Afghanistan, southeast of Kabul and southwest of Jalalabad, near the Pakistan border, it is only reachable by mule train.

## Background briefing
The Tora Bora complex was originally built by extending natural caves, with the assistance of the CIA in the early 1980s. After the destruction of the World Trade Center, it became famous in newspapers as the supposed center of a global terrorist network—al-Qaeda. Diagrams of the caves were printed showing hotel-like corridors capable of sheltering more than 1,000 soldiers, equipped (unlike the rest of Afghanistan) with food, water and electricity. It also supposedly contained a large cache of ammunition, such as anti-aircraft missiles left over from the 1980s. The tunnels were said to be miles long, with exits over the border in Pakistan.

These caves are Osama Bin Laden's last known whereabouts.

## What to see
The battle of Tora Bora took place in the White Mountains of eastern Afghanistan in late November and early December of 2001. Kabul had just fallen and a thousand or more al-Qaeda leaders were thought to have fled to Tora Bora, and to be "holed up" (as the US President liked to put it) in the mountains' vast network of caves.

Alas, none of the cave entrances visible today lead to the vast, underground complexes bin Laden was said to have resided in. Although a sniper's post on the ridge above might have

commanded a field of fire of from two to three miles (3-4 km), these caves really are just caves. At best, perhaps they are where Mujahideen fighters sheltered or kept ammunition.

Anyway, American planes have been along and dropped scores of bombs, creating strings of craters [ 📷 ] in the terrain as well as killing, according to the newspapers, hundreds of al-Qaeda fighters. Today however, the caves themselves appear to be largely untouched by all those air strikes, other than some rocky debris over the entrances.

## Useful information
In 1979 the Soviets installed a progressive secular government (one that, amongst other things, accorded women full status and equal rights). In response, the United States developed the caves as bases for radical Islamic fundamentalists in a successful bid to topple the Kabul government.

There's no longer any hope of finding bin Laden in Tora Bora. But visitors can imagine him once in this area, maybe living in the abandoned huts still there, maybe even using a nearby cave as a bomb shelter.

## Risk factor
Travel in Afghanistan is extremely risky. But this is not so much because of the locals who, like most impoverished people, are extremely courteous and considerate to visitors, but because of the presence of undercover soldiers and CIA agents. If you're tall and wear a turban you might also get blown up in a US air strike.

# 5 No Holiday: **Camp Salerno, Afghanistan**

*A short tour of US concentration camps at Kabul, Gardez, Khost, Asadabad, Jalalabad and (if you're still able) Kandahar*

## How to get there
Camp Salerno, on the outskirts of Khost, is a bleak soviet era base in which the 1,200 troops of Operation Taskforce Thunder are billeted in tents and new concrete dormitories.

## What to see
Afghanistan's allure eludes most people, but it has seen a steady stream of foreign occupiers since the 18th century. First came the British, followed by the Russians, and most recently the Americans. In between there was a brief interlude of Afghan independence under the Taliban, who banned music, made beards compulsory (for men) and forbade going to school (for women). Since most rules carried the death penalty there were many people to execute. They even used the goal posts [ 📷 ] of Kabul's soccer stadium to hang them. But it was their collusion with Mr. bin Laden, rather than anything else, which caused their downfall.

Since its liberation though, the country has become the hub of a network of "detention camps" as the US government puts it, or "concentration camps" as they would more accurately be described (none of the inmates are subject to any legal oversight). The camps' inmates are not merely suspected Taliban or even al-Qaeda members from the area, but anyone picked up anywhere in the world. They may have been captured at random, like the BBC's Afghanistan correspondent, Kamal Sadat, who was seized by soldiers, hooded, and warned he would be killed if he made a noise, let alone a broadcast.

Or, like Maher Arar, who was arrested at New York's John F. Kennedy airport, they may have been specifically sought out. Arar, a Canadian computer programmer, was "rendered to the camp on information obtained." Whether captured at random, or kidnapped to order, even US military intelligence officers admit that nearly all of the prisoners are entirely innocent.

But then, these situations are reminiscent of the Salem Witch Trials. Names are tortured out of those already in custody. And silence (let alone denial of guilt) is considered evidence against you, so plenty of names are going to come up. At least Kamal Sadat was released three days after the BBC complained to the US government. Others, such as Mohammed Khan, grabbed in Pakistan, are returned to relatives covered in wheals, scars and a US Army issue body bag. "He was bitten by a snake and died in his cell," explained Colonel Gary Cheeks, sometime head of the Camp, to reporters. Metaphorically speaking, he's right on the money.

## Disinformation point
Curiously, Afghanistan had a more-or-less independent, more-or-less progressive egalitarian government in the 1980s. Attempts by the US, then under Jimmy Carter, to topple this led to increasing Russian intervention, which paved the way for the Taliban. Western subversion preceded the Russian intervention.

## Useless information
On February 7, 2002 President George W. Bush signed a memo confirming the Justice Department's position that "none of the provisions of Geneva apply to our conflict with al-Qaeda in Afghanistan or throughout the world."

## Risk factor
Few Afghanis will go near the bases, but if you persist you can usually find a desperately poor taxi driver to take you close enough to be arrested and so get a proper visit.


# 6 No Holiday: **Bhutan**

*In search of Shangri La*

## How to get there
Several countries claim to be the seat of Shangri La, the mythical mountain paradise, cut off from the world and from time. It is of course an ancient tale, but it was given a name by James Hilton in the poignant novel *Lost Horizon*, which was published in 1933, even as the Japanese were running amok in much of East Asia and clouds of war gathered over Europe. The Chinese claim it on behalf of their reluctant charge, Tibet. The Nepalese do too, even as their country sinks into violent internal conflict. In Hilton's book, Shangri-La is a Buddhist monastery, its inhabitants are opposed to all violence and materialism, and all the wisdom of the human race is stored within its borders. But perhaps the true Shangri-La is not a place, but a state of mind. In which case it is perhaps still necessary to visit the tiny kingdom of Bhutan, high in the Himalayas.

## What to see
Khudunabari camp in Jhapa, one of the seven created by the United Nations Office of the High Commissioner for Refugees (UNHCR), perches on the border between Bhutan and Nepal.

Bhutan itself is squashed between India and China and the British artificially created its "monarchy" in the early years of the 20th century. It is mostly mountainous, and violent storms from the Himalayas give the country its name, which means, "Land of the Thunder Dragon." Fascinatingly, it has adopted a New Age strategy of raising not its Gross Domestic Product, the conventional person's national measure, but its "Gross National Happiness" instead.

Bhutan, according to the King Jigme Singye Wangchuck, needed to concentrate on sharing its rather limited prosperity, rather than increasing it. It also needed to protect its culture, its environment and its animals. An article in *Le Monde* in 2005 reported an international conference marking its success at achieving this, noting that while individual incomes in the country remain as low as anywhere in the world, life expectancy has increased since 1984 from a disgraceful 47 years to a respectable 66. (Although the CIA World Factbook records it as only 55.) A new constitution demands that some 60 percent of the country be left to trees, and that the number of tourists be limited. As Thaku Powdyel, an official at the Ministry of Education, explained, "The goal of life should not be limited to production, consumption, more production, more consumption."

## Useless information
Bhutan is a good internationalist too. It has joined the Biodiversity, Climate Change, Kyoto Protocol, En-dangered Species, and Hazardous Wastes global conventions, and signed, but not ratified, the Law of the Sea. Although we might forgive the omission, since Bhutan is entirely landlocked and has no navy or ships.

## Useful information
Curiously enough, for such a happy country, Bhutan seems to qualify as the country with the highest proportion of its population living as refugees outside its borders. Some 100,000 Bhutanese of Nepali origin fled the country in the 1980s when the religiously and ethnically

distinct ruling class (the "Drukpas" who are a kind of Buddhist, arranged in clans with the King at their apex), passed laws imposing its own language, dress and culture, not to mention compulsory redistribution of land and occasional disenfranchise-ment. These refugees now live in camps in Nepal, run by the UN.

In its tireless pursuit of happiness, in Bhutan it is often compulsory to dress up as a Buddhist—for example when visiting monasteries, or in order to go to government offices, even to schools on certain days. Subversive books, such as non-Buddhist religious texts, have long been forbidden, and there is only one government-run "Buddhist" newspaper. Since 1989, foreign TV and satellite dishes are forbidden too. The jails are full of prisoners convicted of what are classed as "anti-national" criminals, who may or may not be tortured there. Buddhists believe that suffering is part of life, after all.

## Risk factor 
Evidently if the happiness of these long-term refugees had to be counted into the "GNH" of Bhutan, there is a risk that the all-important "headline figure" for GNH would have to be adjusted downwards. And carrying even a text like this into the happy kingdom might incur a prison term.

# 7 No Holiday: **Mount Everest, Nepal**

*Moving some of the mountain left on the mountain*

## How to get there
Fly to Kathmandu, and start walking.

## What to see
Apart from the mountain itself, of course, there is now a very well worn route to the summit to be seen, with quite a busy little settlement at "Base Camp." Gaze out at the piles of old oxygen cylinders, masses of plastic bags, polystyrene cups and old cans of beans, and—if you step off the beaten path—even the odd dead body with its wooly hat sticking up forlornly from the snow.

Mountains draw explorers with the promise of solitude, raw natural beauty and adventure. Up there, above the clouds, far away from the crowd, you can find yourself. Or so people think. Mountain tourism is big business these days, with fifty million visitors spending an estimated $90 billion a year, roughly one fifth of all the money tourists spend worldwide. The European Alps alone account for almost one tenth of all tourist dollars. It's hardly surprising then that in long-established tourist regions in the Alps, the Andes, the Himalayas and the Rockies, mountaineering provides up to 90 percent of regional income.

However, they also leave the mountains a little less raw, a little less solitary and sadly, a little less beautiful. Mount Everest is the "place to see" if you want to appreciate what tourism has done for mountains. Where once rugged bearded explorers staggered up the "South Col" or the "North Face" with stars in their eyes and ice in their whiskers, now schoolchildren (for example, 14 year olds) and various other kinds of "exceptionalists" (for example, first nude couple to pogo-stick to the summit with monkeys sitting on their heads...) line up to make their ascent, and return to "BC" (Base Camp) in time for a snack.

Listen in on this exchange between enthusiastic "Guy" calling on his cell phone from BC ("with a strong cup of Venus coffee in hand") to "Dave" en route to the top of Mount Everest:

*Very good Dave, it sounds like you are all doing well. Five hours to the top of the icefall on the first journey up is quite a good time so well done all of you—I'll have a brew on for you when you get down so give us a call when you get close to the bottom.*

*"Good one, Guy," Dave responds, "talk to you soon, out."*

## Useful information
In his book, *Ethics in the Mountains,* disillusioned mountaineer, Joe Simpson, complains of the other climbers—those who litter the paths, treat the Sherpas and other native peoples with such contempt, and indeed who abandon companions to die when the snows come down unexpectedly.

"Get off Everest, if you cannot or will not clean up after yourselves. There is no maid service on Mount Everest!" wrote one acerbic Internet commentator on the litter problem. But it turns out that nowadays there is a kind of maid service. An optimistically entitled "ecotourist" holiday offers to trail around Nepal and the approaches to Mount Everest picking up the detritus left by those evidently not on eco-holidays.

## Useless information
In the early 1990s, indeed, a big clean-up campaign carted away 33 tons of litter and waste from the Mount Everest Base Camp area. Today, *Adventure Alternative* offers opportunities for a Project in the Himalayas. During your trip you will rebuild a monastery, build a school, install a hydroelectric power station and repair a clinic. And you'll still fit in a quick ascent up Everest "with a difference." Along the way you will be "conducting an ongoing clean-up campaign."

"Even at the Base Camp there is a lot of rubbish which needs to be carried out," (it can't be burned, according to Sherpa tradition) enthuse the organizers. "This is really an important job" and for sure the work will be "highly regarded" both by the local people and those all-important (and evidently very worthy) tour operators.

Unfortunately the Sherpa tradition seems not to have been shared with Dave (I do not know if it is the "same" Dave, evidently most climbers are called Dave) who adds:

"Once we have finished rebuilding the school and the monastery, and the clinic is fully supported and up and running, then we will embark on a big project to repair the trails and put in more incinerators all the way to Base Camp."

Basically, mountains and tourists don't really jive. Even if they desist from using their "snow-cats" or "ski-doos," tourists degrade and stress fragile mountain ecosystems. The mysticism of sacred mountain sites is always lost once they become playgrounds.

## Risk factor
Sanitized though Mount Everest ascents have become, the trip is not entirely without risk. Most interesting of all the "detritus" on the slopes are the bodies of climbers who mistimed their ascents. Naturally, tidying these up is very complicated and generally impractical.

**Trips 8-12**

# India

# 8 No Holiday: **The Great Hedge of India**

*Searching for traces of India's colonial past*

### How to get there
Fly to Delhi and start looking. It was here *somewhere*.

### What to see
China has its "Great Wall" built by the Emperors to keep the barbarian hordes out, and to allow Chinese civilization to flourish. India has its "Great Hedge," built by the British to keep salt out, and enable them to raise taxes.

The British are usually the first to flaunt their own achievements, but they've remained surprisingly mum on this one. During the days of the British Raj a huge hedge was constructed running for thousands of miles across central India, comparable in scale to China's Great Wall. Only this hedge was not to keep out invaders, but to keep out cheap supplies of salt. Within the area enclosed by the hedge, the colonial masters taxed the Indian people for the use of this unassuming, but essential, mineral.

It's not normally one of the main attractions for visitors to India, but that may be because as a giant shrub, it didn't last very long. Although it was to be sure, a VERY BIG HEDGE, stretching for 2,300 miles (3,700 km), constructed mainly out of spiky thorn bushes, on raised embankments, along with some sections in stone.

Roy Moxham, a sometime British tea-planter, spent many happy summers in India tracing its route, but found only one or two sections, like the thorn tress still proudly there on raised earthworks at Pali Ghar, near Chakanagar. Mr. Moxham was put onto the hedge by a footnote in Major-General Sir (gasp! and there's more!) W.H. Sleeman KCB's book *Rambles and Reflections of an Indian Official* (1893) which noted that, "To secure the levy of a duty on salt ... there grew up gradually a monstrous system ... A Customs line was established which stretched across the whole of India, which in 1869 extended ... a distance of 2,300 miles ... It consisted principally of an immense impenetrable hedge."

## Useful information

Salt has a particular significance in India, as it was the issue of salt taxes that started the revolution against British rule. Gandhi led his famous non-violent march to the sea followed by a ceremonial distilling of salt from the water, to demand the right for the Indian people to have salt without paying taxes. Mind you, the campaign was non-violent only on the protesters' part. In May 1930, when a column of volunteers tried to march towards some salt heaps, the British toleration of protest came to an end, and 320 Indians were injured after being beaten to the ground with steel tipped bamboo sticks. Two protesters indeed later died. Over subsequent protests the violence escalated.

But why a salt tax? Since time immemorial, there have been taxes. Taxes on water, on grain, on ale, beards (yes, facial hair), or windows. Naturally, clothes, tools and "goods in general" have all been taxed. These days everything is routinely taxed, with the possible exception of beards. But perhaps the most hated tax of them all was the salt tax. The ancient Chinese invented the tax four thousand years ago, and the French version of the tax—the hated "gabelle"— notoriously included a stipulation that people had to buy a minimum quantity each week—or be whipped or imprisoned.

For the British the choice of salt was a logical one. Since they relied on the help of the rich and wealthy Indian princes and landlords to maintain their grip on this huge and populous colony, they dared not tax *them*. On the other hand, most people in India had little or no money and little or no goods to be taxed.

So the British came up with a new version of that very ancient tax. Levied at a rate equivalent to almost a week's work in every month, it was significant enough to occasion salt smuggling, and that's where the hedge came in. Planted between the salt producing areas and the rest of India and guarded by troops at regular intervals, it was actually very effective.

So effective indeed, that during the great famines at the end of the 19th century millions of Indians died. The British themselves record one and a third million people died in 1877, and another three and three quarters million in the last fifteen years of the tax. Unable to afford enough food to subsist on grain, the peasants continued to be taxed on their meager salt requirements, and fell victim to a host of painful and often fatal diseases, which lack of that simple mineral entails.

Curiously enough, the last person in charge of collection of the tax became one of the founders (and first General Secretary) of the Indian National Congress that would eventually, under Gandhi, end the tax.

## Risk factor

The Hedge used to be very dangerous—for those who attempted to breach it, for those who attempted to live without salt, and eventually for the British Raj itself. But nowadays there's hardly any hedge left, so looking for it should be safe enough.

# 9 Working No Holiday: **Makrana**

*Earn some extra money mining the white gold marble of Makrana*

## How to get there
Fly to Delhi, and Agra, in Rajasthan, and proceed by truck to Makrana, the small city where the beautiful white marble that (amongst other things) makes up the Taj Mahal, is mined.

## What to see
Everyone who goes to India sees the Taj Mahal. The lucky few see it by moonlight, when the ghostly white marble of its carved minarets and turrets give it a particularly ethereal feel. The rest of us can see it at our local take-out place, painted on the restaurant wall. Legend has it that the mogul emperor Shah Jahan wanted a temple built of a stone as pure as diamonds to commemorate his favorite wife, the beautiful Mumtaz Mahal. It took his architects twenty-two years to track down a source of stone of high enough purity. (Nowadays the marble finds its way into mundane buildings like banks and hotels, often abroad.)

But few people visit the mines nearby, where the "white gold" comes from. Here, the women and the men work side-by-side, many of the women in incongruous-looking (given the heavy work) saris and veils. But perhaps the veils help keep out the silica dust, for there are no masks. Which would be useful, as it is said that 97 percent of the miners develop some form of lung disease. Despite the progress in technology elsewhere, the miners here work entirely by hand, climbing up and down ropes to hack out slabs of stone, which are then laboriously hauled up from the mine shafts, about 330 feet (100 meters) deep.

No one seems to know how many people work in the mines, but it is at least 5,000. And there is, on average, one fatal accident every day. But even in death, the miners can help earn money. Bodies that fall to the bottom of the shafts may lie there rotting until the smell obliges the mines' owners to pay compensation to their families. The going rate? About 12,000 rupees ($1,000). A small fortune.

## Useful information
The rate of pay for the miners is ten dollars a week, the hours are generally twelve a day, sixty a week, with half-days every Wednesday and Saturday. Perfect for sightseeing!

## Risk factor
Very dangerous. And the road to the mine is treacherous too.

# 10 No Holiday:
# Bhopal poison factory

*The site of the world's largest (ever) industrial accident*

### How to get there
Fly to Delhi and take the train north to Bhopal. The Shatabdi Express (daily service) connects the two cities.

### What to see
Bhopal is the capital of the Indian State of Madhya Pradesh, named after its famous founder Raja Bhoj. It is believed that in the 11ᵗʰ century, the Raja built a dam (Pal) here, which resulted in the formation of the three lakes found here. Like Rome, it is built on seven hills and teems with art galleries, museums, theatres and libraries. However, it is more famous internationally for another reason. At five past midnight, on December 3, 1984, an explosion at the Union Carbide plant in the Bhopal town center killed nearly thirty thousand Indian civilians.

### Useful information.
Many more people than those killed after the initial blast (estimates run up to half a million) were left ill or handicapped by the chemicals, mainly pesticides, which persist in the local environment, particularly in the drinking water. And Dow Chemical, who took over Union Carbide in 2001, has declined to accept any responsibility for cleanup. Children have been, and continue to be, born malformed or handicapped. But neither group of victims have been entitled to more than token amounts of compensation, generally less than $500 per case. In total, Union Carbide paid just under $500 million to the Indian Government in amends. According to local observers, the government was reluctant to press for more in case it put off future foreign investors.

### Useless information
The plant was built in 1969 and originally had higher safety standards. Alas, due to factors such as the erratic demand for pesticides locally (affected, for example, by the monsoons) the plant ended up stockpiling large amounts of poisons, and began to lose money. In order to correct this, Union Carbide reduced the amount spent on cooling the several thousand liters of highly volatile gases, which then overheated and exploded.

### ♡ Disinformation point
There has been a warrant for the arrest of the then head of Union Carbide, Warren Anderson, issued by Interpol. Curiously enough though, he continues to live today in his comfortable house in Connecticut, untroubled and unchallenged by either the US courts or, indeed, the Indian ones.

### Risk factor
Back in forgotten Bhopal, each monsoon season more of the 8,000 or so tons of poison leeches into the environment, and it continues to exact a further toll.

# 11 No Holiday:
# Kerala, the rice bowl of India

*Inspecting the two hundred and sixty dry wells around Plachimada*

## How to get there
Fly to Delhi and take a train to Palakkad (also known as Palghat) in the southern state of Kerala. Plachimada is a small village.

## What to see
The Kerala region is sometimes called the "rice bowl" of India, but it has long struggled to find a reliable supply of water for irrigating the paddies. For other uses, most of the villagers carry their daily water supply the several miles from wells to their homes, on their heads. But not all of them. One village user has demands for water that run to over 264,000 gallons (almost 1 million liters!) of water a day. Try carrying that on your head!

This villager's "house" (a factory really) is swathed in barbed wire. And it is full to capacity with bottles containing, in addition to huge amounts of precious water, High Fructose Corn Syrup and/or Sucrose, Water, Caramel Color, Phosphoric Acid, Natural Flavors, and Caffeine.

## Background briefing
That's right: like a sponge on the local ecosystem, here sits the Coca-Cola factory. The friendly "think globally/act locally" corporation opened this plant in March of 2000. Quite properly, they asked the local panchayat for permission to use mechanical pumps to extract the ground water. And the company helpfully drilled some new extra-deep wells while they were at it. There is some dispute as to what the villagers themselves had agreed to, and what Coca-Cola did anyway, but the end result is indisputable. The levels of the local water table fell from around 165 feet below the surface to 490 feet down. Suddenly, two hundred and sixty wells, sunk by the locals over past decades to meet their essential needs, ran completely dry.

And, if that weren't already bad enough, Coca-Cola bottling creates a lot of waste sludge that has to be disposed of. The company's original preferred method was to give it to the villagers for use as "fertilizer." But when the "fertilizer" got the reputation for being a health hazard, they tried to pump it into the bowels of the earth down some of their new private boreholes (formerly known as wells). Incredibly (!) this led to new accusations that they had contaminated the underground water supply in the aquifers themselves.

The local people protested at the gates of the mighty corporation, and created such a fuss that the local council withdrew Coke's license. But curiously enough, the state government's response to the local disaster was not to give Coke a fine but a "regional development grant" of some two million rupees. Critics of the policy say the state governments encourage people to drink Coca-Cola, rather than traditional and nutritious local drinks such as nimbu pani, lassi, panna and sattu.

But in fairness to the beleaguered Coke Co., it should be said that if people think they have poisoned the local water, then the state government should also dissuade people from drinking it. Anyway, there are other soft drinks. Like Sprite, Fanta, Thum[b]s Up (a locally popular drink brand) to choose from. But wait… all of these are also Coca-Cola brands made at the same plant.

### Useful information
In December 2003, an initial Indian Court ruling forbade Coca-Cola from extracting ground water at Plachimada. The legal principle advanced by Judge Balakrishnana Nair (which he said was based on "English Common Law") was that,

> *Certain resources like air, sea waters and the forests have such a great importance to the people as a whole that it would be wholly unjustified to make them a subject of private ownership. The said resources being a gift of nature, they should be made freely available to everyone, irrespective of their status in life.*

Water resources were for the public and the state did not have the right to convert them into private ownership. Dream on, Judge!

### Recommended side trips
Another unusual trip around India might be a tour of each of the ninety bottling plants of the world's favorite soft drinks, Pepsi (38 plants) and Coke (52). Coke wins. There's one at Kaladera, a village near Jaipur. There is another near the holy city of Varanasi and another at Singhchancher, a village in eastern Uttar Pradesh, particularly renowned for its contribution to polluting the water and the land.

### Disinformation point
Actually, they're not really "bottling plants," which sounds innocuous, but pumping stations. (Anyway, these days Coca-Cola prefers plastic, which is another environmental disaster story...)

### Risk factor
So how dangerous is Coca-Cola? Despite a 2003 Indian scientific report that their drinks had up to 70 times too many pesticides in them, Coca-Cola and Pepsi say their products are perfectly safe. Dentists might disagree. And the local villagers might still prefer to have their drinking water back.

## 12 No Holiday: **Mumbai, India**

*The Towers of Silence*

### How to get there
Don't take the train to Mumbai—that's for the riff-raff! Instead, make the drive from New Delhi to Mumbai (formerly known as Bombay) on the west coast. It's an easy ride of about six hundred and twenty miles (1,000 kilometers), along a gleaming new highway. India has embraced the great car economy with a so-called "golden quadrilateral" linking India's four biggest cities, at a cost of a little over six billion dollars. That's a lot of money anywhere, but especially in India, where only around one in every ninety people (1.3 percent) has a car, and where there is a vast, yet under-funded, rail network that the rest of the population uses. From the road you can see the ordinary Indians scurrying out of the way to collect firewood, or admire the new "service areas" in what, until recently, was pristine rainforest. In a kind of gratuitous nod to social sensitivity, the government has decided to name part of the new highway after Mahatma Gandhi.

### What to see
Some of India's unusual features, in a world where so much has become bland and mundane,

are the wooden towers upon which vultures quietly peck the bodies of the dead.

Alas, like the "unsightly" rickshaw drivers of Calcutta, and as with so many fine local traditions, this one is fast disappearing. With the vultures now almost extinct, bodies have been piling up, so to speak. But at the Dakhma (Tower) in Doongerwadi, atop Malabar Hills, one encouraging idea is to use solar power instead to decompose bodies still left on the wooden "towers of silence" more quickly than the few remaining, and thus overworked, vultures can manage.

Each tower has its own solar concentrator, [ ] (please do not take pictures of vultures pecking at the bodies themselves, as this is disrespectful) set up about twenty feet high above the ground. It consists of some twenty-seven flat mirrors, positioned to concentrate the sun's rays onto the corpse kept on a stone slab called a "pavi." At this higher temperature, the body simply decomposes faster, but the method leaves the surrounding plants and animals totally unharmed. And as the originator of the method, one Homi Dali, added proudly to one visitor: "Not only that, I have also noticed that birds such as crows and kites comfortably get into the focal area and peck at the corpse."

Although, strictly speaking, a departure from the Parsi community's thousand-year-old history of leaving corpses to decompose slowly under the sun if not eaten by vultures, the community is not protesting.

The solar "concentrators" are built locally, and were also designed locally. They have been designed to ensure that the corpse is never exposed to a temperature of more than 125 degrees Fahrenheit (52 degrees Celsius) and so doesn't burn, which in Parsi scriptures, as in other religious traditions around the world, is considered very bad.

## Useless information
Even better, in its way, and still more "green," is an option being developed for rearing more vultures in a special aviary, where around 100-150 of the unpopular birds will be needed for the Dakhmas in Doongerwadi alone.

## Risk factor
Unless you're sunbathing, the reflectors are quite safe, apart from the occasional risk of falling body parts dropped by vultures.

# The Far East

## 13 No Holiday: **Phnom Penh, Cambodia**

*The spirit temples of the Khmer Rouge*

### How to get there

Fly to Phnom Penh and take a tour-bus to see the ancient temples of the country such as those at Angkor, home to many headless statues. Actually, they are not supposed to be headless, but like much of South East Asia's heritage, they have fallen prey to the Western desire for antiquities. Fortunately, this being Cambodia, as if to compensate, there are any number of little stone temples along the roads and in the villages, many harboring sad little collections of human skulls.

### What to see

If there is not much left at many of Cambodia's ancient temples, there is not much to see either at Toul Sleng, the former prison and torture center in the capital Phnom Penh. At least 12,000 men, women and children (often whole families) were processed here for political crimes, going directly through the "interrogation unit" to the "torture massacre unit." Nowadays it has been reinvented as a museum, although the only really unusual exhibit is its own symbolic collection of skulls. And these are indeed part of a much larger national collection, of nearly two million, most of which are housed in little shrines all round the country. Incised with what the experts call "chopping/hacking wounds" or "blunt impact traumas" these human skulls are practical, legal testimony to the efforts of the infamous Khmer Rouge to return Kampuchea to Year Zero, in the 1970s.

### Background briefing

Cambodia is full of beautiful old stone temples, such as Angkor, near Siem Reap in the north of the country. They were created as homes for the restless spirits of the country, so well known that they have nearly all been visited by looters, who hack the ancient carvings roughly from the walls and decapitate the statues. Actually, it's been quite a tradition for travelers to do this. Drawings of 19th century French explorers show them strapping huge statues to rafts and shipping them down the rivers to the ports for export.

Interestingly, the celebrated French philosopher and writer, André Malraux was convicted of pillaging delicate figurines from one of the most beautiful temples, Banteay Srei. He was sentenced to three years in prison and although he never (of course) served any of this, he was perhaps punished more appropriately by being made France's first Minister for Culture. Punishment indeed!

Under the Khmer Rouge, temples and statues as well as people were targets, although Pol Pot considered them also to be evidence of Khmer power, and in its final days, the army was pleased to use the Angkor temples as a refuge from the invading Vietnamese. But soon after Cambodia's liberation, the temples came under new attack—this time driven not by ideology but worse, by cash. The robbery was (and is) on a grand scale, with gangs operating in light tanks or armored personnel carriers, and using chainsaws to quickly remove what they want. In one raid in 1999, huge slabs of bas-relief from a magnificent temple in Western Cambodia were trucked in a convoy to neighboring Thailand, along a road specifically bulldozed through the jungle for the purpose.

No other country has lost so much of its heritage as Cambodia, with its thousand-year-old temples hidden in the jungles. At least, it seems no one is interested in stealing the human skulls, which rot quietly in their little roadside shrines.

## Useful information
Here's what John Pilger, one of the first Western journalists to visit the "killing fields," described seeing as the plane swept down over Cambodia in 1979:

> Whole towns and villages on the riverbanks were empty, it seemed the doors of houses open, chairs and beds, pots and mats in the street, a car on its side, a mangled bicycle... Beyond, the familiar landscape of South-East Asia, the patchwork of rice paddies and fields, was barely discernible, nothing seemed to have been planted or be growing, except the forest and mangrove and lines of tall wild grass. On the edges of towns this grass would follow straight lines, as though planned. Fertilized by human compost, by the remains of thousands upon thousands of men, women and children, these lines marked common graves in a nation where perhaps as many as two million people, or between one-third and a quarter of the population, were "missing."

In Phnom Penh, at the edge of the forest,

> there appeared a pyramid of rusting cars, the first of many such sights, like objects in a mirage. The cars were piled on top of one another; some of the cars had been brand new when the owners had been forced to push them to the pile, which included ambulances, a fire engine, police cars, refrigerators, washing machines, hairdryers, generators, television sets, telephones and typewriters, as if a huge Luddite broom had swept them all there.

Cambodia is a very peculiar place. Despite never having been at war with anyone, it has had more bombs dropped on it than Japan had during World War II. This was by the US as part of its war on Communism in South East Asia. And that was despite the fact that the Khmer Rouge were communists, as their name implies, of the "national socialist" variety.

Whatever their reasons, the US, its usual allies, and it less usual ones too (the Chinese) aided the black-shirted youth of the Khmer Rouge (later, EVERYONE had to wear black) to topple the gentle government of Cambodia and install themselves in Phnom Penh to implement their radical program. This program entailed: no hospitals, no reading or writing, and most of all, no money! One third of the population perished during this attempt to take Cambodia back to "Year Zero," with the full, but secretive support of not only the West, but China too. Only the neighboring Vietnamese objected, doubtless because under the plan, they were next. If it hadn't been for the intervention, the Khmer Rouge would indubitably have killed off all the Cambodians it missed the first time. Instead, they were driven out and the survivors returned to their homes, starving and ill. Curiouser and curiouser. At this point the United Nations — even the Red Cross — refused to allow emergency food or medical aid to reach the country and the survivors. In all its long dismal history, the UN has only once barred a country from emergency food and health aid — that country was Cambodia.

In fact, for a long time almost the only assistance that trickled to the Cambodians came from private individuals via newspapers and children's television programs. One of the latter was Blue Peter in the UK, who raised money to help save the Cambodian orphans by collecting bottle tops or some such device. In something of a media coup, Madam Thatcher, then Prime Minister and busily involved in the US-led program of attempting to restore the Khmer Rouge to power by rearming their forces in Thailand, was invited on the TV program. She was asked to explain to the nation's children how the British government was working to save the Cambodians from the Khmer Rouge. Save the Cambodians? From the Khmer Rouge? Madam Thatcher's face took on her trademark look of puzzled disdain at these questions. Surely it was obvious, she said, leaning forward earnestly, that the Khmer Rouge included many "reasonable people" in its ranks, and that hence they had to be allowed to be part of the Cambodian government too?

Pol Pot never faced justice, but for that matter, neither did Richard Nixon, Henry Kissinger or (of course) steely Madam Thatcher.

## Useless information
In 2003, the United States signed a convention that outlaws the importing or exporting of illicit cultural artifacts. At the moment though, there is no sign of diminution. The best way to see Cambodia's ancient stone carvings remains to visit the big auction houses, such as Sotheby's in New York or Christie's in London. According to Kathryn Tubb, of the Institute of Archaeology in London, "It's commonly accepted by those of us who work in the field that 80-90 percent of the material on the market is illicit."

## ♡ Disinformation point
Nowadays all antiquities must have certificates of authenticity explaining that they are not really stolen. Naturally, these respected galleries never knowingly deal with illegitimately acquired items.

## Risk factor
Ministers of Culture beware! In some cases, cheap concrete copies of the heads of statues produced to replace stolen ones have also been stolen.

# 14 No Holiday: **Myanmar, [a.k.a. Burma]**

*To the Katha Tennis Club, in search of "1984"*

## How to get there

Fly to Yangon, and then take a train to Mandalay and on to Katha, a small quiet town cooled by mists and generally suitable for tennis. When Burma gained independence in 1948, it was the first nation to successfully break free from the British Empire since the US did so in 1776. The name Myanmar means, "first people in the world."

## What to see

The Katha Tennis Club Building is the center of the plot in George Orwell's first book and influential travelogue *Burmese Days*, based on his time in Burma as a policeman. The building itself is now home to a government agricultural cooperative, but happily the tennis court remains just as it was. [ 📷 ]

The club itself is a simple wooden building under a tin roof, surrounded by a lush garden of purple bougainvilleas. In the book, the hero shoots an elephant on the tennis court. Orwell felt that the setting illustrated the inequalities and injustice of Colonial rule. (Not the shooting of the poor elephant, the tennis court.)

## Background briefing

Orwell is perhaps the most famous political travel writer of them all. *Animal Farm* was his witty yet powerful parable of the collapse of Communism into tyranny. Its lessons still haunt those who preach the "all animals are equal, but some animals are more equal than others" brand of socialism. Alas, this darker picture of a future totalitarian society has become fodder for reality TV producers, as a jovial "Big Brother" gives witless youth instructions on how to run their household.

George Orwell was a very serious fellow, and drew on just the kind of depressing travel experiences that we are trying to revive here. He spent time *Down and Out in Paris and London*, he visited Russia, and then he spent five "boring" years in Burma. There, just nineteen and fresh out of English public school, he was in charge of gathering intelligence on criminal gangs, watching while the then-British protectorate collapsed into violent crime and indiscriminate murders. It may have been this network of spies and informers that informed some of the sinister vision of *1984*.

Mr. Orwell started his tour of duty in Mandalay at the Police Training School. In *Burmese Days*, the city is described as dusty, hot and famous for "Five main products all beginning with P, namely, pagodas, pariahs [that is stray dogs], pigs, priests and prostitutes." Most of these are still there, although prostitution is discouraged. But in any case, he was soon sent off to the delta region of Burma, which is criss-crossed with steamy canals full of particularly nasty mosquitoes and (scarcely any better) armed gangs.

At the time Orwell visited, Burma had the highest rate of crime of all the colonies in the British Empire. Indeed, the largest prison in the whole of the Empire was built near Yangon at Insein. It housed both conventional criminals and political ones (those who campaigned for independence from the British, for example), a tradition carried on by the Burmese government today. Orwell wrote in his 1936 essay entitled "Shooting an Elephant":

> I was all for the Burmese and all against their oppressors, the British. As for the job I was doing, I hated it more bitterly than I can perhaps make clear. In a job like that you see the dirty work of Empire at close quarters. The wretched prisoners huddling in the stinking cages of the lock-ups, the grey, cowed faces of the long-term convicts, the scarred buttocks of the men who had been flogged with bamboos—all these oppressed me with an intolerable sense of guilt.

Yet in Orwell's time, Burma was at least relatively prosperous, the world's most important exporter of rice. Not so Myanmar today. Since the British left, the country has trudged sadly towards absolute poverty under the absolute power of "the generals." In Myanmar, comment and opinions are officially required to be in "accord with the times" and facts are carefully checked not so much for accuracy, but rather, political complicity with the ruling class.

Orwell's literary efforts clearly defied these expectations. For example, this exchange between a member of the club and the club butler:

"Butler!"
"Yes, master?"
"How much ice have we got left?"
" 'bout 20 pounds, master. Will only last today, I think. I find it very difficult to keep ice cool now."
"Don't you talk like that, damn you—'I find it very difficult!' Have you swallowed a dictionary? 'Please, master, can't keeping ice cool'—that's how you ought to talk."

## Very useless information

• The world's tallest bamboo (more than one hundred feet) grows in Myanmar.

• Myanmar still has the world's largest number of working elephants. The elephants work in the forests dragging logs, unless they are white elephants, which are worshipped instead. This makes them very expensive to own, hence the expression "white elephant."

## Useful information

In those "Burmese days" George Orwell was known as "Eric Blair." The pen name came later. The novel has never been translated into Burmese but is apparently sometimes referred to in the official government newspaper when a point needs to be made about how bad things were in colonial times.

## ♡ Disinformation point

Publishers in the UK, who worried that it might attract legal action, originally rejected *Burmese Days*. Instead, Orwell had to publish it first in the US in 1934, but even then, only after modifications to make it less political. For instance, they changed the occupations of some of the characters from civil servants to businessmen. The book was immediately successful, and the British publisher offered to consider it again, if Orwell made the location less recognizable. To this end, Orwell offered:

*With reference to the possible identification of the imaginary town of Kyauktada with the real town of Katha. I have been unable to obtain a map of Katha, but I have searched my memory and made out a fairly clear picture of it. It was something like my description of Kyauktada, except that (a) I had put the cemetery beside the church, which it was not in Katha, (b) I had put in a pagoda which did not exist at Katha, and (c) I had described the Club as having a garden that ran down to the river, whereas that at Katha, as well as I can now remember, was not actually on the river, though near it...*

## Risk factor

Vacationing in Myanmar holds some cachet, mostly due to its reputation as the world's most secretive dictatorship. Actually, though, the military leaders of Myanmar held elections in 1990, but canceled them after the results were both unsatisfactory and also not at all "in keeping with the times." Ever since, the pro-democracy activist Aung-San Suu Kyi is periodically arrested and released as a kind of "democracy barometer" for the country. (At the time of writing she is back under house arrest again.)

# 15 Working No Holiday: **Plet Me, Vietnam**

*Digging up mines in Vietnam's central Highlands*

## How to get there

Fly to Hanoi and take the famous Ho Chin Min Trail, which the Vietnamese used to smuggle food and weapons along during the long "American War."

## What to see

In 1965 the Ia Drang valley was the site of the first major battle between the US Army and the Vietnamese. It was bloody, but inconclusive. Partly as a result of this, the US took to dropping weapons from the air. B52s carpet bombed whole landscapes, villages, towns and forests alike with conventional explosives and the infamous napalm. One of the photographs that came to define the war was of one young girl, her clothes burnt off by the chemical, fleeing her village after it had been wiped off the map.

Actually, the forests recovered from the bombs and napalm, but they could not survive the arrival of capitalism. Cashews, coffee, tea, and chocolate beans have replaced the trees, the elephants, the monkeys, and even the hill tribes themselves, the people called the Montagnards ("mountain people") by the French colonial rulers, who started the process by clearing vast swathes of the forests for rubber plantations.

But don't go to see the vanishing forests, focus instead on the much more mundane landscape which is home to the landmines. Vietnam, like so many other countries bombed by the US, has a munitions legacy that continues to kill thousands each year. Here, in the Central Highlands, migrant workers use portable mine detectors, hired (not loaned!) by the Vietnamese army, to search for shell casings and live bombs in the dusty red earth.

As an added bonus, you can visit the many recent graves of those who found bombs the hard way!

## Useless information

These days Vietnam is losing one or two thousand civilians a year to landmines. Angola, Mozambique, Somalia, Afghanistan, and Cambodia, on the other hand, are struggling to adapt to an estimated 30 million landmines, making vast areas of land unsafe and unusable.

Yet landmines have a particular symbolism for the Vietnamese. They were the "arme de choix" (favorite weapon) of the Viet Cong, helping them to (literally!) level the war's playing field. Indeed, for all their associations with high-tech bombing raids these days, mines have been central to nationalist struggles against mighty imperial powers in South East Asia and Africa.

In Vietnam, the Americans particularly favored a mine known as the Claymore, which was detonated on command. But they also had a soft spot for smaller self-detonating mines, which they scattered during the late 1960s and 1970s in "area-denial strategies" across not only Vietnam, but neighboring Laos and Cambodia too.

Alas for the US forces, the Viet Cong became adept at not only finding the enemy mines, but also at digging them up and recycling the explosives. The Claymore was particularly prized. In one province, after American forces had planted 30,000 mines in a 15-mile (24 kilometer) antipersonnel barrier, the VC lifted an estimated 10,000 mines. The "insurgents" were even able to make anti-personnel mines out of the American cluster bombs. It is estimated that 90 percent of the material used by the VC to manufacture mines, including explosives, came originally from the US military.

And today the re-use and recycling continue—now by hunters, fishers, smugglers and scrap metal dealers. In 2002, poachers in Pu Mat National Park used landmines to kill both endangered animals and park rangers. One fisherman told papers that, in his village, everyone was keen to use mines for fishing "as you can retrieve so many more fish with them."

## Useful information

Some of these mines may be actual antipersonnel landmines laid during the war. In most cases, however, they are improvised devices made from explosives extracted from war-era bombs and shells. "Bomb hunters" can search for and dig up this ordnance, selling the metal to scrap dealers and the explosives to other intermediaries, who then supply the hunters and fishermen. At a price of up to 1.5 million dong ($100) per disassembled bomb, it's much better business to scavenge for mines than to grow mangoes (regardless of the danger)!

## Risk factor

There are reports of injuries and deaths at all stages of this mine recycling process. In Vietnam in 2004, approximately two thousand civilians were killed by bombs—thirty years after the last one was dropped.

# 16 No Holiday: **Shaoshan, China**

*The true start of the Mao Trail*

## How to get there

Fly to Beijing but be prepared to spend the next few days on trains in order to reach Changsha in the Hunan province. Once in the station though, you'll get a flavor of Mao when the station clock chimes "The East Is Red" on the hour. This tune was composed during the Cultural Revolution in the Chairman's honor. But Mao's home town is still another three hours away, at the end of a railway line constructed in the 1960s to serve up to three million visitors a year.

## What to see

This is Shaoshan, a pleasant village surrounded by carefully managed rice paddies—much like a million other Chinese villages. Except in December 1893, here Mao Zedong (a Capricorn) was born. The oldest of three brothers in a humble peasant family, he would later become a teacher in a girls school, save China from imperialism and capitalism, etc.

Yet today Shaoshan's splendid, Soviet-style station, with its giant portrait of Mao, stands largely empty, looking somewhat forlorn. The peeling cornflower blue walls and the weeds might make you overlook the place altogether.

Still, there is at least a good afternoon to be had here. In Shaoshan itself, a short march away, there's a fine new statue of the Great Helmsman giving a cheery wave and a futuristic Mao Zedong Memorial Library—both inaugurated by President Jiang Zemin in 1996.

Alas, the village itself has eschewed socialism somewhat in favor of shops full of Mao statues, Mao busts, Mao plates, Mao medals, Mao badges, Mao T-shirts, Mao tie-clips, Mao alarm clocks, Mao cigarette lighters and Mao yo-yos. Mao everything…

## Useful information

Mao's house is preserved like the shrine it is, albeit everything is labeled as if by an overzealous curator: "Mao's Brother's bed," "Kitchen where Mao Zedong helped his mother with her chores," "Pond where Mao Zedong swam" and so on. The rapturous effect is enhanced by paintings of a handsome young Mao offering early advice to his family around the kitchen stove, or leading his disciples. There is a 2-Yuan entrance fee.

## Useless information

The People's Republic is justifiably proud of its late Chairman, Mao, even if officially he is now recognized as having been wrong 30 percent of the time (and wouldn't it be fine if such assessments could be made in time to affect the policies...).

Mao's birthplace is the starting point for serious Mao aficionados, a highly auspicious location not far from what the Chinese call Confucius' hometown. Then there is another grand museum in Yanan, the northern town, which was a strategic base of the Communists during the long fight against the "Nationalists" and their Western backers, as well as the base for the anti-Japanese war, which of course, still continues to today.

## Risk factor

No risk. In fact, plenty of Revolutionary Guards are around to ensure nothing untoward occurs.

# 17 No Holiday: **Tiananmen Square, China**

*The summit of the Mao Trail*

## How to get there
Fly to Beijing. Get a moto-rickshaw to the Square.

## What to see
Beijing. Tiananmen Square. The name is now synonymous in Western minds with the events that unfolded here in 1989, but the ill-named Square of Heavenly Peace—the largest public square in the world (2,887 feet by 1,640 feet, or 880 meters by 500 meters)—has been at the very heart of Chinese history for centuries. Since the Ming Dynasty this has been where emperors would issue decrees to their subjects. And indeed, it was the place that Mao came to make all his pronouncements, such as that heralding "Great Leap Forward," which unfortunately resulted in the collapse of agricultural production and mass starvation in the countryside. Or there was the Cultural Revolution, which unfortunately resulted in complete anarchy, the collapse of education and manufacturing, and (again) mass starvation in the countryside. Nonetheless, an impressively large portrait of the late Chairman smiles benignly down from the Gate of Heavenly Peace (over the increasingly capitalist Chinese people). And it is here that the Great Helmsman finally came to rest, in a tomb known as the Maosoleum (no kidding).

## Useful information
If Mao's house is a little too easy to visit, Mao's tomb is a substantial wait. Even first thing in the morning, a line will snake around to the southern side of the square.

## Useless Information
Under Maoism, life expectancy in China rose from 35 years in 1949, to 68 years at the time of his death. This undoubtedly was a "great leap forward." In such a poor nation, the approach was based on education and prevention, and some older Chinese people can still recite a poem Mao wrote about schistosomiasis and the successful eradication of the water snail responsible for it.

## Risk factor
How dangerous is Tiananmen Square? According to China's own official Academy on Environmental Planning it is, like the rest of Beijing, "very dangerous." However, the real risk, whatever the views of Western Human Rights monitors, is not from People's Revolutionary tanks, but from much more mundane vehicles.

For if visitors used to marvel at the throngs of thousands upon thousands of bicycles in Beijing, proceeding chaotically but yet systematically across the city's wide boulevards, now Beijing is famous for another reason. Invariably covered in a blanket of yellow smog, it now claims the world's most dangerous levels of carbon dioxide. Since the year 2000, the number of vehicles

clogging the capital's streets has more than doubled to nearly 2.5 million. It is expected to top the 3 million mark just in time for the Olympics in 2008. China is already the world's second largest producer of greenhouse gases (the United States is the top) and on a World Bank list of the planet's 20 most air polluted cities it features 16 times.

Acid rain now falls on a third of China's vast territory, as well as many of its neighbors, and 70 percent of rivers and lakes are no longer safe for drinking. Government policy, as in the West, is to prioritize road building and even to ban bicycles from certain routes. It is a surprisingly uncritical endorsement of the development strategies of the disastrous car-friendly economies of the capitalists. The political implications are also becoming apparent as serious health issues emerge. Scores of birth defects are being linked to chemical factories and have been a significant factor in recent waves of popular protests.

# 18 No Holiday: **Shantou, China**

*The shrine to the Cultural Revolution (and the wrong end of the Mao Trail)*

### How to get there
Tucked away in Guangdong Province, on the fringe of Chinese society, with a semi-abandoned air is a "shrine to the Cultural Revolution," which, although it sounds nice, actually tore China's villages, towns and families apart a generation ago.

### What to see
You might expect long patient lines of several thousand visitors clutching their digital cameras (like at Tiananmen). Instead, here there is just one lone watchman and a handful of school

children. The building presents a traditional Chinese face to the world, with a facade topped with green glazed pan-tiles with curly ends. The words "Never let the tragedy of the Cultural Revolution repeat itself!" in Chinese script surmount two fine portraits of an imperial looking Mao. It is situated on a peaceful hillside, alongside shrines to other Communist icons, such as Deng Xiaoping, who was one of the first victims of the purges.

The middle of the wall holds a quotation from an official document agreed on at a party conference in 1981, one supposedly settling all the serious historical problems since the founding of the Chinese Communist Party. The wall states: "History has already judged that the so-called Cultural Revolution was an internal riot launched by the leader of China. It was made use of by the anti-revolutionaries who brought severe disasters upon the Party, the whole nation and the Chinese people."

Nothing but the faint sound of birds nesting on surrounding hilltops disturbs this Mao site—part museum, part monument—a first careful acknowledgement of one of the darker chapters in China's recent past.

Inside the circular pavilion that is the site's centerpiece, the walls are lined with a series of grey slate tiles, each depicting a scene from the Cultural Revolution. The first one quotes a 72-year-old Mao incanting: "Under heaven, all is chaos."

The panels then function like a newsreel as the events unfold. There are images of the rallies in Beijing that August, with millions of fervent people waving their *Little Red Books* in adulation. Then the pictures record the full "madness" of the times. In one panel, they show the Beijing Garden where Rong Guotuan, then China's world champion table tennis player, was hung to death.

## Background briefing
The Cultural Revolution was a period in which a faction centered around Mao's wife, but calling in support Mao himself, attempted to outmaneuver reformists in the party (like Deng) by unleashing the power of individual communists throughout the country. Mao symbolized this reinvigoration of the revolutionary spirit in 1966, by undertaking his famous swim in the mighty Yangtze River.

But in the anarchy that was created, self-proclaimed guardians of the revolution were able to report, punish or even kill anyone else. And an estimated one million people were swept away on a wave of destruction, particularly the intellectuals, the doctors, and even Mao's favorite workers, the teachers. During this period, the Great Helmsman himself, as the images in the shrine make clear, diminished from the brilliant political philosopher seen in the pithy sayings of the *Little Red Book*, to an elderly relic, inarticulate and irrelevant.

The memorial is a private initiative of the former mayor of Shantou, Peng Qi An, and is largely privately funded, albeit with support from, amongst others, the City Council. Peng lost his own brother to a revolutionary mob in the years of turmoil.

## Useful information
The Chinese people have suffered greatly under foreign invasions, both Western and Japanese. The invaders set up trading zones by armed force, massacring many Chinese people with impunity, robbing the country of its treasures.

Since World War II the US and its allies have waged proxy wars against China on several occasions, most notably in Korea and Vietnam, and came within a few hours of launching a nuclear attack on the Chinese. Instead, the US has used chemical and biological weapons against the Chinese mainland, albeit covertly. Unable to collapse the regime by military means, it has chipped away at it, using the techniques of internal dissent, and by appropriating the language of human rights and democracy to advance its agenda.

## ☐ Disinformation point

The famous novel *Wild Swans* by Jung Chang claims to expose "the horrors of life under Maoism," as the London *Sunday Times* put it. The book is not only the "biggest grossing non-fiction [well, it's only docu-fiction anyway] in publishing history" but also the book of which "even Mrs. Thatcher confessed she was a fan." Books like this are part of the Cold War being waged between the West and Communist China. *Wild Swans* is essentially a weapon.

To many Westerners Mao is perceived as a kind of cross between Stalin and Hitler, and China itself is seen as something between a vast Gulag and a political prison. *Wild Swans* is grist for the mill. The London *Sunday Times* describes how Jung Chang's youthful experience as a farm worker, village doctor and electrician (or in the "forced labor" camps as the paper puts it) was so awful that it gave her breast cancer some twenty years later when she came to write about it.

Yet in her book, the worst moment she remembers is "standing on the street corners with an umbrella hoping an old lady would pass so that I could escort her home." Apparently this was madness, this thinking of the community rather than just of herself. She seems to have recovered nicely from the atrocity though, in her luxurious home in London's Notting Hill Gate.

Since *Wild Swans* is a mish-mash of self-serving half-truth and innuendo, it is as well that it is classified as a biography. We all like to see ourselves a little better than we really are. And many of us evidently need to see others as a little worse than they really are too. Her next book, *Mao: the Unknown Story*, on the other hand, tried to pass itself as serious history, and came heavily criticized by "day-job" historians. They pointed out that the long but non-specific lists of sources for various groundbreaking historical discoveries (for instance, they claim that the "Long March" was completely unnecessary) fell woefully below the standard rightly required for even a work such as *No Holiday*.

Ironically, as Jung Chang was given a scholarship by this poor nation to travel and to study abroad, she benefited from Maoism. But doubtless she would enjoy this late addition to the Mao Trail. Not quite so well supported, and perhaps not so obviously part of Mao's biography, it sheds light on what happened during that other "30 percent of political errors" which occurred in steering the Middle Kingdom from abject poverty and ruination at the hands of the Western and Japanese invaders, to relative prosperity and independence.

## Risk factor 

There is a small risk of becoming interested in bad novels about the Cultural Revolution.

# 19 No Holiday: **Beijing, China**

*The 798 Factory*

## How to get there

Whilst you are in Beijing, ask the rickshaw driver to take you to the Tense Space Studio of Factory 798 in Beijing's Chaoyang district, east from Yansha Bridge and left at the traffic lights.

## What to see

Factory 798 is a relic, what remains of the massive North China Radio Equipment factory, which covered over 11 million square feet (one million square meters) and employed 20,000 people. At one time, these workers would have been summoned by martial music at the crack of dawn, to toil over valves and circuit boards until nightfall, with only a few hours off at midday for the famous Chinese Tai Chi exercise drills. Here and there in red painted Chinese script are entreaties to "construct the Factory into a Big School of Mao's Thought" and selected aphorisms from the now elusive *Little Red Book*.

Now some of the older buildings, made of beige square bricks, have become arts and crafts workshops, operating on a different, rather more relaxed, timetable. The factory was built with numerous courtyards and these are today places of tranquility with cicadas chirruping on the trees. Cafés and art galleries mark the landscape.

The most famous part of the complex is the Tense Space, 11,000 square feet (1,000 square meters), which offers both the red slogans and on one side the original factory machines. In the center are some life-size Chinese figures of monks sweeping—distinctive for their red hue. Today, as China experiments with capitalism, the space and these figures are popping up in advertising campaigns.

## Useless information

The European Union sent its Culture Commissioner to visit who commented, in the much translated form that it was released in, that it was fine to see that "in its endeavor to become an international metropolitan city, Beijing is also trying hard to explore the possibility of maintaining its characteristics."

It's encouraging to many to see the New China celebrating its history and also extending opportunities for individuals to express their own ideas and creativity. And we should not be too disappointed to see that, like almost all the interesting and unique buildings of this huge country, there is a plan to knock the whole lot down and put up new construction instead.

## Risk factor

Typically, in China you can try to protest but you would run the risk of being considered "splittist," and if you're not put in prison, you'll certainly be made to feel a little unwelcome. But just as typically, comes the realization that the artistic center cannot stay as it was, because its success contains the seeds of its own destruction. As the area becomes attractive, people want to move near to it, the property values rise, and the artists inevitably have to move on, and find new abandoned factories and marginal buildings.

# 20 No Holiday:
# North Korea, the Demilitarized Zone

*To the last Stalinist paradise on Earth*

### How to get there

Backpackers are always looking for places less traveled, a sort of perpetually self-contradicting collective trait. But some destinations remain exotic and are sufficiently difficult to reach that they retain a sort of social cachet.

One such destination is North Korea. Described by George Bush Junior as evil, and by the *New York Times* as the place where the poverty is so extreme that the villagers can only survive by eating grass, it certainly sounds exotic.

This is all the more true if you listen to a BBC report from 2003 that described gas chambers used by the North Koreans to deal with dissenters. This hinted at a very unusual alternative holiday destination:

> *In the remote north-eastern corner of North Korea, close to the border of Russia and China, is Haengyong. Hidden away in the mountains, this remote town is home to Camp 22—North Korea's largest concentration camp, where thousands of men, women and children accused of political crimes are held. Now, it is claimed, it is also where thousands die each year and where prison guards stamp on the necks of babies born to prisoners to kill them. Over the past year harrowing first-hand testimonies from North Korean defectors have detailed execution and torture, and now chilling evidence has emerged that the walls of Camp 22 hide an even more evil secret: gas chambers where horrific chemical experiments are conducted on human beings...*

Accurate or not, there may be a good reason why North Korea isn't a prime honeymoon spot.

Nonetheless, the People's Republic does allow some visitors in, albeit always with a wary attitude. So getting there is a difficult quandary. The travel literature is full of people describing how they managed to get in, usually after deceiving the North Koreans of their true purpose, which is frequently to expose the horrors of life under the system.

One young American teacher, Scott Fisher, based in Seoul, managed it by pretending to be interested in the Cultural Festival that the Koreans put on around the time of the World Cup in the South (a source of some bitter envy to the North). The truth is, the North Koreans do like foreign currency and if you want to visit, and are sufficiently discreet about your political position, you can. Just use the official channels.

### What to see

We join Scott Fisher, our guide for the "Journey into Kimland" as he patronizingly puts it, at the main visitor's room overlooking the security strip between the two halves of Korea. Scott takes the opportunity to talk with one of his People's Republic mandatory guides, acknowledging that he is now able to see that the buildings on the North Korean side are indeed real buildings: one of the stories circulating on the Southern side was that they were all sham facades.

> *While looking over the area from the balcony I told Mr. Huk the story I had heard about the building during my first tour on the Southern side. About how we weren't actually standing in a "real" building. His reaction was immediate and will forever serve as my*

*personal definition of "venomous." "Now you can see the lies! The lies of the American imperialists and their South Korean puppets!" He literally spat this out. Foam flew from his lips he was so incensed. "Someday you will discover the truth about everything! They only tell you lies! Lies!"*

Scott decides, as he puts it in his holiday account, "to have a little fun."

*"Ah, yes Mr. Huk, there are many lies in the world. I hope I'm there when you discover the truth also." ... My words had him bug-eyed with rage. Veins popped from his forehead. "Me?! It is YOU who needs to discover the truth. I already know the truth!" "There are many truths. I hope we are together when they are ALL discovered." At this point he'd lost self-control and was right in my face, screaming in a frustrated combination of English and Korean. "You don't know what you are talking about! WE know! YOU don't know!"*

"Yes, and there are some things we know that you don't. Hopefully I can be there when you find them out." Scott replies calmly (in his account). Scott is presumably not thinking along the same lines as Martin Hart-Landsberg who wrote in *Division, Reunification, and US Foreign Policy* that by careful scrutiny of US policy in Asia, the true motivations could be seen as division of the peninsula. This policy set in motion separate political processes in North and South Korea that resulted in a cultural tragedy for the Korean people and turned the peninsula into a potentially explosive trouble spot. Nor does he seem to be thinking of the policy deceptions discussed by Noam Chomsky in *What Uncle Sam Really Wants* where he wrote:

*When US forces entered Korea in 1945, they dispersed the local popular government, consisting primarily of anti-fascists who resisted the Japanese, and inaugurated a brutal repression, using Japanese fascist police and Koreans who had collaborated*

*with them during the Japanese occupation. About 100,000 people were murdered in South Korea prior to what we call the Korean War, including 30-40,000 killed during the suppression of a peasant revolt in one small region, Cheju Island.*

But Scott is right about one thing. There are a lot of different "truths" to be found in North Korea. Two Canadian historians, Stephen Endicott and Edward Hagerman, spent five years investigating archives in the US and China, and discovered the "truth" that the US had been actively developing biological weapons since the end of World War II and that it had tested these weapons in 1952 by bombing parts of North Korea and China with anthrax, encephalitis and other diseases.

At the time, the US strategy was to keep its research secret in order to camouflage germ warfare as "natural" epidemics, endemic to poor countries of the South. In China's Liaoning

Province, eye-witness accounts tell of a comparable number of US plane sorties and refer to unusual concentrations of insects, particularly flies and fleas, following the bombings. Medical personnel records also note the presence of insects alien to the region and highly resistant to the cold. Following the bombings, epidemics of the plague, cholera and anthrax hit the region with a vengeance.

Be that as it may, you won't be able to see that from the DMZ. But Joe Canon, an unusually sympathetic Western visitor, described what he could see from across the Chinese side of the river, before his "Holiday in North Korea" [ 📷 ]:

*I'm standing at the end of the bridge to North Korea. It stops here at the border, in a riot of twisted metal. Ahead of me the piers march in pairs, on across the Yalu River until they reach the other bank. This bombed-out bridge is a tourist attraction: even now, at the end of a hard winter, a steady trickle of Chinese and South Korean tourists make the walk to the end, where you can have your photo taken with North Korea as a backdrop, or gaze at it through a telescope...*

*The Americans bombed the bridge during the Korean War: the Chinese side is intact, but the North Koreans have left theirs in its ruined state, a monument to the destruction wreaked on their country. And to the fact that for them, the war is not over. This bridge, all concrete and girders, is a bleak enough place in winter. But what's going on beneath my feet is positively eerie. Only a few weeks ago, the river was frozen solid. Now, the thaw has begun, but only on the Chinese side. All the hot water and effluent from factories, homes and shops heats this side up. But the water on the North Korean side remains frozen, and the pack ice ends in mid-river, precisely lining the border...*

## Useful information

How poor are the North Koreans? Do they really starve and eat grass? Until the 1980s, North Korea had been ahead of China economically. The quality of its goods was highly prized across the border. The infra-structure was superior, too, with good roads and highways. Unlike China,

North Korea had successfully introduced uni-versal literacy, free health care and education, and had never abandoned a respect for classical Korean culture. Perhaps we should wonder about some of the claims of disaster. After all, aside from the fact that grass is poisonous to humans, no one seems to be able to source the figures. Amnesty International quotes reports, Reuters quotes Amnesty. What is officially admitted, however, it that since 1994, "a series of natural disasters and years of state-run economic mismanagement compounded by the loss of preferential trade with the former Soviet Union and China in the early 1990s have unleashed acute food shortages leading to famine." In December 1998, the Asia Regional Director of the World Food Program (WFP) described the situation in North Korea as a "famine in slow motion" in which the whole country appeared to be underfed.

## Background briefing
Japan occupied Korea in 1905 and annexed it five years later. In 1945, Soviet troops entered the northern half of Korea and American troops the southern half to disarm the Japanese after their surrender.

In 1948, following the formation of the US-backed Republic of Korea in Seoul, the rival Democratic People's Republic of Korea was established in Pyongyang with Kim Il-sung, a Soviet-backed, anti-Japanese resist-ance leader, as its first prime minister. He became president in 1972. In June 1950, North Korean armed forces entered the South in an attempt to reunite the country by force. Chinese troops later joined them to oppose US-led United Nations forces. The Korean War ended with a truce signed in July 1953, but the two Koreas still remain technically at war.

All North Korean citizens are entitled to disability benefits and retirement allowances. Medical care is free and available at peoples' clinics throughout the country. In 1993 there were about 62,100 doctors (around 1 per 370 people). The official infant mortality rate in 2003 was 26 deaths per 1,000 live births.

Nowadays there is great interest in the North Korean nuclear program. But it was only in September 1991, under North Korean pressure, that President George Bush (Sr.) announced the withdrawal of all US nuclear weapons from the South.

## Risk factor
Despite being an excellent opportunity to see two political systems—communist totalitarianism and capitalist totalitarianism—malfunctioning side by side, the Demilitarized Zone still earns its reputation as one of the world's most dangerous places. Step out of line and you could be shot. But better than that, hang about a bit and the next world war could start here.

# 21 No Holiday: **Tokyo, Japan** 🏛

*The Yasukuni Shrine*

## How to get there
Fly to Tokyo and take a taxi.

## What to see
The shrine is highly political, a must-see for all Japanese Prime Ministers. It is also a must-see mine of disinformation and propaganda. Nowadays, movies, novels and comics all celebrate

the heroism of the Japanese army during the "War of Self-Defense," so Prime Ministers must too.

Built in 1869 as part of a nationalistic project of creating a religion around the Emperor's family, the shrine soon filled up with tributes. By the end of WWII, it commemorated the sacrifice of more than two and a half million Japanese who had laid down their lives for this great deity. Wars included those on China, Korea, Taiwan, and of course, the rival Pacific power, the United States.

And the shrine has a special revisionist educational role, as it sidesteps the fact that the Japanese committed many terrible war crimes in the process of imperialist wars on its unfortunate neighbors. Instead it features a museum, which explains the "Pacific War" as evidence of Japan's commitment to freeing countries like Korea and China from the Western powers who were (and this at least is true) then occupying and brutalizing them. One exhibit "demonstrates" how the US government engineered Pearl Harbor as a means to stimulate the US economy. That, it explains "made a complete recovery once the Americans entered the war." Another explains that the so-called "Rape of Nanjing" in which some 200,000 Chinese civilians were killed by Japanese troops, was the fault of the Chinese commanders, and notes piously that, thanks to the Japanese, later "inside the city, residents were once again able to live their lives in peace."

## Useful information

The shrine has no architectural or aesthetic merits, being very large, and reminiscent of a parking garage. Nor is it useful if you want to understand why Japan pays billions of dollars out in cultural and economic assistance to neighbors who despise them.

## Useless information

Immediately after the war, the Allies held war crime trials in Tokyo, which resulted in the execution of some Japanese warmongers, responsible not only for the war, but for massacres of civilians, slave factories and compulsory military brothels. The list included the then Prime Minister. These are all buried at the shine, and subsequent leaders come to lay wreaths in their memory.

By 1948 however, China and Russia had become the new enemy for the US, and attempts to root out war criminals were abandoned. (Even before that, however, scientists and doctors including those responsible for testing poisons on prisoners of war had been quietly poached for "research centers" in the US.)

Since people like Nobusuke Kiishi, who themselves had barely escaped hanging, were a few years later re-installed as Prime Minister, it should not be entirely surprising to visitors that those who were executed should these days be officially commemorated at the shrine as war heroes.

## Cultural side trip

The Museum at Hiroshima offers a chilling portrait of events on August 6, 1945, at the peak of the morning rush hour, when, approximately 1,900 feet (600 meters) above the Shima Hospital at the center of Hiroshima the first atom bomb exploded. Within sixty seconds a giant fireball had destroyed 100,000 people.

## Risk factor

All trips in Japan are a little dangerous due to the vast number of people living in such a confined space. This is especially true of Tokyo, which explains both why one shrine can have so many people buried in it, and why a highly cultured and sociable people every so often launch particularly nasty wars against their neighbors.

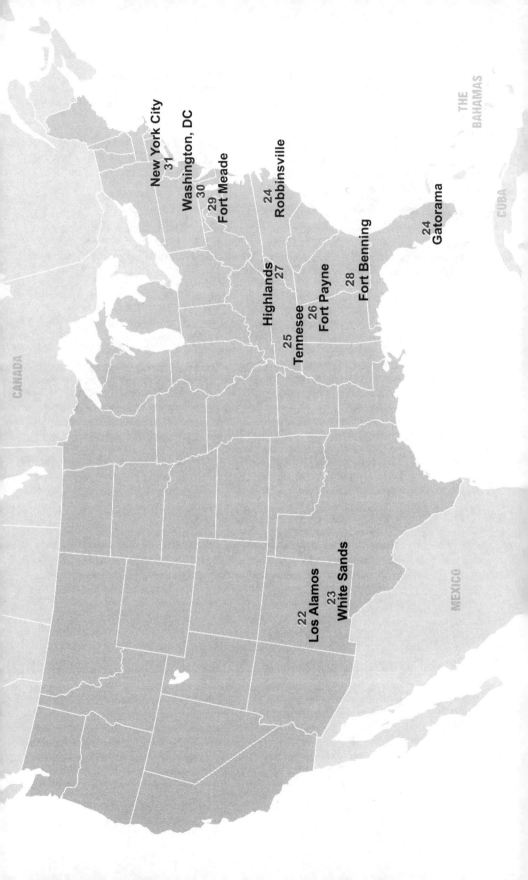

**Trips 22-31**

# U.S.A.

## 22 No Holiday: **Los Alamos National Laboratory, New Mexico**

*The famous nuclear weapons center*

### How to get there

Fly to Las Vegas, Nevada, where it is possible to make large sums of money to offset your holiday costs. In the 1950s, it had another attraction too. When the atomic bombs were being exploded just over the state border, motels here used to advertise the advantages of being able to rise early in the morning to drive into the hills and witness the strange atomic fireballs light up the sky. Indeed, even the most disinterested gamblers were said to have had to cower under the roulette tables as the ground shook after the tests, aside from what it must have done to their calculations of where the ball might end up. But that is all now history. Nowadays, once the coffers are full (or empty), you have to carry on to Los Alamos to savor the "Greatest Show on Earth," the nuclear experience.

### What to see

For starters, there is the brand new Atomic Testing Museum, run in conjunction with the Smithsonian Institution, which has a full size mock-up of a very large T61 bomb (still in the US arsenal) with a nuclear warhead.

It's a pity, of course, on the way, not to be able to visit the US Indian Springs airbase, just past Sheep Mountain, so-called as it is high enough for the summit to be dusted with fluffy snow. It is here that the dreams of war-game arcade junkies come true as pilots control both "practice" nuclear and "real-life" Predator missiles and suchlike in far-off lands like Iraq and Afghanistan. But this is no game and even No Holidaymakers are unwelcome here...

So instead, carry on to the more venerable Bradbury Science Museum, on Central Avenue, downtown. Skip past the various displays on human genetics, ecology studies etc. etc., as these are just so much eye-candy. The history display of the Manhattan Project and the exciting race to have the bomb is much more to the point. Although curiously, the exhibit says the race was against Germany, which gave up as early as 1940, rather than against time, in order to have the bomb ready for trying out before the end of the war. But thanks to The Lab, the bomb was ready, and here the "Fat Man" and "Little Boy" displays celebrate the technical excellence of the bombs that fell on Hiroshima and Nagasaki, killing a couple of hundred thousand men, women and children. As the playwright Harold Pinter said, accepting his Nobel Prize in 2005, the United States is "the greatest show on the road. Brutal, indifferent, scornful and ruthless it may be but it is also very clever."

It is all very interesting, particularly for foreigners, as it shows just how completely unregenerate the US still is about using nuclear weapons, and how very likely it is to use them again. As Pinter went on to confide, "as a salesman [the US] is out on its own, and its most salable commodity is self-love."

## Background briefing

The Los Alamos National Laboratory, run by the University of California for the US Department of Energy, is still at the forefront of US research into nuclear weapons. Naturally this is all secret, but it probably involves research into putting them into space, fitting the weapons into smaller and smaller packages, (thus obliterating the difference between nuclear and non-nuclear weapons) not to forget the "bunker busting" bombs that are needed to "smoke evil-doers out of their hiding places" (to quote President George W. Bush). Whatever. The important thing is that three quarters of the Laboratory's funding comes through something called the Stockpile Stewardship Program for nuclear weapons research.

## ▢ Disinformation point

There are two non-government wall displays on the question of whether the US was right to use the atomic bomb. One by the Los Alamos Education Group relies on sources like the *Albuquerque Journal*, May 17, 1995, which says that the lives of around 400,000 Allied prisoners of war were saved by using the bomb, as the Japanese had issued "orders to execute them all if an invasion of Japan occurred." Interestingly, the bomb's supporters note that the strategy of firebombing the Japanese cities using conventional weapons and napalm was causing "immense loss of life and suffering." These raids stopped when the nuclear ones started, so they think that should be counted as another plus point for The Bomb.

Another display by opponents, simply offers quotes from the various US military chiefs who opposed the decision, essentially a political one, to drop the bomb. General Eisenhower recalled that he had voiced his misgivings to the Secretary of War, saying that, "Japan was already defeated, that dropping the bomb was completely unnecessary." Admiral William Leahy, the Chairman of the Joint Chiefs of Staff also thought that as "the Japanese were already defeated and ready to surrender, the use of this barbarous weapon at Hiroshima and Nagasaki was not of material assistance in our war against Japan at all. In being the first to use it, we adopted the ethical standard common to the barbarians of the Dark Age... Wars cannot be won by destroying women and children."

## Useless information

The post-war 1946 US Strategic Bombing Survey noted that by early 1945 Japan's secret codes had been broken and the US knew that the Japanese government was already planning to surrender. With their navy destroyed, and the country slowly being starved, the Japanese were looking for intermediaries in the Vatican, Moscow, Lisbon, Switzerland and Sweden. Mind you,

President Truman was also aware of plans the Japanese air force had for continued resistance. They were working on a scheme for replacement aircraft built of bamboo and fuelled with oil from acorns.

## Risk factor

A General Groves assured Congress that a team of scientists had found no traces whatsoever of radiation in Hiroshima and that, in any case, radiation poisoning was "a very pleasant way to die." Unfortunately, a month later, an Australian journalist smuggled a report out from Hiroshima past the US censors. This gave a different picture of the day...

> ... Patients just wasted away and died. Then people... not even here when the bomb exploded, fell sick and died. For no apparent reason their health began to fail. They lost their appetite, head hair began to fall out, bluish spots appeared on their bodies, and bleeding started from the nose, mouth and eyes. We started giving vitamin injections, but the flesh rotted away from the puncture caused by the needle. And in every case the patient dies.

# 23 No Holiday:
# Journey to Death, New Mexico

*The less famous Nuclear Weapons Center: an ironic metaphor with bits of green Trinitite too*

## How to get there

Promisingly, as one approaches the White Sands Missile Range, the distinctive radiation hazard signs appear, decorating the barbed wire fence that glitters in the hot desert sun, as its steel links catch the reflections.

At the gates, soldiers in "camis" hand out instructions, brochures and search cars for terrorists. An odd combination of tasks, perhaps, but then White Sands is not only one of the most elaborate, sophisticated army bases in the world, but it's also open to the public. Albeit only two mornings a year, the first Saturday of April and October. So what is there on show?

## What to see

Here, tucked away discreetly in several thousand miles of desert, with only yucca flowers and prickly pears for company, almost everything in the US military's unsurpassed arsenal of mass destruction has been tested. Here the famous Stealth Fighter, such as Serb militants shot down unexpectedly in the former Yugoslavia, and the "Patriot missiles" that failed to destroy Saddam's flying bombs over Israel, were refined and polished. The new "Star Wars" weapons that will save Americans from any rogue nuclear missiles are now being finalized here.

The Missile range is in an area of the desert poetically known as "Jornada del Muerte," which translates, if you will, as "journey to death," although the US Army prefers to re-christen the place simply, "White Sands." Actually, the sand around it is a rather de-pressing grey, but anyway, the site suited them because it was extremely close to Los Alamos National Laboratories, where their atomic bomb was just being finished.

It was here, at what is now known as Trinity Site's Ground Zero on July 16, 1945 that the world saw its first atomic weapon explode, and the bombings of Hiroshima and Nagasaki followed just weeks later. Today, a small obelisk made of shiny black crazy paving is one of America's "Creepiest National Historic Landmarks," as one visitor, Carrie Fountain, put it. Young Carrie grew up in Las Cruces, sometimes nicknamed Bomb Town, not twenty miles from White Sands. Her family had friends and relatives who worked there. She used to be particularly proud of the strange fenced-off circle of sand at Trinity Site. She remembers how poetry readings and prayer service in anti-war commemorative spirit used to be held there.

> It has always seemed fitting that the missile range should encourage such activity, that the circle of scarred earth should serve as a monument to free speech. Indeed, one might argue that the atomic bomb was employed to protect these freedoms. The Trinity Site opening should be a day of contemplation, of mourning, and, most importantly, a day when the site is open to the entire public, including poets and protesters.

But times change. Now Rule number 2 on the list handed out by the soldiers is: "Demonstrations, picketing, sit-ins, protest marches, political speeches and similar activities are prohibited."

Nowadays, in place of peaceniks, soldiers direct streams of tourist cars to a huge paved parking area complete with hot-dog stands, port-a-potties and booths selling T-shirts and baseball caps. Cheaply printed on these is a picture of a mushroom cloud exploding, and the words: "Trinity Site: Home of the First Atomic Bomb."

While Carrie was there, a Boy Scout Troop was too. When she asked the troop leader why they had come, he shrugged, and then explained simply, "Boy Scouts like things that blow up."

And right at the center of Ground Zero now sits just what every Boy Scout expects to see: a replica of the Fat Man bomb—the bomb dropped on Hiroshima—alone on a flat-bed trailer. The day Carrie visited, as a joke, someone had written the words "EXPLODE ME" in the desert dust on the tail.

All that really remains of the original test site is a bit of one of the feet of the melted tower, once one hundred feet high (30 meters), and a small portion of earth, specially protected and preserved. It is a green and glassy mineral called Trinitite, and is what the desert sand nearest the bomb became after it exploded.

Although most of the Trinitite was cleared from the area in the 1970s, small chunks can still be found, false emeralds glinting in the grey dirt. And Carrie concludes that the best efforts of the US Army have been in vain.

> ... When I was a little girl, my grandmother often told me about the explosion, which she witnessed from more than 150 miles away. "I could see the neighbor's house," she said of the moment the pre-dawn sky was lit up, spilling an eerie, greenish light into the front yard. It was silent, no sound, only light. A few minutes later, the sun—the actual sun—rose. In the days that followed, news agencies reported that an ammunitions dump had accidentally exploded. But many years later my grandmother would confide that all along she knew it was something else, something bigger, something awful. So did most everyone in New Mexico. And they were right... More than 300,000 lives were taken by the bomb tested in our backyard.

So she concludes for us, in the best style of the naive student she was (at least prior to the visit), that

> Trinity Site remains an ironic metaphor: one that is particularly American with its confused and conflicting realities; a spot in the middle of nowhere where the entire world changed forever. Its scarred earth should be considered sacred ground—or cursed ground, whatever best speaks to the magnitude of its meaning. Perhaps, most fittingly, America's first Ground Zero should be a place where the public is free to praise or protest, sing or be silent, pray or spit. That's not the place I saw last April. I saw a place that was losing its meaning and turning into just another tourist attraction.

Which is why it belongs in this book.

## Risk factor 

At least according to Carrie, the design, manufacture and testing of America's nuclear weapons here has left countless many with radiation-related illnesses, including but not limited to: "beryllium poisoning, plutonium poisoning, leukemia, and multiple-myeloma, as well as cancers of the breast, bladder, colon, liver, lung, esophagus, stomach, thyroid and skin..." (That's enough, thanks, Carrie.) "No more protests, just hot dogs and souvenirs. Entry rules and RVs. One road in, one road out!" THAT'S ENOUGH, thanks, Carrie!

*William Bartram's Alligators*

## How to get there

Officially the Bartram Trail starts at Russell Bridge on Highway 28 along the Georgia and South Carolina border at the Chattooga River. It stretches for nearly 71 miles (114 kilometers) from the town of Highlands to the Snowbird Mountains, south of Robbinsville. There are roadside markers and the path is blazed in yellow in the Nantahala National Forest. Alas, none of the trip is dangerous.

The trail is named after William Bartram, an English gentleman plant robber, who, back in 1773, when America was still exotic, undertook a botanical survey of the southern states. His account of his travels, full of ripping yarns of dangerous animals, beautiful Cherokee maidens, and above all the "blessed un-violated" spots of the Earth, has become part of the American psyche, part of its national consciousness, a romantic vision of a vanished land. Today, by following the official Bartram Trail, travelers can experience the same landscapes (in a sense) from the comfort of their car.

Special excursions take travelers along historic sections like the Old Post Road to Midway, South Carolina, and down the Cherohala Skyway in North Carolina, highlighting sights like the halfway pond where (as one tourist guide enthusiastically hisses) Bartram and the traders camped in April 1774 [ 📷 ].

But our first stop on the Bartram Trail is Gatorama in sunny Florida. Gatorama sits on Highway 27 in the middle of rural Glades County, about 80 miles (129 kilometers) west of West Palm Beach. A sign promises tourists: "No swimming or sunbathing. Violators may be eaten."

Tourists must then totter down a covered boardwalk over a lagoon crawling with alligators and crocodiles. The two are segregated, crocs on one side, alligators on the other, ostensibly to protect the alligators from the crocs.

## What to see

"Gators, Gators, Gators!" as the publicity bellows remorselessly: "The number one place to see thousands of alligators and crocodiles is at Gatorland, The Alligator Capital of the World!"

Here we can WATCH Gator Wrestlin' (Sorry, only staff can participate), LEARN about local snakes and SEE an array of native wild birds. "Kids, bring your swimsuits and play at Lily's Pad, a very cool mini-water park while your folks enjoy a down home feast at Pearl's Smokehouse!"

Special timetabled shows include the Gator Jumparoo and Up-close Encounters, both of these open for everyone! But here's William Bartram's encounter with the alligator(s).

*The evening was temperately cool and calm. The crocodiles began to roar and appear in uncommon numbers along the shores and in the river. I fixed my camp in an open plain, near the utmost projection of the promontory, under the shelter of a large live oak... The verges and islets of the lagoon were elegantly embellished with flowering plants and shrubs; the laughing Coots with wings half spread were tripping over the little coves and hiding themselves in the tufts of grass; young broods of the painted summer teal skimming the still surface of the waters, and following the watchful parent unconscious of danger, were frequently surprised by the voracious trout; and he, in turn, as often by the subtle greedy alligator.*

And there he is! Subtle beast!

*Behold him rushing forth from the flags and reeds. His enormous body swells. His plaited tail brandished high, floats upon the lake. The waters like a cataract descend from his opening jaws. Clouds of smoke issue from his dilated nostrils. The earth trembles with his thunder. When immediately from the opposite coast of the lagoon emerges from the deep his rival champion. They suddenly dart upon each other. The boiling surface of the lake marks their rapid course, and a terrific conflict commences. They now sink to the bottom folded together in horrid wreaths. The water becomes thick and discolored. Again they rise, their jaws clap together, echoing through the deep surrounding forests. Again they sink, when the contest ends at the muddy bottom of the lake and the vanquished makes a hazardous escape, hiding himself in the muddy turbulent waters and sedge on a distant shore. The proud victor exulting returns to the place of action. The shores and forests resound his dreadful roar, together with the triumphing shouts of the plaited tribes around, witnesses of the horrid combat.*

Horrid indeed, but worse was to come. The wily, subtle alligators decided it was Bartram's turn next.

*My apprehensions were highly alarmed after being a spectator of so dreadful a battle... I kept strictly on the watch, and paddled with all my might towards the entrance of the lagoon, hoping to be sheltered there from the multitude of my assailants; but 'ere I had half-way reached the place, I was attacked on all sides, several endeavoring to overset the canoe.*

*My situation now became precarious to the last degree: very large ones attacked me closely, at the same instant, rushing up with their heads and part of their bodies above the water, roaring terrible and belching floods of water over me. They struck their jaws together so close to my ears, as almost to stun me, and I expected every moment to be dragged out of the boat and instantly devoured...*

*I was opposed upon re-entering the river out of the lagoon, and pursued near to my landing (though not closely attacked), particularly by an old daring one, about twelve feet in length, who kept close after me; and when I stepped on shore and turned about in order to draw up my canoe, he rushed up near my feet and lay there for some time, looking me in the face, his head and shoulders out of water. I resolved he should pay for his temerity and having a heavy load in my fusee, I ran to my camp and returning with my piece, found him with his foot on the gunwale of the boat, in search of fish.*

The scoundrel! Bartram's response should make all true Americans proud:

*On my coming up he withdrew sullenly and slowly into the water, but soon returned and placed himself in his former position, looking at me, and seeming neither fearful nor any way disturbed. I soon dispatched him by lodging the contents of my gun in his head...*

## ♡ Disinformation point

Actually, like the best historical accounts, most of this is the product, not so much of a fevered imagination, as of a fevered desire to sell copies. Indeed, the publisher even adds ears to the picture of the alligator, apparently in order to make it look more threatening. And even though alligators are biologically incapable of growing much past 14 feet, he declares firmly:

> The alligator when full grown is a very large and terrible creature, and of prodigious strength, activity and swiftness in the water. I have seen them twenty feet in length, and some are supposed to be twenty-two or twenty-three feet.

Bartram's Tales are high quality disinformation.

## Background briefing

The American Crocodile (Crocodylus acutus) occupies the northernmost limit of its range in South Florida. Further south, along the coast of Belize, fatal attacks have taken place, but in Florida, emergency calls about crocodile attacks are mainly by residents concerned about their pets.

American alligators are distributed throughout the Southeastern US but the American crocodile is confined to southern Florida. They were almost hunted to extinction, but these days have found safe homes in places such as the cooling ponds of the Turkey Point Power Station.

## Useless Gatorama information

Gatorama harvests about 1,000 alligators annually and sells more than 15,000 pounds (6,804 kilos) of meat a year, most of it over the counter at the Gatorama gift shop. When it opened in 1957, it was one of about 70 roadside tourist attractions in Florida. Now it is among the 20 or so that have survived competition from Walt Disney World, Universal Studios Orlando and other big theme parks. The crocodiles are the color of green olives, with a long snout and an extra row of teeth. They are also a protected species—no crocodiles are served at the restaurant [accusations of prejudice against crocodiles unsubstantiated]. The alligators are darker green, have wide flat snouts, and tongues. They are no longer considered endangered, which is why Gatorama is allowed to kill and sell them. "After watching the reptiles chow down, visitors can sample the creatures themselves." The restaurant serves 'gator ribs and other local specialties…

But farther down the Gatorama boardwalk used to be a "scary-looking crocodile." His cage was lined with skulls, but alas not, it turns out, of past visitors, only of other crocs. Nonetheless, kept in a cage by himself, "Goliath" was shown to the humans with the CAUTION that he might break them in half with a single swipe of his tail. How scary is that! Well, maybe not too scary. After all, Goliath was barely able to see out of his one remaining eye, and most of his deadly tail seemed to have already fallen off…

## Bartramalia collectors pack

Bartram wrote down his exploits both to record the habits and appearance of the animals and plants he saw, and, as a writer, in order to convey the excitement and mystery of the strange new world, but most of all, the same reason he was employed as a specimen hunter by an English aristocrat—for money. And his book was indeed an instant success, influencing nearly everyone, from Romantics such as Emerson, Carlyle, Wordsworth, Coleridge and Ernest Hemingway. Even the 20th-century conservationist, Aldo Leopold, was said to be a great fan.

Bartram's journey took him from the foothills of the Appalachian Mountains to Florida, by way of the Mississippi River. Scholars have called his description of the "pristine natural environment" (more accurately the "pre-European settlement environment"): "the most astounding verbal artifact of the early republic." The artifact consists of two documents: the report of his field journals he prepared for his employer, Dr Fothergill, and the longer and more dramatic account for the public published in 1791. It is this that became the modern *Bartram's Travels*. "At the request of Dr. Fothergill, of London," it sententiously begins, "I embarked on a brigantine... to search the Floridas, and the western parts of Carolina and Georgia, for the discovery of rare and useful productions of nature, chiefly in the vegetable kingdom..."

The tale inaugurated a whole new style of travel writing. However, as a reader noted recently on Amazon.com, the book is "really, really borring," with a double "r," which is perhaps also the tragedy of modern America. Anyway, we shall take this as our recommendation for counting the Bartram trail as a true No Holiday.

## Risk factor 🐊

Low. What?! Even with Goliath! Yes, low. Goliath is a sad old prisoner in a factory farm, not a man-eating crocodile at all. In fact, although crocs have been credited with a few human victims in the Caribbean over the decades, and each year, by tradition, an Australian tourist is eaten, it has happened only once in Florida. That was in 1925, when a hunter shot one four times in the head, enraging the beast to the point where it ate him.

After all, crocs are mostly nocturnal and used to live mainly in hot, dark, mangrove-lined creeks favored by swarms of mosquitoes. So their paths and ours do not need to cross. Except at Gatorama!

# 25 Travel & the American Mind: **A week puttering around the Southern states: II**

*Fields of Strawberries and the black drink of the Cherokee*

## How to get there:
Following the Bartram Trail along Highway 70/79 in Crockett County, Tennessee, on an open stretch of rural highway, is a marker with the unlikely words: "First Strawberries" [ 📷 ].

## What to see
At this point the Bartram Trail intersects with the rather more interesting Cherokee Trail. But we have our minds on higher things than the merely interesting. So it is back to William Bartram, now on his way through the Tennessee River valley, where he describes valleys of crops and pasture, with paths and roads, and Indian villages perched on the hillsides. In one passage he describes a profusion of "flowers and fragrant strawberries, their rich juice dying my horse's feet and ankles."

In fact, long before Europeans knew the sexual pleasures of the red fruit, the American Indians cultivated wild strawberries. And Bartram describes springtime scenes of the Cherokee Indians collecting wild strawberries:

> *Gaining a summit, we enjoyed a most enchanting view; a vast expanse of green meadows, and strawberry fields. Cherokee girls were busy gathering the rich, fragrant fruit, others having already filled their baskets. Approaching them, we discovered that some had stained their lips and cheeks with the rich fruit. Under the watchful eye of their matrons, we were disposed to continue as idle spectators of this sylvan scene of primitive innocence.*

Now much that Bartram described has gone. Many of the rare and unusual trees and flowers, including the Franklin Tree (now extinct) and another tree sacred to the Cherokee used to make a ceremonial black drink have vanished. There aren't many left of the tens of thousands of Cherokee either. But you can still see fields of strawberries. Neat ones, laid out in rows with big signs up inviting you to buy some. Recreate the past from that!

## Useless information
The wild strawberry (*Fragaria virginiana*) of America was successfully bred as an improved hybrid by French botanists in the 1700's. These were crossed with stock from strawberries found in Chile.

## Risk factor 🔖
Picking strawberries is relatively safe, but there is a possibility of getting back trouble (or fat).

# 26 No Holiday: **Alabama**

*Fort Payne and a motorbike ride along "The Trail Where They Cried"*

## How to get there

The Bartram Trail intersects, at least in a sense, here with the Cherokee Trail, not that it's called that, along which each year there is a motorcycle ride. Meet at Harris Cycle Shop Fort Payne, Alabama at 7 a.m. (Sorry, no later, folks!) for the official Annual Trail of Tears Commemorative Motorcycle Ride. "Day to be announced." But heck, if you get the day wrong, or even turn up a bit late, why not do the ride anyway?

## What to see

Cherokee leader John Benge left present day Fort Payne (once known as "Will's Town Mission" for Indian Chief Red Head Will) with a contingent of 1,103 Cherokee for an arduous 734-mile (1,181 kilometers) tramp. Their route went along what is the present day Highway 35 to the top of Sand Mountain, and then across along the present day Highway 75 to Albertville, finishing at Guntersville, then known as Gunter's Landing.

Fort Payne itself is interesting as it was one of five stockades built in Alabama and was the only internment (or "concentration") camp in the state. Captain John Payne supervised its construction. An historical marker now stands in front of the DeKalb County Tourist Association building [ 📷 ].

## Rather shocking information

There were perhaps ten million Native Americans in North America before the Europeans arrived. By 1840 all the eastern tribes had been annihilated or forcibly removed to newly designated Indian Territory west of the Mississippi. And only a handful of that ten million had survived. The story of the Cherokee Indians (*Ani Yun wiya*) is emblematic.

The Cherokee were a unified, peaceful nation of about 25,000 people when Spanish explorer Hernando de Soto first encountered them in 1540. Some three hundred years later, almost to the year, the remnants of the Cherokee were divided, with their culture and civilization annihilated.

Traditionally they lived in villages amongst the valleys, ridges, mountains, and streams of the southern Appalachians—what are now Virginia, West Virginia, Kentucky, Tennessee, western North Carolina, western South Carolina, northern Georgia and northeastern Alabama. They had a highly sophisticated culture based on farming, hunting and fishing.

As the European settlers arrived, the Cherokee traded and intermarried with them. They built European-style homes and farmsteads, laid out European-style fields and farms, developed a written language, established a newspaper, and wrote a constitution. They even began to adopt European customs and the techniques of agricultural economy. But all the while their lands— the foundation for their history, their traditions and their sustenance—were being taken away, piece by little piece. Between 1721 and 1819, over 90 percent of their lands were seized or alienated by the settlers.

But when they tried to stop this, the American Indians soon found that the equal protection that the US Constitution had so proudly declared "...that all men are created equal, and that they are endowed by their Creator with certain unalienable rights, among these the right to life, liberty and the pursuit of happiness..." did not apply to them. Specifically, the Cherokee found that they could not prevent the Europeans from seizing their woods, their lakes and rivers, their fields, their homes. Instead, they were driven from their lands, herded into internment camps, and in due course, marched by force out of their ancestral lands. This is the "Trail of Tears."

The crunch for the Cherokee came in 1828 when Georgia passed legislation pronouncing all the laws of the Cherokee Nation to be null and void from June 1, 1830. At the same time, President Andrew Jackson began to enthusiastically implement a broad policy of extinguishing Indian land titles in affected states and relocating the Indian population. In his 1829 inaugural address, President Jackson had explained the policy.

*My friends, circumstances render it impossible that you can flourish in the midst of a civilized community. You have but one remedy within your reach, and that is to remove to the west. And the sooner you do this, the sooner you will commence your career of improvement and prosperity.*

And in 1830 Congress passed the Indian Removal Act to force those remaining to move west of the Mississippi. In fact, it was Thomas Jefferson who had proposed the idea originally, as part of a strategy for creating a buffer zone between US and European territories, inhabited by American Indians. This would also allow for American expansion westward from the original colonies to the Mississippi River.

Actually, many Congressmen were against the act, including Tennessee's Davy Crockett, who quit politics over it saying, "I would sooner be honestly damned than hypocritically immortalized."

Even General John Wool resigned his command in protest, rather than move on the Cherokee, but a replacement, General Winfield Scott, was soon found to take over and Federal troops and state militias began the roundup. Within two weeks every Cherokee in North Georgia, Tennessee and Alabama had been captured, killed, or had fled.

Altogether, thirty one stockaded concentration camps were specially constructed near Cherokee towns*thirteen in Georgia, five in North Carolina, eight in Tennessee and five in Alabama. As a military report in July 1838 notes, the seven camps in and around Charleston, Tennessee, contained more than 4,800 Cherokee: 700 at the agency post, 600 at Rattlesnake Spring, 870 at the first encampment on Mouse Creek, 1,600 at the second encampment of Mouse Creek, 900 at Bedwell Springs, 1,300 on Chestooee, 700 on the ridge east of the agency, and 600 on the Upper Chatate. Another 2,000 Cherokee were held at Gunstocker Spring near Calhoun, Tennessee.

(Actually, one group of Cherokee did not leave the mountains of North Carolina. This group, including Will Thomas, an adopted Cherokee, who had purchased 56,000 acres, traced their origin to an 1819 treaty that gave them an allotment of land and American citizenship on lands not belonging to the Cherokee Nation. When the forced removal came in 1838, they managed to argue that the 1835 treaty did not apply to them, as they no longer lived on Cherokee lands. This small group became today's Eastern Band of Cherokee and still lives in North Carolina.)

Between 1830 and 1850, about 100,000 American Indians living between Michigan, Louisiana, and Florida were moved west, some of them in chains. Many were treated brutally. An estimated 3,500 Creeks died in Alabama and on their westward journey. Families were separated—the elderly and ill forced out at gunpoint—people given only moments to collect cherished possessions. White looters followed, ransacking homesteads. Overcrowding, poor sanitation and drought took their toll.

The Cherokee pleaded to be allowed to delay the march until the autumn, offering instead to take responsibility for the transfer themselves. The Cherokee eventually left in groups of 1,000 each, most of them in heavy autumn rains that made their wagons unusable. The last party, including Chief Ross, went by water. Private John G. Burnett, of the 2nd Brigade, Mounted Infantry, described the process:

> I saw the helpless Cherokee arrested and dragged from their homes, and driven at the bayonet point into the stockades. And in the chill of a drizzling rain on an October morning I saw them loaded like cattle or sheep into six hundred and forty-five wagons and started toward the west... On the morning of November the 17th we encountered a terrific sleet and snow-storm with freezing temperatures and from that day until we reached the end of the fateful journey on March the 26th 1839, the sufferings of the Cherokee were awful. The trail of the exiles was a trail of death. They had to sleep in the wagons and on the ground without fire. And I have known as many as twenty-two of them to die in one night of pneumonia due to ill treatment, cold and exposure...

But there is a happy ending to this tale. Justice was delayed, but ultimately prevailed. (Although some Cherokee still hanker after a bit more recognition—like maybe having their country back?) In December 1987, President Ronald Reagan signed a bill, and created their own National Historical Trail, one encompassing about 2,200 miles (3,540 kilometers) of land and water routes, over nine states...

## Useless information

The story goes that the mothers of the Cherokee grieved so much that, from that day, a beautiful new flower, a rose, grew wherever a mother's tear fell to the ground. The rose is white, for the mother's tears. It has a gold center, for the gold taken from the Cherokee lands, and seven leaves on each stem that represent the seven Cherokee clans that made the journey.

In a nice touch, the state that stripped the Cherokee of all their rights and liberties by statute, today has adopted the rose as the official flower of the State of Georgia.

## ↳ Side Trip

Memphis and a cruise on the Mississippi for highly optional Day 3 of "The Trail Where They Cried"

After the long motorcycle ride, a more restful cruise can be considered part of the Trail, following the "lucky" groups of Cherokee who got to leave by steamship on the Mississippi River (via a short journey on the Ohio River), south to the Arkansas River. Then down the river to Fort Smith, on the border between Arkansas and so-called Indian Territory. From here though it was back on foot towards Oklahoma and the fate that awaited them there.

Another watery trip idea along the Trail of Tears is a paddle at Moccasin Springs. The site commemorates the loss of yet more Indian lives. Often the Europeans did not like the Cherokee in their towns, so the groups trudging the 800 miles (1,287 kilometers) from their ancestral homes to the reservations were sometimes forced to change their route, and were frequently unable to use bridges. At Cape Girardeau, the Cherokee tried to cross the Mississippi at a point too near the town for the city fathers, who insisted that they cross two miles (3.2 kilometers) north instead. Today a state park commemorates the site where Indians died attempting to cross the ice-covered river.

## Technical details

There was no standard route for the 12 main groups. The route that is officially designated the "Trail of Tears" began at the Cherokee Agency near Rattlesnake Springs and headed northwest to the vicinity of Nashville, Tennessee, then to Hopkinsville, Kentucky, before crossing the Mississippi near Cape Girardeau and then across the Ozark plateau towards Oklahoma.

*Why are there so many trips dedicated to some rich white guy, yet the much more interesting Cherokee Trips are relegated to being side trips?*

It's discrimination. But then there are hardly any Cherokee left, and there is a lot of America to see...

# 27 No Holiday: **Travel & the American Mind**

*The Magic of Magnolia Mountain*

### How to get there
Not only our last section of the Bartram Trail, but the highlight of your US wilderness experience starts in downtown Atlanta. In your rental car, take the highway to Gainesville and then follow route US route 441 to Clayton and on to Dillard. At Dillard, turn right and look out for a sign pointing to Sky Valley and Highlands, North Carolina. It is then just over four miles to Old Mud Creek Road. At a water wheel on the corner, turn right. A narrow, steep paved road with a sign announces "Rabun Bald Trail," although it is in fact a few hundred yards further to the start of the walk proper.

### What to see
From the observation platform atop the 4,696-foot (1,431 meters) summit of the two-mile (3.2 kilometers) climb, where as one poetical tourist put it, "the clouds move in horizontal puffs of grey and white, inviting us to reach out and touch" we can see what Bartram calls the "exalted peak" of "Magnolia Mountain." This is Rabun Bald, Georgia's second highest, set amongst a panoramic view of the Blue Ridge Mountains. As Bartram's deathless prose has it: "The ridges rise higher, the rocks in beds of clay heave their sturdy shoulders through a rich and fertile mould."

On a clear day, looking northeast, you can see for 100 miles. Bartram described seeing nothing but forest made up of magnolia and dogwood.

Nowadays you can also see, looking north through a fringe of red oaks and yellow sassafras, a view of Sky Valley, a growing golf community attached to the popular Highlands, N.C. resort area. To the southwest, there is US route 441, and the ever-widening ribbons of development that have joined up the new towns of Clayton, Mountain City and Dillard. In the 1990s, 14,000 acres surrounding the mountain were proposed for a national park. But now, after widespread logging and road construction, only a third of that is left.

Occasionally, as one guide philosophically puts it, "landscapes seem caught between past and present." Yet, if parts of Bartram's world seem irretrievably lost, "there are sites that can sing to the imagination today just as they did more than 200 years ago. One needs only to walk and listen." And here is one such walker and listener, Richard Hyatt, admiring the remnant forest on the trek up to the observation platform.

"Looks like someone splattered a fresh bucket of red paint," he says, with all the sensitivity of a man who normally runs a sawmill, which it turns out, is exactly what he does. Hyatt, our guide tells us, grew up in Los Angeles, so he appreciates the rural life. He once owned a sawmill in

North Carolina, though, and takes a more pragmatic view of conservation than some outdoors advocates. "Too many people," he says thoughtfully, surveying the view on the way up. "But they have to live somewhere, and they need wood for their houses."

## Useless information
Ryan Adams & The Cardinals have at least preserved the magic of Magnolia Mountain in a song of that name:

> "I wanna go to Magnolia Mountain
> And lay my weary head down Down on the rocks...
>
> ... There ain't nothing but the [truth/tunes] of Magnolia Mountain
> Where nobody ever dies..."

## Risk factor
Part of the trek up Magnolia Mountain is very steep.

# 28 No Holiday: **Fort Benning, Georgia**

*Join the annual protest at the notorious School for Terror*

## How to get there:
Fly or take the train to Atlanta, Georgia, and rent a car and drive to Fort Benning, about 85 miles (137 kilometers) southwest. The Commandant's door is always open to visitors:

> We invite you come to our campus, meet our students and faculty, and see our programs in action. Our motto is "Libertad, Paz y Fraternidad," which means Freedom, Peace, and Brotherhood. Together we will make a difference in the region and the world.

The crazy paving entrance and the pink stucco mansion of the main block look more appropriate to a college summer camp than the school for assassins and torture techniques that it really is.

## What to see
Not that you can see that from outside. But at least every November at Fort Benning there is a protest outside one of the gates, attended in past years by over 10,000 people, some of them bearing crosses with names of civilian victims of Fort Benning's graduates carefully inscribed on them.

Activists like the implausibly named Reverand Bourgeois, who frequently mounts a lonely vigil outside the gate, or Major Blair, help to organize protests throughout the year. Major Blair used to be  one of the school's instructors but then, as the Director of the School himself says of his graduates, with lots of people, "you are bound to get one or two bad apples."

As one of the demonstrators explained to the local paper, the School for Terror is part of a wider US plan, no less than "the military arm of the World Bank in Latin America," as she puts it tidily. "I am doing this not just for Latin American SOA [School of the Americas, then the name for the

School for Terror] victims, but also for people working in sweat shops in Asia. I am really protesting US foreign policy world-wide."

Naturally, the police have already arrested and charged her. The Reverend Bourgeois himself has spent much of the past six years in prison. But he says: "A real patriot is someone who appreciates the positive things about their country and the standard of living in their country, but also can criticize and make sacrifices for social change to make their country one to be proud of."

## Useful information

The School of the Americas has a half-century of history as a training ground for some of Latin America's most notorious war criminals, including Panama's General Manuel Noriega, the many assassins of El Salvador (including those of ArchBishop Oscar Romero) and a junta of Guatemalan dictators accused of genocide. The curriculum includes training in different methods of beatings or executions and medical doctors offer instruction on torture techniques. What! Did the School really hand out torture manuals? Here, the school relies on the defense ably expressed by representative Colonel Glenn Weidner:

> The fact is that there was an administrative error because they were already in Spanish and in use by another unit who had obtained clearance for those manuals to be used, and so they were not properly screened by our translation department, and by the people who brought them to the school in 89. They contain some passages which, if they're taken out of context in some cases, and which in other cases if they were read literally, they could be construed to condone improper practices such as using fear, using blackmail, paying bounties for enemy dead and so on.

So that's a yes, then. And what about all those massacres? The UN found unambiguous proof of the School's role in the massacre of more than 900 people at El Mozote; the Trujillo "chainsaw massacre" of 100 civilians; not to mention several politically sensitive cases, like that of the execution of six Jesuit priests, the assassination of ArchBishop Romero and Bishop Juan Gerardi, and the brutal rape and murder of four US churchwomen.

School of Americas graduates have been implicated time and time again in the murders of many uncounted thousands of civilians, and a few hundred more famous people too, such as the ArchBishop and the Jesuit priests.

Faced with Congressional demands for its closure, the School of Americas changed its name to the genial sounding "Department of Defense Western Hemisphere Institute for Security Cooperation" and stayed open.

Col. Glenn again:

> As Commandant, School of the Americas: I have to clarify that while we are very disturbed when someone does commit a human rights abuse, and who has passed through the school at some time in the past, it is a very small percentage of the total number of students.

Anyway, the new School has now got a "Human Rights option" included in the training, he added. After all, as outgoing Secretary of the Army Louis Caldera said at the closing ceremony for the School, "This school brought our nations closer together in a common quest for peace and prosperity in our own hemisphere. Every country in Latin America—save Cuba—is now governed by elected leaders accountable to their people." Let us honor the graduates of the school, who have upheld American values and "served as a force for good!"

The Principal also had a message for those who accused the school of teaching torture and training dictators:

> Let me say very clearly that any soldier in Latin America, who had even the most remote connection to the School of the Americas, who has ever committed a human rights violation, did so in spite of the training they received at the School of the Americas and not because of it.

Mind you, the school has produced at least eleven military dictators. Even as recently as April 2002, the Venezuelan Army Commander-in-Chief Efrain Vasquez and General Ramirez Poveda—both graduates of the SOA—were key players in an attempted coup against the democratically elected Venezuelan government. Although that could have been in spite of the training.

**Risk factor**
Low, but you might be arrested.

# 29 No Holiday: **NSA Headquarters, Fort Meade, Maryland**

*The brain behind the world's largest intelligence gathering operation*

### How to get there
Fly to Baltimore-Washington International Airport, which these buildings are very close to. Albeit, hidden.

### What to see
The National Security Agency is still one of the shadowiest of the US intelligence agencies. Until a few years ago its existence was a secret (until 1989 the buildings didn't even have so much as a sign in front of them), it was jokingly referred to as "No Such Agency" by government insiders, and its charter and any mention of its duties are still classified.

But it is the world's largest intelligence gathering operation. Its 20,000 employees patiently sift signals intelligence (or "Sigint" as they like to put it) and information security ("Infosec") for the US government. Its biggest overseas supplier of data is Menwith Hill, Yorkshire, in the UK. (No Holiday No. 76)

During the Watergate affair, it was revealed that the NSA, in collaboration with Britain's secret listening post, GCHQ, had routinely intercepted the international communications of prominent anti-Vietnam war leaders such as Jane Fonda and Dr. Benjamin Spock. Another target was former Black Panther leader Eldridge Cleaver. President Carter had to order the NSA to stop obtaining "back door" intelligence about US political figures through its UK bugging operations.

So today things have opened up a bit. Now everyone, not just the enemy, knows about the NSA and its base in Maryland. And there are a number of buildings there to traipse around, at least the outsides of them, all in the severe office block style the US government specializes in. In fact, the style ranges from the mock Greek of the Admin building to a more modernist quasi-nuclear power plant chic for the computer centers. None of it is at all interesting, least of all the National Cryptologic Museum, located next to the NSA's headquarters building.

This is the NSA's public face. Hidden obscurely away in a disused motel at the end of a crumbling road behind a gas station just off the Baltimore-Washington Parkway it couldn't be more anonymous—unless perhaps it did away with the elaborate chain-link fence that surrounds it, topped with barbed wire. Inside it has a dismal collection of artifacts, which are there, it explains, to remind people of "the Nation's, as well as NSA's, cryptologic legacy and place in world history." There are books on cryptography dating from the 16ᵗʰ century, as well as an elegant little wooden cipher machine dating from around 1800, that may or may not (it's a secret) have been Thomas Jefferson's. There are lots of German World War II Enigma cipher machines, the electro-mechanical typewriters with adjustable rotors, as well as a US Sigma machine, the only machine during the war whose codes remained unbroken. There's a large, modern Cray computer.

If its daily activities are all secret, here at least visitors can "catch a glimpse of some of the most dramatic moments in the history of American cryptology," the people who devoted their lives to cryptology and national defense, the machines and devices they developed, the techniques they used, and the places where they worked. "For the visitor," the publicity leaflets promise, "some events in American and world history will take on a new meaning."
One visitor commented:

> Whoever named this place had quite a sense of irony—the surveillance cameras, briefcase searches, constant escorts, and armed guards did not project a particularly "friendly" image. I was hoping to pick up some souvenirs, but when I asked about an employee gift shop they looked at me like I was crazy. One thing that really caught my eye was a poster, which was displayed widely, apparently a security-reminder-of-the-month thing. This was the holiday season, and the poster showed Santa stopped at the gate submitting his bag to be searched. I'm surprised they didn't have the old boy being strip-searched. Anyway, I begged and begged but nobody would let me have one.

Adjacent to the Museum is the ludicrously named National Vigilance Park. The park contains, or "showcases" as the cryptologists code it, two reconnaissance aircraft used for those very worthy secret missions over Vietnam and the Soviet Union.

## Useful information
The 1998 movie *Enemy of the State*, starring Will Smith and Gene Hackman, portrayed the NSA as an evil Big Brother spying on Americans! Its plot involved the NSA's deputy director overseeing the murder of a congressman who was opposing a bill that the NSA wanted passed. Astonishingly, or not, George W. Bush's administration admitted in 2006 that it had indeed instructed the NSA to spy on Americans.

## Useless information
Like the CIA's own Spy museum in Langley, Virginia, the National Cryptologic Museum was originally created to "give employees a place to reflect on past successes and failures." Actually the CIA's museum is much more interesting, with the entrance graced by a bronze statue of Wild Bill Donovan, the founder, and decorated by 83 stars. Not, as foreigners will imagine, for each of the countries the US has quietly turned into client states, but for each of its agents who have died on active service. But anyway, the CIA museum is only open for dignitaries and its own agents. Only they can share the frisson of excitement at the "fish robot," the pigeon camera, the letter from Stalin's daughter asking for political asylum, etc.

However, the National Security Museum threw its priceless collection of code making and code breaking exhibits open to all and sundry in 1993. It is thus apparently the first and only public secret museum.

## Risk factor 🎖
Orange.

# 30 No Holiday: **Washington, D.C.**

*The garage where Deep Throat gave away a President*

## How to get there

Fly to Washington, home to run-of-the-mill political sites like the FBI Headquarters and the White House. But don't delay there; hail a cab to head east, past the famous Watergate Building and across the Potomac River. The multilevel garage is about ten minutes away, at the junction of Wilson Boulevard and North Nash Street.

## What to see

The garage is suitably anonymous. There is not even a large blue "P" sign to symbolize something of political interest. (Or parking, of course.) But Level D, four levels down in the multi-story building, is where one Mark Felt, sometime Deputy Director of the FBI, secretly briefed the *Washington Post* journalist, Bob Woodward, and brought about the impeachment of President Nixon.

The walls are whitewashed with bright red pipes, and stenciled location markings. "32" marks the exact spot where the rendezvous took place. Alas, the upkeep of this historic spot is rather erratic, and it is often strewn with litter.

## Useless information

The garage rendezvous was immortalized in the film *All the President's Men*, long before its real life counterpart was publicly acknowledged. Curiously, as the meeting point was just by a ventilation shaft, conversations could have been easily overheard. Albeit probably with some words indistinct or missing. Not as bad though, as the famous "Oval Office Tapes," starring President Nixon, that Mr. Felt advised the journalist to look into, with its famous eighteen and a half-minute gap. This revealed that Tricky Dicky had been ordering political burglaries, which in those days was considered to be A BAD THING. Ah, lost innocence!

## Risk factor

So, is it safe then to meet in garages in Washington, D.C., or was Deep Throat (Mr. Felt to you) taking a bit of a risk? After all, back in 1998, Washington, D.C. briefly had the prestige of being the United States' most dangerous city, and—even sexier—was officially the place you were most likely to be murdered in the whole world.

A widely reported survey conducted by the British government of twenty European and nine North American cities found the capital of the Free World way out in front in the crime league with a murder rate of 69.3 per 100,000 population.

That made Washington nearly two hundred times more dangerous than the rival political capital, Brussels, home to the administration of the European Union, with a miserly 0.4 murders per 100,000 citizens. Even deaths from its infamous chocolate couldn't push the Belgian total up much. By way of comparison the well-armed communities of strife-torn Belfast—the most dangerous city in the UK—managed a death rate barely a twentieth that of Washington's.

But in fact, more recent analysis of the statistics by Morgan Quitno Corporation (all 369 cities and 330 metropolitan areas in the US, ranked in a 28-page $4.99—cancel that!—now $1.99 document) relegated Washington to near the bottom of the rankings. The consolation for the risk-seeker is that en route to Washington they can at the very least detour through Camden, New Jersey, the new holder of the United States' "most dangerous city" title.

# 31 No Holiday: **Bronx Zoo, New York**

*Finding racism and supremacism in New York*

## How to get there

New York's Bronx Zoo is in the center of the great internationalist city, the melting pot of America (okay, it's in the Bronx, not Manhattan, but it's close!). Zoos—like museums—are political places, packed with hidden messages. Sometimes the messages are not so hidden either. It was here that Otto Benga, a representative of the diminutive African forest people, or "pygmies," was put on display in a cage with the introduction: "The Missing Link."

## What to see

Naturally, Otto is no longer there. But his grave can be tracked down in White Rock Cemetery, at the corner of Harvey and High Street in Lynchburg, Virginia, where he is thought to be buried alongside his "benefactor," Dr. Verner. The sad little plot has a wooden post at each corner and a clay pot in the middle. It looks like a child's grave alongside a larger mound of earth.

## Background briefing

In 1904, an American missionary named Samuel Verner bought Otto in a slave market in the Belgian Congo. Otto was there after his village, his wife and most of his tribe had been killed by the ominously named "Force Publique"—a group of mercenaries working for the Belgian government—that then administered the region. Verner took him to New York to display at the St. Louis World's Fair. After this, Dr. Verner took Otto home, but as everything Otto knew had been destroyed, he found it hard to settle back in. So in 1906, the two returned to America. It wasn't easy to know what Otto could do there either, but it was decided he could work at New York's famous zoo. To start with this was real work, looking after the animals, especially the primates. But soon the head of the New York Zoological Society, one Madison Grant, had the new zoo-keeper put on display in a cage alongside his animals, with the placard reading:

> *The African Pygmy, Otto Benga. Age 23 years. Height: 4 feet 11 inches. Weight 103 pounds. Brought from the Kasai River, Congo free State, South Central Africa by Dr. Samuel P. Verner. Exhibited each afternoon during September.*

Indeed, the exhibit was very popular with New Yorkers, who "made for the monkey house to see the star attraction in the park—the wild man from Africa. They chased him about the grounds all day, howling, leering and yelling. Some of them poked him in the ribs, others tripped him up, all laughed at him."

Or so the *New York Times* reported on September 18, 1906. But soon pressure from the Religious Right coupled with Otto's occasional use of his bow and arrow to injure his tormentors, made the future of this fine exhibit problematic. Through what the paper called "a storm of protest among Negro ministers in the city," the Mayor, George McClellan, stood firm, backed by the *Times*, which on September 12, 1906, penned in its inimitable style:

> *One reverend colored brother objects to the curious exhibition on the grounds that it is an impious effort to lend credibility to Darwin's dreadful theories . . . the reverend colored brother should be told that evolution . . . is now taught in the textbooks of all the schools, and this it is no more debatable than the multiplication table.*

(Funnily enough, the *New York Times* continues to this day to bang away in favor of Darwin's Theory of Evolution in its editorials.)

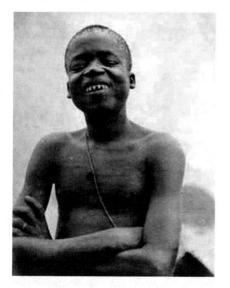

Alas for the *Times*, pressure did soon oblige the zoo to forego this educational attraction and Otto went to the Howard Colored Children's orphan Asylum and then to a Church home instead. There he learned English and helped the younger inmates to learn about the countryside and hunting. But all the while he grew more and more depressed, and on checking the price of steamship tickets to Africa, concluded he would never be able to return home. One day he sneaked off on his own, built a ceremonial fire, performed a ritual dance and shot himself in the head with a borrowed revolver.

### Useless information

The taste for displaying black people as curiosities still lingers. Many small town museums all round Europe and America still include their curious stuffed indigenous person, although now, usually, these turn out to be recreated using mannequins and shop dummies. Only in 1999, amid much protest, did the Francisco Darder Natural History Museum in Banyoles, near Barcelona, Spain eventually repatriate the mummified body of "El Negro," an unfortunate member of the Khoisan tribe whose body had been misappropriated by grave robbers for display in Europe in the late 19th century. And only in 2002 were the remains of the "Hottentot Venus," an African woman whose pronounced buttocks were considered a scientific curiosity in Paris, allowed to leave France to an eventual resting place in South Africa.

### Risk factor

All visitors to New York will be able to admire the elegant green statue, holding the flame of liberty that promises the huddled masses the chance to become whatever they want. And nowadays even the slums have been gentrified, so the once popular "ghetto tours" no longer exist. But that reflects the incredible property values of Manhattan—not a disappearance of social divisions. New York remains a city where politics, work and educational opportunities all depend on race—just as they do in the rest of the world. If, these days, foreign visitors are unlikely to be put in cage in the zoo, there is certainly a continuing small risk for black visitors that they may find themselves caged at the local police station.

## Travel advice for those considering leaving America

Most of the destinations in this book are not in America. That's fine if you don't happen to live there, but if you do, it might be off-putting to be told that most countries in the world are far too dangerous to visit (let alone to live in). Take the US Consular advice sheet for travelers to Mexico, for example, which describes the world's seventh most popular tourist destination, in unrelentingly grim terms. But actually, the trouble may have started as soon as you entered Mexico, if you tried to take your car, as under Mexican law, it may be confiscated. Even if you have a permit and can continue, then all political holidays are still out as "activities that might be deemed political" are banned by the Mexican Constitution to foreigners.

For anyone not put off by that, and surely most tourists would want to include political activities at some point, the advice note has other warnings. Crime, "often violent" in Mexico, is at "high levels." Armed street crime is a problem in all of the major cities. Victims have been raped, robbed of personal property, or abducted and then held while their credit cards were used at Automatic Teller Machines.

Additionally, kidnapping is "at alarming rates." So-called "express" kidnappings, an attempt to get quick cash in exchange for the release of an individual, have occurred in almost all the large cities in Mexico and appear to target not only the wealthy, but also middle class persons. Even if no one has been kidnapped, extortionists may still call you up, often posing as police officers, and demand payments in return for the release of an arrested family member, or to forestall a kidnapping. The Consular advice note observes sagely that prison inmates often place these calls using smuggled cellular phones.

Tourists are warned they should not hike in backcountry areas, nor walk on lightly frequented beaches, ruins or trails. At least, that is, not alone. Bars and nightclubs are not safe either as they are "havens for drug dealers and petty criminals."

If you decide to abandon your holiday and try to leave, but you don't have your car, or you did take it but had it confiscated, bear in mind that "armed robberies of entire busloads of passengers" occur and that "robbery and assaults on passengers in taxis are frequent and violent in Mexico City, with passengers subjected to beatings, shootings and sexual assault."

So the furthest many Americans ever get instead is the much safer New Mexico.

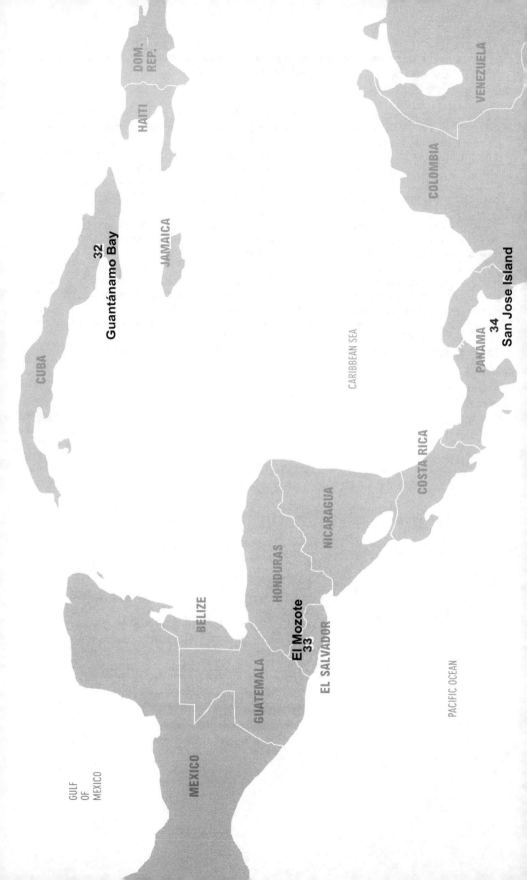

GULF
OF
MEXICO

MEXICO

CUBA

32
Guantánamo Bay

HAITI

DOM.
REP.

JAMAICA

BELIZE

GUATEMALA

HONDURAS

El Mozote
33

EL SALVADOR

NICARAGUA

CARIBBEAN SEA

COSTA RICA

VENEZUELA

COLOMBIA

PANAMA

34
San Jose Island

PACIFIC OCEAN

**Trips 32-34**

# Caribbean &
# Central America

## 32 No Holiday: **Guantánamo Bay, Cuba**

*The most famous of all the Cuban bays*

### How to get there

For years and years you used to be able to just wander in and out of the US Navy Camp on the South Eastern tip of Cuba. But that all changed after the Revolution. Nowadays Americans are not even allowed to visit any part of the island—at the risk of a $10,000 fine. Those who really want to see Cuba have to employ a "roundabout route" (like maybe fly to Pakistan and join the Taliban). But for non-Americans, the easiest way to see Camp Delta is still to go to Havana and then down to Guantánamo Town, notable for its French-style architecture. There, for a couple of US dollars, they can hire a driver for the day, and be driven up a steep rough road to the Loma Malones observation point. This is a little rock shelter under a canopy, complete with a tourist-standard public telescope.

### What to see

And from the little observation refuge, it should be possible to see far below, set amongst one of the wildest and least hospitable landscapes of Cuba, a kind of Wild West fort, complete with wooden stockades and watchtowers flying the Stars and Stripes. If you're lucky, through the telescope you may also see US soldiers frog-marching prisoners, clad in their famous orangey-red jump-suits, from their cells to the interrogation rooms.

The land surrounding the bay is dry and baked by the sun, and there is a fringe of cacti to the northwest, a relic of Fidel Castro's attempts, in the early 1960s, to discourage Cubans from fleeing to capitalism. The inhabitants of the base call this the Cactus Curtain, a sly reference to the more famous Iron one. Their idea was that on one side there were people living in perpetual fear and misery, whilst on the other was a world of freedom: singing, drinking and laughter in the bright sunshine. (Only it is not clear if they appreciated then which side of the curtain they were living on.)

One American student at the lookout, who had sneaked into the country by her own roundabout route, gives the flavor. "It looks so boring," she complains, "just like Los Alamos."

Boring, yes. But "Guantánamo has become an icon of lawlessness... dangerous to us all," as Amnesty International said in a statement marking the third year of Guantánomo's new role as a concentration camp and torture center. For that reason alone, it is well worth stopping off, if you're in Cuba, for a look.

## Useful information
Guantánamo Bay, a useful haven from the Caribbean hurricanes, served for years as a base for pirates, such as the dreadful Rosario. Columbus discovered it shortly after America, and named it Puerto Grande, but left after just one night, after deciding there was no gold there.

So when the US captured Guantánamo Bay in 1898, it was not from the Cubans, but from the Spanish, and with the assistance of Cuban soldiers. Only in 1958, after the Communist Revolution, was the base segregated from the rest of Cuba.

But the Camp continued to be quite a desirable posting, a friendly little town of more than 10,000 residents, with its own schools and hospitals, and of course clubs. The transition of Cuba from capitalism to communism at the end of the 1950s, the Cuban Missile Crisis and even the Bay of Pigs invasion, all passed it gently by, even if the base lost most of its Cuban employees as US-Cuban relations soured. The official history of the Camp records events like the day in 1948 that "a set of new chimes for the Chapel was installed and dedicated" or the day that a mini-earthquake "left cracks in the pavement." The chimes, it notes incidentally,

were purchased with money contributed through good-will offerings from personnel, and as for this earthquake, the "Residents of the Base were badly frightened as their homes shook so hard that small objects fell off the shelves, but there was no panic." Ah! Innocent times!

## Useless information
The Base's history as a prison predates the US War on Terror. It served as a holding camp for would-be refugees from Cuba, captured elsewhere and returned pending a decision on their "final status."

But when the first 20 shackled and blindfolded prisoners arrived at Guantánamo on January 11, 2002, they were kept in open-air pens like animal cages. These however can no longer been seen as they have been replaced by prefabricated cells with steel-mesh doors, and a maximum security block for 100 high value prisoners. Alas, after all this expense, the US Supreme Court ruled that Guantánamo prisoners still had some legal rights and could challenge their detentions in US courts. (Suspects are usually now sent instead to CIA facilities in countries beyond the Court's gaze, like Pakistan, Uzbekistan, Jordan, Egypt, Thailand, Malaysia, Indonesia and Diego Garcia—Britain's own Guantánamo Bay.)

The American Civil Liberties Union obtained documents under a Freedom of Information Act request that showed that the United States holds hundreds of suspected al-Qaeda members at Guantánamo, captured in Afghanistan or elsewhere. They also recorded that these prisoners were routinely shackled in a fetal position on the floor for up to 24 hours and left in their own urine and feces. One report described an interrogation in which a prisoner was wrapped in an Israeli flag and bombarded with loud music and a strobe light. Another described a barely conscious prisoner who had torn out his hair after being left overnight in a sweltering room. Altogether, the reports showed that Guantánamo had lost its innocence.

Appropriately enough, the United States' 100-year lease ran out a few years back and now the existence of the base itself is in violation of international law.

**Risk factor** ▨
Be careful crossing the Cactus Curtain.

# 33 No Holiday: **El Salvador** ♔

*To the deserted village of El Mozote*

**What to see**
The relentlessly hedonist and strictly apolitical *Lonely Planet World Guide* describes El Salvador and its capital as "not the prettiest place in the world" since the central valley around the capital is a pollution trap.

> *Shantytowns abound and the streets are lined with people selling everything from bruised fruit to Velcro gun holsters just to get by... The city's central landmark is the domed Cathedral Metropolitana, where ArchBishop Oscar Romero is buried. [But the Guide doesn't manage to say how he died, assassinated by the US-trained "anti-communist" militia.] The cathedral faces onto the principal plaza, the Plaza Barrios. Nearby, the red-velvet opulence of the Teatro Nacional dates from 1917... The Museo Nacional David J Guzman holds most of the country's notable archaeological finds,*

*and the Jardin Botanico La Laguna is an attractive garden built on what was once a swamp at the bottom of a volcanic crater...*

Yes, yes, but where to go? Well, the Zona Rosa is the "ritziest and most exclusive restaurant and nightlife district" but better is to get to the closest beach to the capital, La Libertad, "about an hour-long trip by bus." This, *Lonely Planet* describes as a "been there done that" surfer destination "with some of the best waves rolled out by the Pacific Ocean." Unfortunately, if you don't surf, "there's not much else to do in this small seaside town full of dried, diced and just plain dead fish—all emitting a pungent, salty smell."

Mind you, there are plenty of other things to smell in the forest...

*In the Montecristo cloud forest, oak and laurel trees grow to 30 meters (98 feet), and their leaves form a canopy impenetrable to sunlight. Ferns, orchids, mushrooms and mosses coat the forest floor, and the local wildlife includes rare and protected spider monkeys, two-fingered anteaters, pumas, agoutis, toucans and striped owls...*

And there are other things, some of them not so nice either. But we'll let journalist Mark Danner take up the story, and lead us to El Mozote, "the Thistle." Its story, he says, is the central parable of the Cold War. Surely worth a stop.

## How to get there
Fly to San Salvador, rent a car and head off to the forest. Mark Danner again:

*Heading up into the mountains of Morazán, in the bright, clear air near the Honduran border, you cross the Torola River, the wooden slats of the one-lane bridge clattering beneath your wheels, and enter what was the fiercest of El Salvador's zonas rojas— or "red zones," as the military officers knew them during a decade of civil war—and after climbing for some time you take leave of the worn blacktop to follow for several miles a bone-jarring dirt track that hugs a mountainside, and soon you will find, among ruined towns and long-abandoned villages that are coming slowly, painfully back to life, a tiny hamlet, by now little more than a scattering of ruins, that is being rapidly reclaimed by the earth, its broken adobe walls cracking and crumbling and giving way before an onslaught of weeds, which are fueled by the rain that beats down each afternoon and by the fog that settles heavily at night in the valleys.*

## What not to see
*Nearby, in the long-depopulated villages, you can see stirrings of life: even in Arambala, a mile or so away, with its broad grassy plaza bordered by collapsed buildings and dominated, where once a fine church stood, by a shell-pocked bell tower and a jagged adobe arch looming against the sky—even here, a boy leads a brown cow by a rope, a man in a billed cap and blue-jeans trudges along bearing lengths of lumber on his shoulder, three little girls stand on tiptoe at a porch railing, waving and giggling at a passing car...*

*But follow the stony dirt track, which turns and twists through the woodland, and in a few minutes you enter a large clearing, and here all is quiet. No one has returned to El Mozote. Empty as it is, shot through with sunlight, the place remains—as a young guerrilla who had patrolled here during the war told me with a shiver—espantoso: spooky, scary, dreadful. After a moment's gaze, half a dozen battered structures— roofless, doorless, windowless, half engulfed by underbrush—resolve themselves into a semblance of pattern: four ruins off to the right must have marked the main street,* and a fifth the beginning of a side lane, while an open area opposite looks to have been a common, though no church can be seen—only a ragged knoll, a sort of earthen platform nearly invisible beneath a great tangle of weeds and brush.

## So what is it with El Mozote?

In 1992, as part of the peace settlement established by the Chapultepec Peace Accords of that year, a United Nations Truth Commission investigating human rights abuses committed during the war in general, and ten year old newspaper reports of a massacre at El Mozote in particular, supervised the exhumations of the little village by a team of forensic scientists. This is what they found.

• "All the skeletons recovered from the site and the associated evidence were deposited during a single temporal event." (The physical evidence recovered at the site excludes the possibility that the site could have been used as a clandestine cemetery in which the dead were placed at different times.)

• "The events under investigation are unlikely to have occurred later than 1981." (Coins and bullet cartridges bearing their date of manufacture were found in the convent. In no case was this date later than 1981.)

• "In the convent, bone remains of at least 143 people were found. However, laboratory analysis indicated that, "there may, in fact, have been a greater number of deaths. This uncertainty regarding the number of skeletons is a reflection of the extensive perimortem skeletal injuries, post-mortem skeletal damage and associated commingling. Many young infants may have been entirely cremated; other children may not have been counted because of extensive fragmentation of body parts."

• "The bone remains show numerous signs of damage caused by crushing and by fire."

• Most of the victims were minors. The experts determined, initially, after the exhumation, that "approximately 85 percent of the 117 victims were children under 12 years of age" and indicated that a more precise estimate of the victims' ages would be made in the laboratory. The experts noted that, "the average age of the children was approximately 6 years."

• The weapons used to fire at the victims were M-16 rifles. As the ballistics analyst described, "two hundred forty-five cartridge cases recovered from the El Mozote site were studied. Of these, 184 had discernible headstamps, identifying the ammunition as having been manufactured for the United States Government at Lake City, Missouri."

By early 1992, and the peace agreement between the government and the guerrillas that finally allowed the exhumation, the United States had spent more than four billion dollars funding a war that, over twelve years, cost seventy-five thousand Salvadorans their lives. By then, too, the bitter fight over the future of El Salvador had largely been forgotten in Washington—the United States had turned its gaze to other places and other peoples. But El Mozote may have been the largest massacre in modern Latin-American history. That in the United States it had been reported at the time, was denied and the truth allowed to fall back into the dark, makes the story of El Mozote, in Mark Danner's phrase, a central parable of the Cold War.

## Risk factor 

Nowadays, very safe. That's the thing about razing settlements to the ground.

# 34 No Holiday: **Panama**

*Looking for old cans on San Jose Island*

## How to get there

Fly into La Paz, and rent a motorboat. San Jose Island is in the Gulf of California (also known as the Sea of Cortez) a long, narrow body of water squashed between Mexico and the Baja Peninsula. (Early arrivals may want to fit in some scuba diving or snorkeling before the trip begins.)

The area is part of the "Gulf of California Islands Flora and Fauna Protection Area." Unique species such as the San Jose rabbit (*Sylvilagus mansuetus*) inhabit the islands alongside more than seventy types of amphibians, reptiles, birds and pretty mammals such as the Juancito (little squirrel), the Babisuri (Ring-tailed cat), the Black Hare and the Sand Snake. San Jose appears to be an untouched tropical paradise with Boa constrictors, parrots, and iguanas abounding in its forests.

But Isla San Jose is both a paradise found—and lost. Plans to make it into an ecotourist resort have come and gone, as finds of rare animals amongst the giant cacti or in the incredible blue lagoons alternate with discoveries of rusting bombs of mustard gas and drums of cyanide.

## What to see

Visitors to the island recently have reported finding remnants of the "Project" everywhere. Rusted US Army tractors and unmarked metal drums lay abandoned near beaches. A wharf, built to unload thousands of gallons of chemicals as well as bombs and other supplies, still thumbs its nose at one of the beautiful bays. Inland, there's even the concrete skeleton of an American military chapel in the middle of the jungle. During a short visit in 2001, David Pugliese found remains of discarded mustard gas bombs on the side of a dirt road and a US-made chemical weapon cylinder in the grass beside the path to the beach.

For, tropical paradise or no, hundreds if not thousands (the exact number is still a state secret) of chemical weapons tests were conducted on tropical San Jose Island, Panama, by the United States Army. The first tests started in the 1920s and were then supposedly related to defending the Panama Canal.

But the bulk of the poisons derive from the Second World War. Concerned about the heavy resistance American troops found in attempting to recapture tropical islands from the Japanese, General William Porter, head of chemical warfare for the US, believed he could kill or incapacitate entire Japanese garrisons, cheaply and efficiently, by saturating their bunkers with mustard gas, phosgene, and various other poisons. Although of course the Geneva protocols outlawed such weapons.

To prove his theory, General Porter needed a tropical island. Which is where San Jose comes in again. Canada, then at the forefront of chemical warfare production and experimentation, offered 50-pound mustard gas cluster bombs as the ideal method of dispersing the chemical, and the San Jose Project was given the green light.

Between May 1944 and the end of 1947, the US government conducted more than 130 tests on San Jose. Nearby Iguana Island was sprayed with various chemicals too. To start with, the island was divided into six target areas, made up of overlapping squares about one square mile (2.6 square kilometers) each. The chemical agents tested included: mustard gas, phosgene, cyanogen chloride, hydrogen cyanide, and butane. (One small and presumably public-spirited activity for No Holidaymakers is to try to find old canisters of each kind.)

To help observe how lethal various methods of attack, extra rabbits, as well as goats from Ecuador, were brought in on a boat. José Alsola, a Peruvian who worked on the island, clearing vegetation for paths and an airstrip, described what happened next: "They put those gases on them. The skin fell off the animals, they died, and they ended up cooked. The animal was red, red!"

Soldiers from the Canal Zone were tested too. One of the tests sought, as the army researchers put it, "to determine if any difference existed in the sensitivity of Puerto Rican and Continental US troops to H [mustard] gas." The soldiers quickly developed problems breathing, and had to be rushed to nearby Gorgas Hospital. One of them complained to a medical aide that his buddy had "almost choked to death." The aide then asked the doctor, "What's wrong with them?" And the doctor said, "It's that damn mustard gas!" Eventually, the tests showed no difference; both groups of men writhed in pain, their skin burned and they became covered in hideous lesions.

After the war, from 1953 to 1957, the United States experimented with the detonation of chemical mines and warheads filled with live nerve agent. At least some of the mines were filled with the VX nerve agent, one of the military's most deadly products. Ten milligrams of VX agent constitutes a lethal dose, so each VX mine theoretically contains enough nerve agent to kill nearly half a million people or, failing that, rabbits or goats.

## Useful information
The current owners of the island have asked the US State Department to conduct a review of the island for contamination, and are building tourist cabins, a swimming pool, a bar, and a dining room overlooking the Pacific Ocean. They hope tourists will be able to explore the island on motorcycles and carts, without supervision.

## Risk factor
Unfortunately, although the United States government acknowledges having buried chemical warfare agents in the Panama Canal area, it declines to disclose any details citing concern that such information could assist terrorists.

**Trips 35-37**

# South America

## 35 No Holiday: **Rio de Janeiro, Brazil**

*Ripping yarns of squatter towns and drug wars.*

### How to get there

Fly down to Rio, where Favela Tours organizes visits to areas like Rocinha, Brazil's largest "favela" or squatter town, with a population of over 150,000 people squashed into an area of only one square mile. Here the tin shacks are piled one upon the other. As government policy originally was to wait for the squatters to move on, they typically lack services like drinking water, electricity and of course, sewage. There are hardly any jobs or schools, and they are havens for crime, especially drug crime. Until recently the government largely ignored them. But now, they have begun to get attention. The government is rooting out the criminals, putting in services, and most importunely, the favelas are now on the tourist circuit.

One visitor, Wendy O'Dea, explains why:

> I knew what most people know about this city: it's full of long, beautiful beaches with sun worshippers in tiny swimsuits, the people are vibrant and beautiful; and the city knows how to throw a serious party about this time each year, Rio's infamous Carnaval. I didn't know that in Rio I could find some of the best sushi I've ever eaten, soar through the air in a city that is one of the world's best for hang gliding, and stroll through run-down slums—mini cities within the city that house a subculture that is both frightening and fascinating.

For tourists driving from Rio de Janeiro airport to the center of Rio not only immediately see the famous view of Sugar Loaf Mountain and Christ the Redeemer, but also the less celebrated

views of the squatter towns, clinging to the rocky hillsides.

## What to see

Here the mean buildings are pockmarked with bullet holes and armed gangs of bandido youths patrol the streets at night looking for rivals to blast away. To mark out their territories, the gangs lay concrete pillars or burnt out cars across the streets, and paint murals on the walls. The emblem of choice these days is, of course, Osama bin Laden.

If you're lucky, you may find someone to tell you about the system:

> *The chief of the traffic [gang] called everybody together and there was a long conversation from midnight until 3 am. It was decided that one of the gang had broken its rules. "We shot him right there, in the school. He just kept quiet. He knew he was going to die . . . First we shot him, then used an electric saw to cut him up and put parts of him in a suitcase. His torso was left in the road. It is a way of imposing respect." Other informers are frightened and the community knows not to grass.*

It sounds pretty bad, but even if there are an estimated seventeen million illegal weapons in Brazil, "they are used in confrontations with the police or other bandits. They are not used to assault you on Copacabana beach"—or at least according to Antonio Rangel Bandeira, the coordinator of the arms control program in the city.

Tour guides echo this sentiment, telling their clients, "You're completely safe when you're in a favela. The violence that takes place in the favelas is not directed at tourists."

The reassurances would have been better both if there had not been so many of them, and if I hadn't just happened to read, in the newspaper, under the heading "Rio de Janeiro," about a thirteen-year-old girl who had just confessed to flagging down a bus. Now this, in itself, is not such a bad thing, but it had been part of an attack ordered by a drug baron, and her gang mates had poured gasoline over the bus, blocked people from getting off, and set it alight. Five travelers died.

And in any case, the rules about only targeting gang members do not apply to the police, who are notoriously corrupt in Brazil, do not respect the "beach code," and will shoot people anywhere. In 2003, the state police killed 1,195 civilians during operations. And this is a common theme in South America where the war on drugs, like the war on terror elsewhere, seems to have removed all constraints on the so-called security forces.

Perhaps thinking of this, one guide tells visitors confidentially, "I brought a tour by this corner not long ago—and there was a long line of police at the intersection. Concerned, I slowed down to inquire if there was a problem and the policeman told me there was no problem—they just really liked the food!"

So it seems these tours are safe enough. But is it really ethical to pay money to look at poor people? Wendy says that, "Admittedly, it did feel somewhat voyeuristic, but most people went about their daily business—hanging laundry, shopping at the daily street markets—paying little attention to the foreigners slipping in and out of their midst."

Anyway, the tourists were reassured to learn that part of the day's fee of about $20 goes towards sponsoring local schools.

## Useless film
An art house film, *Ciudad de Deus* (City of God), is set in these self-same drug-ridden slums. It is not likely to generate much business for Favela Tours as it is unrelentingly violent.

## Risk factor
But hang gliding is dangerous, regardless of where you are.

# 36 No Holiday: **Bolivia**

*The start of the Che Trail*

## How to get there
Fly to Buenos Aires, Argentina, rent a powerful motorcycle and get a large-scale map of the whole of South America.

## What to see
Ernesto Guevara, as his parents always knew him, and earnest by nature he was too, was born and brought up in Argentina, and his major work was helping foment Cuba's excellent revolution (although he tried to encourage many other generally less successful insurgencies too). He once said, "The true revolutionary is guided by a great feeling of love," but nevertheless decided to also write several Maoist works on the tactics of guerrilla warfare.

> *The guerrilla band is an armed nucleus, the fighting vanguard of the people. It draws its great force from the mass of the people themselves. The guerrilla band is not to be considered inferior to the army against which it fights simply because it is inferior in firepower. Guerrilla warfare is used by the side which is supported by a majority but which possesses a much smaller number of arms for use in defense against oppression.*

## Useful information
There is one official Che Trail and several unofficial variations, including one, which follows the

hair-raising ride of Che and his friend Alberto (who, interestingly enough, is still alive, and working as a doctor. But then, he never was a revolutionary.) on their iconic motorcycle, "the Mighty One," through blue, half-remembered mountains and one-horse towns. This longer trail stretches from Buenos Aires to Santiago, and then on through Chile, Peru and Colombia to finish eventually in Venezuela. During his travels, Che became more and more aware of the chronic inequality in South America, a continent in which the domination of multinationals, like United Fruit, is maintained only by the exploitation and misery of the people. In a letter to his aunt Beatriz he wrote: "In El Paso I traversed the vast domains of United Fruit. Once more I was able to convince myself how criminal the capitalistic octopuses are. On a picture of our old and bewailed comrade Stalin, I swore not to rest before these capitalistic octopuses are destroyed."

The travel company, Journey Latin America (based in London) will take you on a three-week recreation of the experience for some $5,000 (that's about seven years hard earned wages at local rates), "not including riding any motorbikes," as they reassuringly put it. Since, long as it is, their trail does not include Bolivia, where Che was killed, it does not seem very promising, and indeed probably has more to do with the success of the film *The Motorcycle Diaries*, celebrating the Che thing, than any serious biographical, let alone political, concern. As Chip Mascorro, of US based Moto Discovery, puts it, the Che Trail is just "another marketing hook." Fortunately, Stephen Spielberg is said to be working on a new film rather better researched, using Che's own diary as a guide.

## Useless information
The professional fashion photographer Alberto Diaz Gutierrez took the famous image of Che, "The Heroic Guerrilla," in 1960. Despite its wide merchandising, Che refused to take any fee from it.

In March 1964 Che represented Cuba at a UN conference on trade and development in Geneva. He traveled to Beijing and China, then to Paris, Algeria and Moscow. In December he returned to the UN General Assembly to denounce Western imperialism, singling out the Congo in Africa as an example of the damage that can be caused by Western meddling in the affairs of underdeveloped and newly independent countries.

"We would like to see this Assembly shake itself out of complacency and move forward," he began before continuing excellently:

> We would like to see the committees begin their work and not stop at the first confrontation. Imperialism wants to turn this meeting into a pointless oratorical tournament, instead of solving the serious problems of the world. We must prevent it from doing so... Much progress has been made in the world... But imperialism, particularly US imperialism, has attempted to make the world believe that peaceful coexistence is the exclusive right of the Earth's great powers... It must be clearly established, however, that the government of the United States is not the champion of freedom, but rather the perpetuator of exploitation and oppression against the peoples of the world and against a large part of its own population.

## Risk factor 
Less risky than it used to be.

# 37 No Holiday: **Valle Grande, Bolivia**

*The end of the Che Trail*

### How to get there:
Tour operators in Santa Cruz today offer special "Che Guevara itineraries," but independent revolutionaries can try Bolivia's bus network at least as far as Valle Grande, after which a four wheel drive vehicle is required to reach La Higuera itself, 19 miles (30 kilometers) southwest. During the rains of December through March the roads are impassable.

### What to see
A generation ago, they had him shot in secret, his hands cut off, and his body hidden at the end of Valle Grande airport's runway. But today the Bolivian government is sponsoring an official "La Ruta Che," which allows tourists to follow the "path of Guevara's last march," as they put it, into the village before he was killed.

It was in La Higuera that Che was placed under guard in the schoolhouse, along with other captured rebels. At noon the following day he was executed there. His famous last words are supposed to have been, "Shoot, coward, you are only going to kill one man." One man or not, the army used some four bullets.

Graham Greene said of Che's death: "Was this the end of forlorn hope, the fight against odds?" But in the famous poster, Che promises: "Other hands will carry on the struggle." Regardless, El Comandante's trail ends in Bolivia, in a little hilltop village. A large white bust of the illustrious revolutionary, complete with carefully carved beret with the trademark five pointed star, stands as monument to his otherwise ill received efforts to change this desperately poor land into something better. Devoutly, the villagers have put a wooden cross alongside, as if to ward off evil spirits.

Down a dirt track is a hut, where a small door painted with the words "Museo Historico del Che" houses one of the trail's main attractions, a small treasure trove of Che photos, old newspaper cuttings and other revolutionary memorabilia.

One visiting journalist, Kevin Hall, spoke to Susana Osinaga who was a young nurse on October 9, 1967, when she washed Che's blood off her grocery's wall. The wall today is covered with icons of Jesus, the Virgin Mary, various Roman Catholic saints and a picture of Che. "They say he brings miracles," she explained, which the journalist thought very odd. But then, relief agencies such as Britain's Department for International Development are now spending sums like $600,000 locally to promote what they call "Che Tourism."

Projects include a "Che Eco-Challenge," accommodation for backpackers, and road, sewage and electricity improvements. And that is a kind of miracle, although in La Higuera itself there is still no electricity and the number of families has dwindled to about half of what it was when Che was imprisoned there.

Manuel Cortez, a poor La Higuera farmer who lived next door to the schoolhouse where Guevara was executed has not lost his faith. He also explained his belief to Mr. Hall, "It's like he is alive and with us, like a friend. He is kind of like a Virgin (Mary) for us. We say, 'Che, help us with our work or with this planting,' and it always goes well." That the revolutionary should be resurrected in this popular form is not so odd, "He suffered almost like Our Father, in flesh and bone."

Manuel took his visitor to a special unmarked Che site, where a stream trickled and birds chirruped amongst purple flowers. This is where Che and his band of revolutionaries took their last stand, against 1,800 US-trained and armed Bolivian troops directed by advisors from the CIA.

## Useless information

CIA documents record many other missions in South America, such as the 1964 Panama Canal flag incident; the 1964 coup d'etat in Brazil; the 1964 presidential election in Chile; the 1966 coup in Argentina; the 1968 coups in Peru and Panama and support for insurgencies in Ecuador, Peru, and Venezuela.

Another CIA file includes a debriefing of CIA operative Felix Rodriguez—present in the little schoolhouse that fateful day—that reveals that it was he who informed Che Guevara that he was to be executed.

## Useful information

Today, the Bolivian Highland and Amazon Indians, who make up over two thirds of the country's population, live under the heel of a small European elite, legacy of the colonial era, which, until recently, banned them from town centers, and compelled them to be sprayed with things like DDT "to remove bugs." They are still likely to be banned from restaurants, and on the vast white owned soy farms, they are treated as little better than slave labor. In fact, overall, the population enjoys an average income of rather less than $2 a day, even though Bolivia has South America's second largest gas fields, valued at at least $250 billion. But these were long ago handed over to transnational companies such as British Gas, Respol (of Spain) and Petrobras (from Brazil), on especially generous terms agreed to by Bolivia's famously corrupt politicians. And so now, the energy riches flow smoothly out of the country with scarcely a trickle diverted to national coffers for small things like education or health. Indeed, so little money goes to Bolivia proper, that since the mid-1980s the country became one of the favorite test-beds of the International Monetary Fund for its radical free market policies.

Not for nothing is Bolivia today experiencing a new round of revolutionary ferment, with (at the time of writing) its President forced to step down and the streets of Samaipata paralyzed by strikes and blockades.

## Risk factor

On October 18, 1967, Castro delivered a eulogy for Guevara to a million people assembled in Havana's Plaza de la Revolución.

"They who sing victory over his death are mistaken," Castro proclaimed. "They are mistaken who believe that his death is the defeat of his ideas, the defeat of his tactics, the defeat of his guerrilla concepts... If we want to know how we want our children to be we should say, with all our revolutionary mind and heart: We want them to be like Che."

Yet there is small risk of becoming like Che.

# Oceania

## 38 No Holiday: **South Surin Island, Thailand**

*The island where (nearly) everyone survived the "people-eating sea"*

### How to get there
Fly to Bangkok and take a connecting flight to the Andaman coast. South Surin island is about forty miles offshore.

### What to see
The island is home to the Moken people, who have continued to live in houseboats or in thatched huts on stilts, fishing and diving for sustenance even as their neighbors in mainland Thailand have embraced Western capitalism, and replaced the natural jungles of South East Asia with concrete ones.

For academics, the most interesting thing about the Moken people is that their ability to see underwater is so remarkable that several research reports have been written on it. Better still, they couldn't come up with any reason for it (so more research needs to be done). A second, more interesting, thing is that they believe the sea has a spirit. In fact, they believe that all things have spirits, and have a complex series of rituals, centered around totem poles, to communicate with them. But the intriguing thing about them is that they are still there. This is because they are prepared to follow messages delivered in ways other than via totem poles. For example, when the tide suddenly changes, and rapidly recedes a long way out, they interpret this as the message "run for the high ground of the hills." For the sea has become a "people eating sea," and running from it is the only thing to do.

Thus it was that on December 26, 2004, when the tsunami killed two hundred thousand others,

it caught just one member of the Moken people, a lame elderly man who was too slow to escape on his own and was missed in the rush.

## Useful information

There are a few thousand "water people" living in the region, and most of these are now in regular contact with the mainland and the tourist dollar. The Moken in particular try to keep away from that, but after the tsunami, the Thai government's national park rangers visited and offered to help with rebuilding. So now there are plans to include a souvenir shop for visitors to the now famous island where (nearly) everyone survived.

## Useless information

Sadly, Thailand today is run by an increasingly autocratic and brutal clique of men in suits who worship, of course, only money. The long peaceful history of the "Kingdom of Siam," with its national religion of Buddhism, has become a short story of profit and exploitation. Typical of this is that many of the poor coastal communities destroyed by the tidal wave, like Nam Khem, are being replaced with concrete villas—not for the original inhabitants, but for tourists.

## Risk factor 

People-eating waves are rare, but they do eat a lot of people when they come.

# 39 No Holiday: **Manila, Philippines**

*Quiapo church and its famous outside stalls*

### How to get there
Quiapo church is an old Spanish Catholic one, right in the center of Manila, on a busy road surrounded by side streets full of stalls and little markets. It provides a landmark, within strictly Catholic Philippine society, of hope for women with unwanted pregnancies. It is here that they head for drugs that may enable them to terminate the pregnancy.

### What to see
This of course does not happen in the church itself, although inside there is supposedly a life-size statue of Jesus, said to perform miracles (say solving the problem of an unwanted pregnancy) if you pray to it. Rather, just outside the church are dozens of stalls selling concoctions made of herbs and roots that are supposed to induce menstruation, or the shedding of the womb walls, which leads to abortion. And then there are stalls selling commercial drugs, such as one really intended for ulcers, which was so effective that the local anti-abortion group had it banned from official sale in the country. (As a result it now sells only on stalls like these at the much higher black-market rates.)

### Useless information
It might seem odd that Catholic churches in the Philippines should have this role, but it is also appropriate. After all, it is only because of the political power of the Catholic church in countries like the Philippines that the governments provide no official methods of help with unwanted pregnancies. And in the Philippines, there are a lot of them. The World Health Organization estimates that there are three quarters of a million unsafe abortions there each year, and the country's own Department of Health records 100,000 hospital admissions as by-products of abortifacient drugs or back-street abortion clinics.

### Risk factor
The street markets of the Philippines are quite friendly and safe, although the same evidently cannot be said for even excellently alternative herbal remedies if they are designed to cause abortions.

### ↳ Cultural side trip
The Museum of Mrs. Marcos' Shoes

### How to get there
While you're in the Philippines' capital, browsing the wares of the Quiapo church markets and so on, "just looking" of course, there is a small and relatively safe political tour available in Marikina, of the Shoe Museum and its selection of a few of Mrs. Marcos' 1,600 pairs.

### What to see
The museum contains shoes from famous people, but the selection that is of most political interest is that of Imelda Marcos, sometime beauty queen, Minister of Human Settlements, and of course, devoted wife of the former dictator. Mrs. Marcos opened the museum herself, with these words:

> *This museum is making a subject of notoriety into an object of beauty... They went into my closets looking for skeletons, but thank God, all they found were shoes, beautiful shoes. More than anything, this museum will symbolize the sprit and culture of the*

*Filipino people. Filipinos don't wallow in what is miserable and ugly. They recycle the bad into things of beauty!*

Anyway, Madam Marcos' shoes include some by Givenchy, Chanel and Christian Dior, all size 8 1/2, and most of them worn only once. Many, never at all. Alas the most famous pair, plastic disco sandals with three inch high flashing battery-operated heels, are mysteriously missing, along with an estimated $700 million dollars from the national treasury.

## Background briefing
After Ferdinand and Imelda were toppled from their lofty perch (in 1985), they fled to Hawaii, reluctantly handing in several million dollars worth of jewelry on the way. Back home, in the ever-impoverished Philippines, (the majority of the population lives on less than $2 a day) the new President, Corazon Aquino, ordered Mrs. Marcos's shoes to be put on display to, as she put it, show everyone their "extravagance." As President Aquino, of course, is a woman, we must consider this to be a little bit of cattiness. In any case, it scarcely seems to have worked. People *like* the Shoe Museum. And since the death of her husband in exile, Mrs. Marcos has returned to the Philippines, stood for the Presidency a few times, and even been elected to the Philippines House of Representatives.

## Useless information
Gems the size of golf balls were impounded by US and Philippines customs offices when the Marcoses fled. At first the officials apparently left the gems lying around casually on their desks, as they were so comically large that they assumed they were all glass or plastic fakes.

## Risk factor
Small risk of becoming "Imeldific"—the term coined by Mrs. Marcos herself for gross extravagance.

# 40 No Holiday:
# Bikini Atoll, Marshall Islands ☢ 💣 👑
*Swim in the expanded lagoon of one of the prettiest Pacific Island nuclear test sites*

## How to get there
The Marshall Islands are a string of 29 coral atolls in the Pacific Ocean, just north of the equator. The most famous of them is Bikini Atoll. They were directly administered by the United States for decades, until becoming a nominally sovereign state in 1986 with the signing of the Compact of Free Association with the US. There is a military airstrip on Johnson Island.

## What to see
The Marshall Islands in general, and Bikini Atoll in particular, are famous for their nuclear tests. Half a century later, Bikini Atoll looks again like a tropical paradise, a jewel in the ocean where palm trees framing a blue-green lagoon sway in the breeze. During the tests, many people living on and near Bikini and Eniwetok atolls were forcibly evacuated to other islets. Since these were isolated and barren, the move involved the destruction of their traditional "canoe" culture of fishing and gathering fruit, for a new US one of ration stamps and processed food handouts. For those evacuated, it seemed a great injustice, scarcely made any better by the fact that 239 people were left behind to face blast radiation after the first hydrogen bomb. This was the 1954 BRAVO test—the United States' biggest bang ever. The islanders still remember seeing the

"second sun," an intense fireball a thousand times more powerful than Hiroshima, and the 20-mile-high (32 kilometers) mushroom cloud.

It was followed by hurricane-force winds that stripped the branches and coconuts from the trees. To the delight of the planners, a small fleet of empty ships, including the USS Saratoga and the Nagato, Japanese Admiral Yamamoto's flagship, were engulfed in the nuclear explosion and plunged to the bottom of the lagoon. And a plume of radioactive fallout spread quickly toward Rongelap, an un-evacuated island nearby. A fine powder fell like snow on the islanders (not that they had ever seen snow), and anyone whom it touched later became nauseous and their skin went red and peeled off in layers... In the years that followed, the islanders would measure the health effects in numbers of cancer deaths and birth defects in each family.

The islanders that were evacuated were promised it would be for a short period only. In 1967 some 150 people were indeed returned to Bikini, only to be evacuated again when it was discovered that radioactive Caesium 137 had contaminated everything. Caesium 137 has a half-life of thirty years, so for it to drop to safe levels would take a good few generations.

Tourists can now visit Bikini Atoll, but are warned against swallowing anything. Dive enthusiasts like to swim around the lagoon looking at the sunken US and Japanese aircraft carriers, warships and submarines.

But for the islanders, the novelty has worn off and there is not much to do. On Ejit Island, where most of the Bikini Islanders ended up, bare-foot children play outside shanty homes.

## Useful information

There are many beautiful romantic Pacific Islands, even if when you've seen one coral beach, framed by swaying palms, you've seen them all. But not all Pacific Islands have been used for testing nuclear bombs.

Although there are more than you might imagine. The two thousand plus tests world-wide average out to one test every 9 days for the last fifty years. Indeed, between July 16, 1945 and September 23, 1992, the United States conducted (by official count) 1,054 nuclear tests (not to forget its two nuclear attacks). That works out for the US as the equivalent of one test every 17 days, versus one every 23 days for the Soviet Union; one every 63 days for France, while even plucky little Britain afforded one every 349 days. (In addition, The Valiant aircraft that dropped the first British H-bomb on May 15, 1957 is now in the RAF Museum at Hendon, North London, fully restored in its anti-flash colors.)

The peak testing years included the height of the Cold War, when the major changes in weapon design occurred. During this time, tests were grand operations, involving huge numbers of people. (By the time of the last test series—Dominic I—some 28,000 military and civilian personnel were involved.) Explosions were carried out in all environments: above the ground, under the ground, and underwater, on top of towers, on barges, from balloons, in tunnels and fired by rockets hundreds of miles up into the atmosphere. It is estimated that some 9,259 pounds (4,200 kilos) of plutonium has been discharged into the atmosphere as a result.

The tests took place not so much everywhere in the world, but everywhere in the world remote from strong national governments. For the Western democracies, Pacific Islands with few voters held a particular attraction. The unfortunate Bikini Atoll, Christmas Island, Eniwetok and Johnston Atolls were ideal for the US and UK (when it wasn't respectively New Mexico or Australia), while for France Malden Island and Mororua and Fangataufa Atolls were convenient (when it wasn't Algeria).

The Soviet Union preferred to use the Arctic Islands of Novaya Zemlya (the only currently open Russian test site) and anyway had lots of remote republics to use too (over 400 tests in Kazakhstan, Uzbekistan, Turkmenistan and even a couple in the Ukraine).

Other Marshall Islands tests included the "Kickapoo" series of June 1956 which worked its way through Aomon (Sally) Island, Runit (Yvonne) Island and Rujoru (Pearl) Island all in Enewetak Atoll; followed a month later by Dog Island at Bikini Atoll, then back to Enewetak, and Eberiru (Ruby) Island briefly before "Tewa," which left a crater in the Bikini reef 4,000 feet (1,219 meters) in diameter and 129 feet (39 meters) deep.

On November 1, 1952, the United States detonated the first hydrogen device, code named "Ivy Mike," near the island of Elugelab in the Eniwetok Atoll. It left a crater deeper than the height of the Empire State Building. Then back to Bikini for the test known as "Cherokee" in May 1956. This was the first US airdrop of a thermonuclear weapon and was mainly intended to impress the Soviet Union.

On a technical point, the easiest Doomsday Machine to construct is the cobalt bomb cluster. Each cobalt bomb is an ordinary atomic bomb encased in a jacket of cobalt. When a cobalt bomb explodes, it spreads a huge amount of radiation. A small number of these bombs could extinguish all animal life on earth. (Other than the insects.) The final "Flathead" test of June 1956 at Bikini Atoll lagoon was a test of just such a dirty bomb.

Restoration of the Bikini Atoll was attempted in 1969 but the vegetation was found to be too contaminated and highly toxic. Although, the Pentagon optimistically reported that after the tests, "All of the test islands have been swept clean and Elugelab in particular is completely gone, nothing there but water and what appears to be a deep crater."

## Risk factor

A 1997 study by the National Cancer Institute concluded that due to 80 million person-rads (number of persons x dose in rads) of total exposure, roughly 120,000 extra cases of thyroid cancer can be expected to develop, resulting in some 6,000 deaths. But that risk is the same risk wherever you are, worldwide.

# Australasia

## 41 No Holiday: **Outback Art at Carisbrooke Cattle Station**

*Searching for disappearing Aboriginal art*

### How to get there
Fly to Adelaide, and take the train across the center of Australia. (That's just for fun.) Get out at Alice Springs and fly in a light aircraft to Hughenden.

### What to see
The cave painting of Ardèche and other areas in the Pyrénées on the border of France and Spain are well known—and justly celebrated. The images of hunting wild bison are vibrant and beautiful. And they are old, thousands of years old. But the cave paintings of the Australian aborigines go back thirty or forty thousand years—and this is part of an unbroken tradition. Like the European cave painting, the images are steeped in ritual, but the range is far wider. For the Aboriginal dreamtime encompasses all of time and all of creation.

Our guides are John and Katy, who reveal their finds in their Travel Log, for Sunday July 13, 2003:

> *We start the day, pre-dawn as usual, with brekkie at the excellent Wirrilyerna cattle station, near Boulia. The brekkie was damn good as well. Ahead of us was a 700 kilometer (435 miles) journey to Hughenden, somewhere in the middle of nowhere. The day was broken up by 3 interesting stops. Firstly at a place called Middleton, population 3!! I kid you not. This place seems typical of many outback settlements in that it is gradually disappearing. Middleton's heyday was back in the 20s or something. It was a prosperous farming/mining town and stop off point with a*

*population in the hundreds. Since then it has declined to an elderly couple and their daughter.*

Yeah, yeah, 'nuff said, but what about the flippin' cave art!? John and Katy again:

*Our second stop was at Carisbrooke Cattle Station where we met the owner who gave us a tour down a gorge to show us some Aboriginal art, reckoned to be a few thousand years old. Then we had a barbie and a quick tour around his 50,000 acre station, small by local standards and small enough for one man and his family to run!*

## Useful information
All over Australia are traces of Aboriginal history—or rather traces of traces. For although the art is both unique and extremely historic, the Australian government seems happy to see it replaced by quarries, roads, or just anything really.

The art that is fast disappearing relates to the "Dreamtime," or the Creation Period in Aboriginal traditional history, when the Ancestral Beings formed the land and created the people, plants and animals. The Ancestral Beings rose from below the Earth to become various parts of nature, humans, animals, lakes and streams, rock formations and the sky.

Every corner of Australia has an associated "Dreamtime" story, and often carvings or paintings to record it. Some, such as Murujuga Island on the northwest coast of the Pilbara in Western Australia, are amongst the world's largest and most significant collections of ancient rock-art engravings and date back tens of thousands of years. Here alone, hundreds, if not thousands, of carvings cover the rocky landscape. The area also includes many formations of standing stones, the largest occurrence in Australia.

But since the 1960s the island has been connected to the mainland by an artificial peninsula, and under the care of the Federal government, the art is rapidly disappearing. It is expected to be gone completely within the next 25 years. In its place are being planned some giant gas processing plants with associated port facilities, water-desalination plants and quarries.

As the Australian government has a policy of "assimilating" the Aboriginal people, as it puts it, into the modern world, the caves will need to be assimilated too. Anyway, they tend to remind people that the Aboriginals have been in Australia rather longer than the white people they are now supposed to emulate. So that may be why there are no plans for protecting, let alone celebrating, so many of the world's oldest and most mysterious paintings and carvings.

## ⛝ Disinformation point
Aboriginal art is sometimes only dated from the 1970s, when a teacher at the tiny town of Papunya, about 150 miles (241 kilometers) from Alice Springs, gave some modern acrylic paints to Aboriginals and asked them to paint a mural on the wall in the school. "Fair dinkum, mate." However, this was the start of modern Aboriginal art, which now provides the most positive interface between the various kinds of Australians.

## Risk factor 
So today, if you want to see Aboriginal cave art, you may have to track down the minor finds on private land, such as at Carisbrooke Cattle Station—and endure the rituals (the barbie) first.

# 42 No Holiday: **Murdering Creek, Australia**

*In search of the lost peoples*

## How to get there

Fly to Sydney or Brisbane, then onward to Mudjimba airport in the bustling suburbs of Maroochydore. This sub-tropical region of Queensland once contained vast numbers of globally rare species, but now consists of endless high-rise holiday apartments, stretching along the coast for hundreds of miles. Somewhere along here is where the eco-tourist must stay to fully savor the changes. Behind the coastal fringe of development lie large areas of paperbark trees, scrubby regrowth on land systematically cleared of native plants, animals and peoples.

Travel by four-wheel drive up the David Low Highway and turn off after Coolum towards Eumundi on the Sunshine highway. On your left you will see the road sign for Murdering Creek. Follow this single carriageway to where it ends in the middle of a quiet patch of eucalyptus forest. You must now leave your 4x4 and walk along an unmarked path.

*Note*: You do not need a four-wheel drive for any of this, but people in Australia, as elsewhere, like to think they do.

## What to see

What the guides say:

> Picture an area of sweeping shiny beaches bordered by beautiful blue water. Picture majestic mountain ranges and refreshing radiant rainforest. Picture scenic drives along ridges and through valleys, overlooking coastal panoramas and vast fruit plantations. Picture tranquil hillside villages famous for local arts and crafts. Picture fun filled family activities and attractions. Picture perfect weather with winter temperatures a warm 25 degrees Celsius (77 degrees Fahrenheit). Aim for action with abseiling, skydiving or sea kayaking. Surf, swim, scuba dive or sail to your heart's content. Tee off on some of Australia's top golf courses. Indulge in the finest freshwater and saltwater fishing and bushwalk through national parks. Steep yourself in the region's rich history...

And this last is what we must do. However, the early history of Australian settlement is surprisingly sparse, given that it is well within the era of publishing and newspapers. In fact, often the first clue to a local area's true history, as opposed to its recently imagined one, is the legacy of place names. So it is that the official history of the Sunshine Coast, with its tales of heroic early settlement, can still offer clues of another and darker story of now vanished peoples.

The Sunshine Coast is now a chain of luxurious holiday resorts, in the prosperous Maroochy region of what is now southeast Queensland, but not so long ago it was still the northern frontier of the colonies in New South Wales, and home to some of the most friendly and accepting Aboriginal tribes. The two modern settlements of Eumundi and Obi Obi are named after those friendly Aboriginals. And indeed many Aboriginal names are still retained for the towns, the hills and the creeks.

There are still some native people in Australia, despite an official policy of assimilation that the Yorta Yorta tribe challenged in court as tantamount to genocide (and included, for instance, the forcible adoption of indigenous children by white parents). But you won't find too many of them in southeast Queensland, for 40,000 years perhaps the heartland of all the ancient Aboriginal peoples. There isn't even an Aboriginals shop in central Brisbane, although some artists, such as the multi-facetted Terry Saleh, can be tracked down on the outskirts. But Terry is not a member of the Gubbi Gubbi people. For them, we must return to the clues of the place names.

Maroochy itself is an Aboriginal word meaning "red bill" after the red bill of the black swan that lives along its river. And Murdering Creek lies between Mount Coolum and Peregian, both areas accepting and recording the original inhabitants' terminology. Coolum, is from Gulum or Kulum meaning "blunt" and reflects the shape of the mountain, while Peregian comes from the Mangrove seedpods found along the waterways there. But "Murdering Creek" is a new name, and one not only reflecting recent history, but also condemning it. In many other areas of Australia, in contrast, similar deeds have been either deliberately forgotten—or worse, repackaged and celebrated.

Fortunately, our particular area is part of the Lake Weyba reserve and as we leave the coastal strip, soon the sounds of the forest return and you could almost imagine you are in pre-European Australia. The creek itself is dark with the characteristic blood red color of the soils, and the paperbark trees peel their white skins slowly giving a haunted and desolate effect.

## Background briefing
Every November, in Australia, there is a "National Sorry Day," and there is indeed much to be sorry about. Half of all indigenous males do not live to see the age of 46. Native peoples suffer 12 times the rate of infectious diseases than the settlers. Babies born to indigenous parents are four times more likely to die than those born to whites. 93 percent, [i.e. almost the entire native population] suffer from hearing defects due to lack of primary health care. Yet, health funding for Aboriginals is almost non-existent. Communities have little or no access to doctors, medical advice or medicine. Resource deals struck between indigenous peoples and their governments in Australia contrast sharply with those in New Zealand, Canada and the United States. The greatest and most disgraceful contrast is: there aren't any deals. Australia's indigenous people remain without recognition of their existence, let alone their rights.

## Useful information
For every Australian who's "sorry" there seem to be at least two (including a member of Australia's parliament) who aren't. The latest best-seller down-under is a political tract euphemistically styled as a history, claiming that the genocide of the indigenous peoples never occurred, and that there were never any settlement victims to feel sorry for.

But there are other sources. Mr. Murdoch's antipodean newspaper and television networks do not promote them, but they are at least based on facts. A Mr. Bull wrote one such account relating to Murdering Creek less than a century after the event, (that is in 1950) but it was published as a pamphlet only in 1982. Bull lived locally and had contact with people who would have been around at the time of the massacre. The immediate background to the event was several massacres, the killings of Murries at Teewah beach, and the "clearing" of the Dawson Valley where other Murries had been fighting a sort of guerila war against the white invasion of the grasslands. It seems that the Gubbi Gubbi people were effectively penned up in the marshy and less productive land of Lake Weyba by Mount Emu, after being forcibly evicted from their traditional and more productive lands.

Now let Mr. Bull retell the murderous story:

> ... A party of eight men was organized by a policeman and the manager of the station... one of the party was to go well around the eastern part of the lake with a

*swag on his back and billy in his hand. When well around he was to enter the water and walk in the direction of the creek fairly close to the edge, but far enough out to attract the attention of the blacks. On a nice high-level piece of ground at the junction of Lake Weyba and Weyba Creek there was always a large number of blacks camped.*

*... As soon as he entered the lake they saw him. Many of them got into their canoes and came towards him, but in front of him. He pretended not to see them at first until they got fairly near to him... When the correct distance between them was reached he pretended to see them for the first time and he jerked his body every step to make the blacks believe he was hurrying. When he got opposite the creek he left the water and went up the creek past the other seven men [lying] in ambush with guns fully loaded. The blacks followed "swaggy." When the last black got opposite the waiting men, all seven opened fire. Most were killed outright, some badly wounded. As those not shot turned and ran for the lake another [round] was fired at them and the murder, which was a little carnage, was completed. I never heard how many were murdered, but I was well acquainted with some of them who lived and reared their families in Tewantin. I never heard the year the murder took place, but that is the story of how Murdering Creek got its name.*

There was never any police investigation of the massacre. Indeed, the first prosecution of a white for killing a native Australian was not until 1883, long after the "indigenocide" proper had finished. The killers instead returned to their homes in nearby Tewantin, and prospered. You can see their triumph now in the plantations, the villas and the golf courses.

### Risk factor

Low, but you might be bitten by one of Australia's deadly spiders or snakes. For travelers with darker skin, additional risk of being denied hotel accommodation or taxi travel.

# 43 No Holiday: **Auckland, Aotearoa**

*A dinghy ride around Auckland Harbour*

### How to get there

Fly direct to Auckland, stay at the Kingsgate Hyatt and rent a rubber dinghy.

On the return trip, use a boat to get to Noumea, scuttle this in the Coral Sea, and board a French nuclear submarine to get back to Tahiti, where you can catch onward flights to Paris.

### What to see

New Zealand, or Aotearoa as it should properly be called nowadays, is a land of snowy mountains, crystal lakes and steamy geysers, all still largely untouched by the modern world. It used to have a reputation as being rather dull, but since the blockbuster *Lord of the Rings* trilogy was shot there, it has managed to cast off some of that drizzly character.

Nonetheless, it *is* generally cold and wet, and No Holidaymakers will need good quality waterproof jackets and—for the full option—wetsuits. While at the Hyatt, you may want to ask to stay in the same room used by Colonel Louis-Pierre Dillais (alias Jean-Louis Dormand, alias Head of Operation "Satanic"). This has a fine view of the harbor.

And, it's not there now, but back in 1995, the view would have included the Greenpeace protest boat, Rainbow Warrior. This former fishing trawler, with its colorful rainbow stripes, was docked here as part of a series of protests against the testing of nuclear weapons by France in Polynesia. (Nowadays it lies at the bottom of the ocean acting as an artificial reef.)

But what is there to see in Auckland Harbour today? Not much, although some tourists climb the 1950s bridge, and there is maritime museum, which has a machine to make the floor sway, so maybe a dinghy ride would be fun after all. It is best done in the early evening, after dark. The important thing is not to see things, but to not be seen.

The route is across the grey, misty harbor from Mechanics Bay to Marsden Wharf. It's about a 1.2-mile (1.9-kilometers) paddle, so you may (and this is fully in keeping with the original trip made by French secret agents Jacques Camurier and Alain Tonel) use a motor until the last few hundred feet. Those set on a full-scale reconstruction of the experience, will at this point select a small boat to dive under and—having obtained the necessary government approvals—place two explosive charges against the hull. Then drive back across the harbor and watch the fireworks!

### Useful information
The French government spent a lot of time planning and rehearsing "Operation Satanic" (curious choice!) at their Aspretto base in Corsica, France. They thought the trip needed at least 13 secret agents, including Christine Cabon, alias Frederique Bonlieu, who worked full-time for the DGSE in Paris and at least part-time for Greenpeace and fed information about the activities of the Rainbow Warrior home to headquarters. The rowboat and motor were flown out from Britain, the bombs and diving equipment came from Noumea, and the secret agents came from all over. Posing variously as tourists on a mid-winter diving voyage or Swiss tourists on their honeymoon, they took elaborate observation of the harbor for several weeks, including, no doubt, several dinghy rides.

After the first bomb went off under the Rainbow Warrior, the little boat immediately began to sink, but those onboard managed to scramble ashore. After all, most of Greenpeace is staffed by ex-commandos, and many of them are also secret agents. So, for example, as well as the French DGSE agent, there was an ASIS agent from Australia, and such people are good at getting out of sinking boats. Unfortunately there was also one environmentalist, Fernando

Pereira, a Portuguese photographer who was there just to film the protests for the Amsterdam daily *De Waarheidalong*. He bravely, but unwisely, stayed on the boat to try to save his cameras and films. The second bomb probably killed him outright: it blew a hole the size of a garage door in the side of the hull right by his cabin.

## ⌖ Disinformation point

The thinking behind the French operation in New Zealand is still unclear. New Zealand had annoyed both France and—yes!—America for its anti-nuclear stance and opposition to nuclear testing in the Pacific. An official French "disinformation" inquiry, while admitting French agents were involved, grandly denied the government had ordered it. The buck did not reach, let alone stop at the Elysée Palace. However, further revelations did oblige Defense Minister Charles Hernu to resign and the DGSE chief, Admiral Pierre Lacoste, was eventually dismissed.

The scandal, which the French press quaintly dubbed "Underwatergate," damaged France's image around the world, but Greenpeace's then somewhat flagging fortunes and finances soared.

## Risk factor

There is little risk for environmentalists in visiting Auckland Harbour. Even those traveling on false passports and carrying bombs can offer the New Zealand police a perfectly good explanation, notably, that you are there as part of a conspiracy to blow up a boatload of civilians and are acting for a foreign power. You will then, like the French secret service operatives, be flown home business class.

**Trips 44-60**

# Africa

## 44 No Holiday: **Madagascar**

*Town somewhere in Madagascar*

### How to get there

Fly to the capital, Antananarivo. This was founded as a fortress in the early 17ᵗʰ century by the Merina tribe. Madagascar is about the size of France (its former colonial ruler) and Belgium put together, but as there are hardly any proper roads or modern buildings outside the capital, getting around is both much more difficult and much easier, as there are only a few places it is possible to go. Nonetheless, a local guide is essential, which is fine if you hire a taxi driver on arrival. As one relic of French colonialism, the taxis are all 2CVs, the cheap little Citroen cars with the side windows that flop up whenever you go over a bump. (In fact, it's easier to leave the windows open.)

### What to see

No one remembers Madagascar. Nature herself forgot the island, allowing most of the animals and plants there to develop quite differently from the rest of the world. Here there are the forests of baobab, the strange desert tolerant trees that appear to be growing upside down, huge trunks with small branches like roots pointing to the sky—and hardly any leaves. Then there's the lemurs, a bit like monkeys, whose name means "nocturnal spirit," and the last known home of the most famous bird of them all, the dodo. Famous because it is extinct. Not many people remember that the dodo came from Madagascar, and not many know about all the other unique and vanishing species of the island, slowly being turned into a red desert by the usual international interests of "clearfell logging" followed by cattle ranches.

Nor does Madagascar feature much in the history of slavery, although it was one of the major sources of slaves, as the dominant tribes of the island captured and sold their countrymen to the European traders. It was in 1896, fed up with resistance to their activities, that France declared Madagascar a French colony and deported the Queen and Prime Minister, first of all to the island of Reunion, and then to Algeria. A secret society dedicated to re-affirming Madagascar's own cultural identity was formed in 1913, calling itself the "Iron and Stone Ramification" and this was brutally suppressed. But resentment took on a more serious militant form in 1947, when a couple of hundred demobilized Madagascan soldiers, fresh from helping to liberate Europe, (where General de Gaulle decreed they should not be permitted to sully the parade through Paris on Victory day) led several thousand spear-brandishing Madagascans Zimbabwe-style in attacks on the settlers and their farms and businesses; and indeed perhaps a hundred Europeans were killed. But the uprising failed to attract widespread support as most of the islanders were pacifists by nature.

Nonetheless, the newly-returned-to-democracy French responded with 30,000 troops, aerial and offshore bombardments, mass arrests and torture, and arbitrary executions. The Army estimated that they killed about 100,000 people, although no one seems to have counted very carefully.

But nor yet are their victims completely forgotten. Scattered around the country there are a number of simple memorials to the "pacification."

This being Africa, and Africa being very poor, the memorials are made of cheap concrete blocks, with scrap iron adornments sticking out. One in particular consists of three tall concrete blocks on a concrete pedestal painted green with "29 Marsa 1949" on it. Ironically enough this color is technically called "French Court": the color used traditionally on the walls and wood paneling in chateaux.

As a visitor notes in their weblog: "In 1947 this town (whose name I cannot remember) was the site of a massacre."

## Useless information
In 1954, six of the original rebels were sentenced to death, but pardoned. In 1960, they became a part of the first independent government of Madagascar.

Albert Camus wrote soon afterwards:

> If the French calmly take on board methods sometimes used by some of their compatriots against the Algerians or the Malagasies, it is because they live, quite unconsciously, in the certainty that they are in some way superior to these peoples, and that the choice of the means used to reflect this superiority is of little importance.

## ♡ Disinformation point
Later on, it emerged that the trigger for the rebellion came from an underground political group covertly run by the British, aiming to subvert the French. Naturally it was the Malagasies (the Madagascans) who paid the price.

## Risk factor 🖼
Some risk of getting lost.

# 45 No Holiday: **Manzini, Swaziland** 🐴 🏛

*The Royal Palaces and the Peoples' Beehives*

## How to get there
Swaziland is a former British colony of 1.1 million people, squashed between South Africa and Mozambique. The easiest way to get there is to travel via South Africa.

## What to see
Royal Palaces are always popular with tourists, and Swaziland has quite a few, even if they're not all that fancy, to be honest. But then Swaziland is one of the world's poorest countries, with a quarter of its one million citizens relying on food aid. So that should be taken into account before writing the buildings off as uninteresting. Actually, more interesting then the Royal Palaces are the traditional and everyday homes of many Swazilanders, the curious beehive woven huts. These strange houses look a little like igloos in that they are round like half domes, with no windows, just a low down door that it is necessary to crawl through to enter.

## Useless information
So, let us be more positive. Since often the only money that stays in Africa is what the government officers and their relatives spend there (rather than dump in their offshore bank accounts), the sort of government spending demonstrated by the ruler of Swaziland, King Mswati III is most encouraging. In the last few years he's spent $700,000 on eight Mercedes cars with the usual conveniences such as cocktail fridges and air-conditioning (and gold plated number plates) all of which need washing (jobs for locals) particularly as Swaziland has almost no paved roads. Africa's last not-quite-absolute monarch has built and maintained not one but thirteen "Royal Places" if not quite "Royal Palaces" (one for each of his wives). Within Swaziland, the male citizens admire him for his virility, although he has some way to go before he emulates his late father, who boasted 99 brides. Not entirely coincidentally, Swaziland has been hard-hit like many African countries by the AIDS/HIV virus, with two out of every five adults infected with it. (The continent's second worst figures.)

In 2004 the international press picked up the story in the Swaziland newspapers of the King's latest request to the country's parliament for $15 million. Purchased in time for Christmas that same year, a Daimler-Chrysler car equipped not only with television but more importantly a DVD player, refrigerator and solid silver champagne service is truly a sight worth seeing. [📷] Even though much of the money spent on the building and upkeep of those Royal Palaces eventually goes to Swazilanders, or maybe Filipinos. Poor people anyway.

Alas, the country receives a mere $20 million dollars or so of aid a year, which is barely enough to pay for the King's needs. In 2003 he had to abandon plans for a $30 million executive jet.

## Risk factor 💥
Commentators warn small-mindedly of local people being covered in dust as the King's convoy sweeps elegantly past.

# 46 No Holiday: **Molapo, Botswana**

*Hunting the Basarwa in the Kalahari*

## How to get there
Rent a jeep in Swaziland to get you due west to Botswana and the Central Kalahari Game reserve. (It's over 600 miles (967 kilometers), so take extra gas and water).

## What to see
The Kalahari Game reserve is one of Africa's most famous, and celebrated. Its rolling swathes of grasses and brightly colored wild flowers are home to herds of antelope preyed on by jackals and hyenas. Tourists come here to stay in the lodges and have carefully sanitized hunts for rare animals. So far, so conventional. Our holiday, however, is a bit different. It involves hunting for the rare Basarwa people. They are a small but resilient race, skilled at surviving in near desert conditions. For 40,000 years, the "Bushmen" have roamed the Kalahari, living off the animals, as well as harvesting the rich supply of berries and plant roots that grow there. But in recent years they have become increasingly hard to find. In Molapo, for instance, at the heart of the Kalahari, where once over 1,000 of them lived; by 2004 less than sixty remained. It seemed that a new kind of predator had been active in the park. And indeed, it turns out to be the case. It is the Botswana government that has been around and busy, systematically shutting schools and health clinics, cutting off water supplies and terminating social security payments. According to one observer from the BBC, concrete has been poured down the Bushmen's desert wells, and expulsions have been accompanied by beatings and torture. All in an effort to clear the area of the stubborn Basarwa.

## Useful information
The Kalahari Game reserve was made a national park in 1961, in part to protect the Basarwa or "San" people's traditional way of life. Of Botswana's 1.6 million people, there are about 60,000 Basarwa, who have a distinct appearance, with lighter skins, high cheekbones and their own musical language, involving complicated clicking sounds. But President Festus Mogae considers them a "stone-age people" with no place in modern Botswana. And if you say different, he'll have you thrown out of the country or put in prison.

Now almost all of the Basarwa live outside the National Park, in shanty towns dominated by beer halls. The government says they were persuaded to move out in order to take part in "modern economic activities." It thought that their hunting was a threat to the game in the park, which is there to be hunted by fee-paying tourists instead. And then there are the diamonds...

## Risk factor
Low, although a white hunter might shoot you. Or a De Beers security guard...

# 47 No Holiday: **Angola**

*The site of the Battle of Cuito Cuanavale*

## How to get there
Carry on in the Jeep, heading due northwest across the Angolan border.

## What to see
It's not very famous at all, and not many people go to visit it. But it was here in the scrublands adjoining this small Angolan town that Angolan forces alongside 50,000 Cuban troops, under El Commandante (Che Guevara), decisively defeated the South African army.

It was Africa's greatest battle since El Alamein, involving tanks and fighter planes, and on it appeared (at least) to hinge the future of the continent. Certainly, it resulted in the South African withdrawal from Angola and Namibia.

Castro was aware that behind South Africa stood the United States and Britain. The battle appeared to have strategic implications, ensuring the survival of black governments in these countries, along with that of Mozambique, and that the days of apartheid South Africa would be numbered.

As Che put it: "Let the flag under which we fight be the sacred cause of benefiting all humanity, so that to die under the colors of Vietnam, Venezuela, Guatemala, Laos, Guinea, Colombia, Bolivia, Brazil... is equally glorious and desirable for an American, an Asian, an African and even a European."

Alas, Angola remains one of the world's poorest countries, and conditions for the black people of Mozambique and Namibia are scarcely any better. But it is still an interesting historical site.

## Useless information
For most of the 20th century, swathes of Southern Africa were part of tiny Portugal's imperial circle, which included not only Angola but also Mozambique and Guinea-Bissau. At its peak, 50,000 Portuguese troops were active in Angola alone. And in due course, Portugal lost more soldiers in her African wars than the US would lose in Vietnam. But in 1974 Portugal's right-wing dictatorship collapsed and the new socialist government decided to withdraw immediately, leaving Angola's diamonds and oil for others to fight over.

During the 1980s, apartheid in South Africa came under increasing attack from African nationalist movements such as the African National Congress. One response was the Total Onslaught Strategy under P.W. Botha. As well as creating secret pacts and alliances with both friendly regimes and bandit forces, South African commandos were sent to carry the war to wherever the ANC was to be found: Matola, Lesotho, Swaziland, for example. But most of all, to Angola. A full-scale invasion was launched into this unfortunate land, reducing towns like Ondjiva, Ondangwa and others to sticks poking up out of rubble.

In the north, the independent African revolutionaries of UNITA (ideological opponents to the other communist liberation movements) were co-opted to help collapse the Angolan government. Angola seems to be irredeemably corrupt, and Maoist one-party ideologies do not seem to have stopped its leaders from salting away a slice of the country's oil and diamond riches in partnership with the usual Western multinationals. But more to the point was that in 1964, during a mass meeting of African liberation movements at Dar-es-Salaam, Tanzania, the leader of UNITA, Jonas Savimbi, publicly disagreed with our hero, Che "El Commandante" Guevara. The problem was Che wanted African revolutionaries to use Cuban methods, rather than African ones, which were more relevant, Savimbi claimed. Certainly, UNITA would later show itself to better able even than the South African forces to abduct villagers, butcher infants and massacre convoys of civilians. They also burnt fields and killed cattle, and mutilated corpses as part of psychological warfare.

After a particularly bloody period of such acts, Savimbi boasted to the world press that soon he would, "eat lunch in Malange" and shortly afterwards (allowing for digestion perhaps) "declare independence."

But that bravado was before the Battle of Cuito Cuanavale.

### Background briefing
In the south of Angola, in their eagerness to reach the capital Luanda, the Angolan Army had surrounded the South African Army with its elite Cuban battalions. Six thousand troops were encircled near the little town of Cuito Cuanavale and threatened with total annihilation. And that would not go down well with the South African voters. A flurry of diplomatic negotiations between the countries really running things in the region—the South Africans and the US on one side and the Russians and Cubans on the other—took place. The result was the so-called "14-Points Agreement." In return for the safe passage of the encircled white troops in Cuito, the South Africans would allow elections leading to Namibian independence. Other provisions committed all the countries to cease harboring rebel forces and to respect each other's territorial integrity.

Nelson Mandela himself later acknowledged the debt of South African majority people to Cuba when he embraced Fidel at his presidential inauguration.

### Risk factor
Since the death of Jonas Savimbi in 2002, the countryside has been a lot quieter. And the new government of South Africa doesn't invade much either. So that's something.


# 48 No Holiday: **Morogoro, Tanzania**

*A visit to a shoe factory*

### How to get there
Fly back to Africa's Eastern coast and Dar-es-Salaam. Morogoro is about 93 miles (150 kilometers) back west again, but is well worth the trouble.

*What to see*
The factory, an Italian initiative funded in 1980 partly by the World Bank, is one of the biggest shoe factories—not only in Tanzania, not only in Africa—but in the world! It cost more than $30 million to build. Such international generosity! Such largesse!

*Useful information*
Unfortunately, Tanzania does not have suitable leather to make the shoes, nor suitable shoe designers, nor suitable shoe markets. So the factory, at its peak, only managed to reach 4 percent of its operating capacity, at which rate it was losing $400,000 each year it was kept

open. In any event, it ran for ten years before the funds ran out, in 1990. So today, the factory is an elephant graveyard (not many shoes to see).

## Useless information

But who gives all this aid? Between 1984 and 2003, the self-styled G7 of the "World's most powerful economies" dispensed some $400 odd billion to Africa, the largest chunk of it from the European Union, which is in fact more than two and a half times more generous than the United States in terms of international aid. That might be a plus point for the US, though. As the American development economist, Thomas Dichter, wrote in a report for the South African Institute of International Affairs, the best thing for improving life for Africans would not be for Mr. Blair (the globe-trotting UK Prime Minster of the 1990s and alas early 21$^{st}$ century too) *et al* to promise to double aid, but rather to halve it. And after they'd done that, they should send more than half the experts home, and close down or shrink most of the hundreds of organizations in the "development aid business."

## Risk factor

Very dangerous for investors.

# 49 No Holiday: **Lake Turkana, Kenya**

*The Fish Freezing Plant in the middle of the desert*

## How to get there

The Lake is about nine hours by bus from Nairobi. Nicknamed the "Jade Sea," it is the largest volcanic lake in the world. Crocodiles and hippos play in the shallows (although not normally together.)

## What to see

Lake Turkana is in the middle of a desert, so it might seem an odd place for a freezer plant. Not to the Norwegians though. In 1981 they provided money and (Norwegian) experts for a huge fish-processing factory, just like the ones so useful back home in Norway. With temperatures in Kenya regularly exceeding 100 degrees Fahrenheit (38 degrees Celsius), diesel powered generators were installed to provide energy for maintaining freezing conditions, and even if the cost of this exceeded the income from the fish, it was not allowed to be an insurmountable obstacle. Alas, from time to time, Lake Turkana also shrinks as rainfall fluctuations reduce the inflow of water. A drought such as this during the mid 1980s killed off all the fish.

## Useless information

The nomadic herders who where brought in to work at this plant viewed fishing as a low status profession, suitable only for those incompetent at herding. This kind of typically African "irrational" local tradition is often said to be a big problem in development projects. However, since after the plant closed, the herders were left worse off than before (now totally dependent on outside aid) maybe the irrationality was not all on one side.

## Risk factor

Dodgy job security.

# 50 No Holiday: **Addis Ababa, Ethiopia**

*The International Airport, Addis Ababa*

### How to get there
Fly straight there. Bole International Airport is located 5 miles (8 kilometers) southeast of Addis Ababa, Ethiopia. It is the larger of the two international airports located in Ethiopia, the second being the Lideta Airport, which is located to the southwest of the capital.

### What to see
This is a magnificently modern, gleaming glass and steel structure stuffed full of fashionable boutiques selling the usual airport necessities like silk ties and Belgian chocolates. But they are necessities if you want to attract Western experts! And even as Bob Geldof's "Band Aid" alerted the world to the tragic images of Ethiopian children dying in the parched fields, in Addis Ababa, the restaurants were full of the aid experts and development professionals wining and dining the Ethiopian ruling class. Such people, unlike No Holidaymakers, do not travel rough.

In 2001, an expansion plan was announced for the airport at a cost of $130 million. This involved the construction of a new runway, as well as five taxiways linking the new runway to the existing runway and various practical safety improvements. It also involved the construction of a new steel structure to house the airport terminal, a parking garage, a shopping complex and restaurants. This made up about two-thirds of the total bill of $75 million with a British firm, Fitchner, in charge of the project management and a Kuwaiti company as the contractor.

The new terminal is capable of handling six to seven million passengers each year, although at the moment the airport receives only about one twelfth as many as that. This is comfortably more even than the number of international development experts expected.

Today the ultra-modern glass structure dominates the skyline of the area. The "shining glass structure is an architectural and artistic masterpiece, functional and beautiful at the same time," according to its owners. On the other hand, the existing terminal, which had served customers very well for years, is now relegated to serving domestic flights.

### Useful information
Ethiopia is a country of 72 million people, with a Gross National Product so small that it works out at about 40 cents per person, per day. Not of course that it is distributed equally—there are plenty of rich people in Ethiopia, quite a lot of money for waging wars against its even poorer neighbor, Eritrea—and even a bit for its airport.

Remarkably, ever since the 1980s when Band Aid highlighted the plight of the 60 million or so rural Ethiopians (who make up five out of every six of the population) aid has made up a good third of the country's income. And not all of it goes straight back to the donors in the form of arms deals! Apart from the essential proportion carefully saved in offshore bank accounts for the use of the quintessentially African "socialist" ruling elite and their relatives, there has been cash for a few grand, national projects, like the airport. (Financing for these facilities has come through low interest loans from a variety of donors, the largest being Kuwait and the African Development Bank.)

The authorities hoped that the expansion of the airport would turn Bole into the aviation capital of Africa. The provision of easy international connections is a key element in the ambition of Addis Ababa to become the African hub of a global network. Good air connections are believed to be essential in attracting business to the capital.

## Useless information

At the time of Band Aid and the famine, Ethiopia was implausibly, but formally, under a Maoist dictatorship (Mengistu Haile Mariam's), the practical sign of which was that all the land was nationalized and the channeling of all resources into armaments for the conquest of Eritrea was seen as the main national requirement. The Maoism never extended to industrialization strategies, nor to population control and certainly not to any rural initiatives such as basic educational and health care.

Nowadays the country is officially more democratic and not at all Maoist, but funnily enough the government still owns all the land and seems to have a hand (or a family member) in all the major businesses. So the money that is poured into Ethiopia for infrastructure by the donors continues to flow through the government's hands and then (slightly reduced of course) on to the usual benefactors: transnational companies and arms dealers.

The fact that the government owns all the land is, however, the main explanation both for the change of Ethiopia's once fertile lands into semi-arid desert and the collapse of food production in the country.

When Band Aid shut itself down, it had officially raised $144,124,694, or just about the same amount of money as the government wanted for the new airport.

## Let's be positive about this

If the Band Aid type donations were politically naive, and inadvertently supported the war on Eritrea, at least many of the projects the money was spent on, being ground level crisis intervention such as emergency feeding and emergency health, were valuable—and certainly would not have been financed otherwise.

And support for the airport comes from Amr Mohammed Al-Faisal, writing about the project for *Arab News* on July 11, 2004:

> *When I visited Addis Ababa last week, I was pleasantly surprised to see how nice it was. The city has wide, well paved, tree-lined avenues and comfortable first-class hotels. Although it is a poor city, the people there have done well with the meager resources they have available. An example of this is Addis Ababa Airport where a new terminal has just been completed. The new building is very beautiful and well designed, and cost, I was told, less than $100 million. The new terminal at Karachi airport, Pakistan, which cost about $250 million, gave me the same impression—a lot can be done on a modest budget. These projects contrast sharply with our airport here in Jeddah, which cost more than $4 billion 20 years ago but is badly designed. It will cost another fortune to renovate it.*

## ↳ Ethiopian side trip:

The Political Monuments of Addis Ababa

## How to get there

But whilst visiting Bole International Airport—why not take a side trip to see some of Ethiopia? The airport is 3 miles (5 kilometers) from the city center and a free shuttle bus runs into the city. It is a very political capital, with much for the No Holidaymaker to see.

## What to see

The town itself boasts numerous patriotic statues and memorials of a vaguely political nature. Abune Petros Statue at Arada, marks the spot where the Ethiopian patriarch courageously faced the firing squad in defiance of the fascists, while The Freedom Tower at Arat Kilo, and the Martyr's Statue at Sidist Killo commemorate the victories of Ethiopia against both the genocide committed by the Italians and the political treachery of the British.

Piquantly perhaps, the Menelik Monument, near St. George's cathedral, is intended to recall the battle of Adwa in 1896 where Africa was supposed to have triumphed over colonialism. Not to forget, the Tiglachin Monument, which proudly commemorates the war against Somalia.

Revolutionary parades are held every September in a natural amphitheatre nearby to mark the 1974 communist revolution. Portraits of Marx, Lenin, "Angels," and Ethiopia's own Comrade Mengistu used to adorn the square, but have now sadly gone.

The infamous Haile Selassie's Grand Palace is located north east of Churchill Avenue at the end of Colsen Street, whilst his second residence, Jubilee Palace, is on Menelik Avenue, just near the Ghion Hotel, celebrated for its Italian style coffee. But Haile Selassie's palaces are simple stuff compared to the headquarters of the UN Economic Commission for Africa. Africa Hall is a magnificent building with huge stained glass windows depicting the suffering of the people of Africa. It is said to be a symbol of African independence and revival, just like the thermal springs to the west of it. Alas, these springs are now diverted to a private bathing complex.

Another, as the Ethiopian tourist board puts it, "major attraction" is the old Imperial Lion Zoo, where the last few Ethiopian lions can be seen waiting out their twilight days.

### Useful information
The name "Addis Ababa" means "new flower," and Addis is a flower that grows very high, at 7,900 feet above sea level in the Entoto Mountains. At 8,000 feet (2,440 meters), Addis Ababa is the third highest capital in the world. Ethiopia used to have no less than six capitals at six different locations, with King Menelik moving between them as available trees and hence fuel wood became exhausted. Addis itself was on the point of being abandoned when fast-growing eucalyptus trees were introduced from Australia.

Addis Ababa strives to be an administrative center not only for Ethiopia but also for the whole of Africa. The headquarters of the UN Economic Commission for Africa was established here in 1958 and is the base for the Organization of African Unity's (OAU's) secretariat.

Administration-wise, Ethiopians have their own methods though. For example, very few streets have names in Addis Ababa, and those that do may not be the same as either the ones on the map or the ones people use. "Africa Avenue," for instance, on the map is popularly known as "Bole Road," and "Has Biru Avenue" as "Debre Zeit Road." Likewise, people in Ethiopia use a different calendar from most of the rest of the world, the Julian calendar (which has thirteen months, 12 of 30 days and one of just five!) rather than the more usual Gregorian one, with the Ethiopians running about seven years behind. This means that when it is 2006 in Europe, it is 1999 in Ethiopia.

# 51 No Holiday: **Ugoli, Nigeria**

*The Ajaokuta Steel Mill*

## How to get there
Fly across the heart of the Dark Continent to its own small airport, near Ugoli, changing at Lagos.

## What to see
The plant is such a magnificent project that once built, it cost an extraordinary $40 million a year just to mothball, which is exactly what the government did. It never produced any steel; if it had, the Western countries would have been obliged to keep it out of their markets by tariffs anyway.

With an average income of less than one dollar a day, many Nigerians may be desperately poor, but the country itself is a huge and wealthy land in terms of mineral and energy resources. So a steel mill must have seemed like a good idea. Certainly the government was pleased to receive some $4 billion dollars to build one. And the ever-generous donors did not seem too bothered that nearly half of the cash went to the circle of cronies surrounding the country's then dictator, Sani Abacha. Not that that had anything to do with the important modernization deals (with the Western transnationals over concessions to exploit the oil fields, the mineral concessions, the arms deals and so on), which were being all signed up.

## Background briefing
Ever since oil was originally found in the Niger delta in the 1950s and in more recent years in offshore fields, Africa's largest country has been awash in money. Yet the 100 billion barrels of oil produced so far have provided only about 50 cents a year in benefit for each of the country's 115 million citizens. But that figure does not include the rather more impressive sum—no less than $350 billion—shared among just a few of the Nigerian elite, oil dollars carefully salted away in offshore accounts.

Coincidentally, that's almost as much money as the whole of sub-Saharan Africa received in "aid" over the last 40 years. The British government has led the campaign to have more aid money directed at Nigeria, successfully negotiating in 2005 an additional $30 billion or so of debt relief, most of which, as usual, goes to relieve the Western banks.

## Useless information
The total spent worldwide on weapons rose above $1 trillion in 2004, the first time since the height of the Cold War. A small, but not inconsequential, part of that trade consists of British arms sales to the impoverished and not-so-impoverished countries of Africa. Of the latter, Nigeria has always been a good friend of the UK, ordering in 2004, for instance, £93 million worth of armored vehicles and large caliber artillery. Other arms deals that year took the UK above the £1.76 billion a year mark and included useful things like:

- £53 million received from Angola, for armored cars.

- Licenses for military exports granted to Eritrea, Ethiopia, Algeria, Sudan, Zambia, Uganda, Malawi, Namibia and Somalia.

- £201 million from South Africa for components needed for a high-tech air force.

## Risk factor

It is not just governments and large multinationals that can lose money in Nigeria. In fact, individuals can too, and surprisingly large numbers have, traveling starry-eyed to its capital, Lagos, to complete transactions, in which they will receive (no strings attached!) large "unclaimed funds" of deceased millionaires or defunct lotteries. Here's one emailed invitation, just came in as I was writing, for instance:

> During our investigation and auditing in this bank, my department came across a very huge sum of money belonging to a deceased person who died on November 2000 in a plane crash and the fund has been dormant in his account with this Bank without any claim of the fund in our custody either from his family or relation before my discovery to this development. Although personally, I keep this information secret within myself to enable the whole plans and idea be profitable and successful during the time of execution. The said amount was sum of $ TWENTY TWO MILLION THREE HUNDRED THOUSAND UNITED STATES DOLLARS.

Mind you, stranger things happen... Maybe worth looking into, carefully of course. And fair enough, some of the meetings do end up with checks being handed over—signed the "Central Bank of Nigeria." FOR MILLIONS OF DOLLARS! But no one has ever managed to find a bank to cash one. Other meetings end up more straightforwardly, with the optimistic traveler being attacked and robbed.

Perhaps surprisingly, given that the original invitations are issued by plausible sounding bank officials and the like, even those who have been robbed at an unsatisfactory meeting, fall again for the next lot of people now saying that they are real Nigerian government officials, or police officers, and offering to help them "get their money back." For a small fee, of course.

Having been lured to Nigeria to a rendezvous and robbed, it might seem odd that people would now still obediently do as they are told, even pay substantial fees, to help with the "investigations." But that's human nature. The US Department Of State says it is: "... kind of like gambling. You get in so deep you keep putting money in to get something out of it."

And perhaps that's why the Ajaokuta Steel Mill still receives generous funding, and is always supposedly about to start being a "very profitable proposition."

# 52 No Holiday:
# Rwanda Genocide Outings:

*Stay at the Hotel of a Thousand Hills*

## How to get there
Fly direct to Kigali.

## What to see
The Hotel of a Thousand Hills, or Hotel Des Mille-Collines as it should properly be known, as Rwanda is an area of French influence, became famous in *Hotel Rwanda*, a film about the Rwandan Genocide. It was here that the Hutu owner of the hotel, at great risk to himself, rescued and hid several hundred people, using food and cigarettes as bribes for smuggling

them in under the very noses of the militias seeking to kill them.

That is how the Hotel wants to be remembered. Yet it is also the place where—as all around them the Hutu dominated government prepared, publicized and implemented its plans for a "final solution" to the Tutsi problem—the ambassadors, soldiers, and international experts who backed the regime laughed and drank and made free with local prostitutes, even as the bodies piled up in the streets around them.

## Background briefing

In his classic account of events at the Hotel Des Mille-Collines in the last days before the killing reached a frenzy (driving even the Whites from the poolside), Gil Courtemanche records:

> The killers were becoming less inhibited, less cautious and less anonymous every day. They proclaimed their extermination plans on the radio. They laughed about them in the bars. Their ideologues, like Léon Mugaser, were inflaming whole regions with their speeches.

After every rally, Interahamwe (Hutu militia members) militiamen rampaged through towns and villages "burning, raping, crippling, killing with their Chinese Machetes and their French grenades." International experts came to note the damage, listen to terrified eyewitnesses, dig up bodies from mass graves, while the organizations themselves carefully declined to draw conclusions.

During the visit of the International Commission of Inquiry in January 1993, Captain Pascal Simbikangwa, in full view of the Commission, threatened witnesses from the Rwandan Association for the Defense of Human Rights and Public Liberties with death, while the UN Special Rapporteur noted during the 1993 massacres the "phone system had suddenly 'broken down' (in the areas involved) ... and had curiously become operational again without any needs for repairs."

By no means the first well-documented trial massacres were in mid-March of 1992, in a small town called Bugesera following a government radio broadcast made by Ferdinand Nahimana. Perhaps 200 Tutsis were killed and over 10,000 were displaced. Another well-documented massacre in the last week of January 1993 in Gisenyi cost the lives of at least 300 Tutsi.

These were practice runs for the genocide proper, and involved chopping off heads, hands and feet with machetes, with the women being raped in addition. People sought refuge in churches, pathetically seeking a sanctuary that was not respected. These too became charnel houses of blood and death.

All the time, the partying continued at the Hotel Des Mille-Collines. As one philosophy professor there said, "The blacks are always killing each other." That's philosophical!

## Useful information

Expect to pay $100 a night (or a year's average income for locals) at the Hotel.

## Risk factor

Not risky at all—now.

# 53 No Holiday:
# Rwanda Genocide Outings II:

*A tour around Kigali*

## How to get there
Step outside the hotel.

## What to see
In Kigali you can visit the United Nations Building on Revolution Boulevard, and just opposite the barracks of the Presidential Guard, where the final list of 1,500 key political figures—politicians, businessmen, priests, human rights workers, journalists—was decided. The Zero Network was to kill them as soon as the President was assassinated, which he was on April 6, 1994.

## ♆ Disinformation point
The French newspaper, *Le Figaro*, bravely reported later that the surface-to-air missiles used to shoot down the President's helicopter had been covertly supplied by the French army, flouting the arms embargo in effect. The government said (disinformation!) that the US had supplied the missiles while then trying to make it look like the French had.

Radio Mille-Collines announced openly that this attack was the signal for an African-style Holocaust of the Tutsi, with squads of warriors blocking roads around settlements and working their way through whole towns with lists of "cockroaches" to be exterminated.

And you can walk down "Justice Avenue," which was piled high with the bodies of Hutu moderates and Tutsis in general...

## Useful information
Rwanda is a tiny, mountainous nation in the Rift Valley of south-central Africa, one of the most densely populated areas of the world, with fertile plains and lush green volcanic hills, home to the famous mountain gorillas. It was quite a catch for the German and later Belgian colonists, who set about dividing the people into two groups: the majority were Hutu, who they said were darker and "therefore more primitive," and the minority Tutsi, who were richer and better educated. It was these that the colonialists thought might have been from North Africa originally, and who they promoted as a kind of governing caste. The legacy of this, of course, was a deep resentment of the Tutsi by the Hutu. Just as in Nazi Germany, where the first step was drawing up lists of Aryans, Slavs and Jews, when the Belgians imposed an identity card system on the Africans, giving the "ethnic" identity of each person, the groundwork for a future genocide was laid.

In 1963, newly independent Rwanda suffered vicious fratricidal fighting, largely carried out at the behest of the Hutu government, and this continued on and off until the 1991 peace agreement imposed on the country by outside nations. Under this, the two "racial" groups were to disarm, and to share power. But some had other ideas.

However, it takes time and money to prepare a holocaust. For a start, millions of Tutsi and thousands of key moderate Hutu civil servants and intellectuals had to be identified, their names and addresses recorded, their executions timetabled and allocated. The killing squads had to be given training, and weapons, usually machetes (for Rwanda is a poor country), had to be purchased and distributed. The time and the peace-accords were provided by the UN, the money was supplied by the World Bank, and the racist ideology was often supplied by priests of the Catholic Church.

All the while, as Gil Courtemanche relates, the UN (through its commander, General Romeo Dallaire) had a mandate to use very proactive powers including "the tracking of arms caches and neutralization of armed gangs throughout the country" but chose to avert its gaze from both the plans and the actual killings.

And the plans were well known. On December 17, 1993 the journal *Le Flambeau* even described in some detail the then Rwandan government's plans for a "final solution" comparable to that of Hitler. "Political adversaries and defenseless populations" had been identified and would be slaughtered. "About 8,000 Interahamwe sufficiently trained and equipped by the French army await the signal to begin the assassinations among the residents of the city of Kigali and its surroundings."

A year later, the Canadian General at last acted. Some would say it was because he was worried about "covering his back" from charges of not fulfilling his mandate, by not following up detailed accounts from his own staff of the massacre at Bugesera. He wrote a memo (January 1994), suggesting that he could—if the UN bosses approved—intervene to seize the arms caches before the government had finished its planned distribution. But, the UN did *not* approve. After all, to act would risk the political co-operation of the government. No matter that the government had an obviously murderous plan.

Yet if the story of Rwanda is one of Western complicity, deeply rooted racism and inhumanity, it is also a story of great resilience and compassion. The international community (let alone the UN) did not stop the killing. But a small, dedicated and largely Tutsi army drove the Interahamwe out of Rwanda to Congo, (where the French now stepped in to protect them, the Interahamwe army, of course, not the innocent civilians). On the day the killing stopped, the UN had not fired a shot in response to the 20th century's last genocide.

Today, thousands of village tribunals hear confessions and seek the truth—but they will not get near the leaders of the genocide who were evacuated by the French government to the Congo and to Paris, as part of "Operation Turquoise," where they continue to wine, dine and plot.

Nor can they demand answers from those within the UN who could have acted, who should have acted, but chose to do nothing. The official UN report conveniently decided to blame the "lack of commitment from the major powers in the Security Council, especially the United States," a finding that must have pleased the French who armed and trained the militias, the Canadians who had the immediate practical power to intervene, but refused to use it, and most of all Kofi Annan, who, as Under-Secretary-General for peacekeeping at the time, had formal responsibility (and commissioned the report). Annan was promoted to become Secretary-General—no reckoning with the relatives of the victims for him!

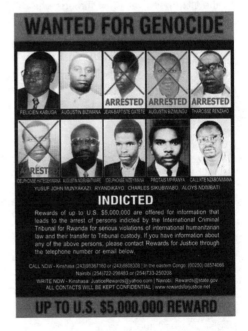

Even so, within Rwanda a remarkable process of reconciliation has begun, another side of the African spirit, with the survivors of the madness of their murderous neighbors trying to rebuild the land of a thousand hills—with the help of just those self-same neighbors too.

## Risk factor

Today, the killing fields are back as pastures. Although remnants of the Interahamwe, led by veterans of the genocide *are* active on the borders, operating from their French-supplied bases, if you visit Rwanda today, the only gorillas you are likely to come across are the furry kind.

# 54 No Holiday:
# Rwanda Genocide Outings III:

*To Kigali College, and then to the country for a different kind of lesson*

## How to get there
Step outside the hotel.

## What to see
Another poignant sight in Kigali is the site of the technical school, L'Ecole Technique Officielle, where 100 Belgian soldiers kept a machete-wielding mob at bay. At least they did while they were there. For in keeping with the general UN policy, the Belgians decided to evacuate their forces.

As the UN troops withdrew through one gate, the genocidaires moved in through the other. Within a few hours, over 2,000 men, women and children who had fled there seeking UN protection were dead.

## Useful information
Here, international wrangling at the UN bore its bitter fruit. With Britain and Belgium demanding out, with the French still aiding the killers, and the Americans worried about being "sucked in," the international community decided to abandon the people of Rwanda at the very moment when they were being exterminated.

Overall, in spite of his earlier inaction, we should give some credit to Romeo Dallaire, who finally maneuvered to keep his forces at nearly twice the size authorized (500 troops). And by merely sitting there, they managed to save the lives of an estimated 20,000 to 25,000 Rwandans.

Mind you, when France sent 500 soldiers to evacuate its own citizens and Akazu members on April 8 and 9, Dallaire's UN troops received orders reminding them not to help save threatened Rwandans, but only foreigners.

"You should make every effort not to compromise your impartiality or to act beyond your mandate," wrote Kofi Annan and Iqbal Riza in an April 9 telegram, "but [you] may exercise your discretion to do [so] should this be essential for the evacuation of foreign nationals."

Today there is another kind of political lesson to be learned from Rwanda. The Interahamwe soldier who led the assault on Kigali College was one of the first people tried and justly convicted by the war-crimes tribunal. For the school year of 2004, the Rwandan Ministry of Education chose the theme "La part de l'enseignant dans la lutte contre le divisionnisme et l'idéologie génocidaire" ("The role of the school student in the fight against the divisiveness of the ideology of genocide").

And today, travelers who tour around the country can only be impressed by the warmth and courage of the people, so soon after the cataclysm. Genocide sites and memorials dot the country, (such as Murambi Technical College where 50,000 bodies were found) yet also ten times as many new signs of beginnings, new reconstructions, involving all Rwandans. As one of the rangers showing westerners to the mountain gorillas put it:

*We can't ignore it, it's part of our history and we want people to know about it, but it's in the past. We're in the process of healing, moving on, looking to the future.*

# 55 No Holiday: **Southern Sudan**

*The Rumbek Bookshop*

## How to get there
Fly to Rumbek itself. The southern capital of what used to be Sudan, the more famous one is Khartoum. Rumbek is some 373 miles (600 kilometers) to the South West, heading towards Congo and a big swamp.

If Rumbek is a suitably unlikely place for a No Holiday destination, even so, it seems to have had more than its obvious share of media attention. But then Rumbek provides a touch of local color to the story of Sudan, independent since 1956, an otherwise rather dreary tale of the twenty-year-long civil war that has resulted in two to three million deaths.

## What to see
Rumbek bookshop is a very small shop in a very small town, with a very, very small stock of books. Yet it has some cachet as perhaps one of the most widely reported bookshops in Africa.

## Useless information
"If Jerome K. Jerome were alive today, he would be proud. Over a century after he wrote it, *Three Men in a Boat*, his quintessentially English comic novel about accident-prone Victorian gentlemen paddling down the River Thames, is a bestseller in southern Sudan." Or so quipped *The Economist* in January 2004, under the witless headline: "The people of southern Sudan are starved for reading matter."

This might seem implausible, the London-based business magazine continues, with a chuckle, as southern Sudan is the scene of Africa's "longest-burning civil war." Its people have lived for decades "in fear of death or enslavement." How could they relate to a comedy about chaps in red-and-orange blazers sculling to Hampton Court and getting lost in the hedge maze? Indeed, we might add, not that the paper does, how could they read about it, given only 15 percent of the population of southern Sudan is literate?

Nor does *The Economist* report that the Commission of Education had in fact supplied 415,000 books to primary schools in southern Sudan the previous year. The first batches of books even went through Rumbek (as well as Maridi) from where they were distributed more widely. They included about 370,000 pupils' books, 40,000 teachers' guides and 7,000 handbooks. And the plan was to increase this to a million books in the subsequent years.

But let's return to *The Economist*, which has found an obliging "man-in-the-bookshop" to complete the piece. He reveals that he has sold eight books, and five of them were *Three Men in a Boat*. "People find this book a bit hard to understand... but for now we have to rely on the Ugandan distributors to send us what they think is appropriate." Doubtless this is intended to strike the reader as rather droll, as is the fact that a friend of the bookseller enjoyed the book so much that he named his goat "Montmorency" after the dog that accompanies its three heroes down the river. A final whimsical observation at the end of the piece claims that Rumbek Secondary, one of the few remaining secondary schools in the south, is considering making *Three Men in a Boat* a set text this year. But given that the school must have several thousand students, this seems unlikely—unless there are unsuspected truckloads of Jerome K. Jerome heading for Rumbek bookshop.

## Useful information
In 2003, southern Sudan had just 1,700 schools for its 1.4-million school-age children, according to the UN, of which less than a quarter went to school. And just six percent of teachers had any formal training; most are volunteers. When the north-south war flared up in 1983, many of the teachers were obliged to join the armies. Schools became barracks and targets of war, with the result that after the war, the entire system needed to be rebuilt from scratch.

But one problem which financial aid has little effect on is the cultural resistance to the education of female children. Only in Afghanistan under the Taliban were fewer girls given even the most basic education than in Sudan. Girls in Sudan are often considered fit only to do household chores, not to learn, and are obliged to marry at 14. Social structures such as the dowry of cows (which go of course not to the girl, but to her closest male relative) mean that those with other plans are under pressure not only from their fathers but also their uncles and brothers too. Any girl not married by 17 is considered a spinster.

The UN has been setting up new schools, including all-girl schools. At these schools, girls attend classes in the morning, and then go home for the rest of the day to do the chores. Thus keeping one tradition alive.

## Risk factor
The bookshop is not risky, but since Bill Clinton's cruise missile strike on Sudan's main medicine factory, visitors must realize that pretty much all of Sudan could be a target.


# 56 No Holiday: **Day 2 in Southern Sudan** 🏛 👑

*Rumbek Business Center, Market and UN Office*

## What to see
Although most of Rumbek's houses are just temporary wooden shacks and its airstrip is just a line of red earth in the scrubby forest, since the partition of the country under the peace deal, foreign donors have pledged 4.5 billion dollars (3.7 billion euros) for reconstruction projects,

and much of that is flowing through Rumbek. Indeed, Rumbek is at the heart of something of a post-war investment boom.

Rumbek market used to be a barter-only affair consisting of a few stalls selling scraggy looking chickens and bits of old land mines made into ornaments. But now No Holidaymakers are promised a bustling center of free enterprise. The traders will certainly expect hard cash for items like pink Joe Boxer underwear, Casio watches, and even the fresh fruit. That's despite the fact that, just like Ethiopia during the drought that prompted the pop world to launch "Live Aid," you only need to go just outside the town, to see there is still something of a problem with food shortages.

## Useful information
Two years ago, no less than 200,000 people starved to death in what was described then as the worst food crisis in Sudan in a decade. A decade earlier (1988), a quarter of a million Sudanese perished during the famine.

"The main problem here is malnutrition, which is also the key cause of many diseases," a health official in Rumbek told the UN, adding that most children have not received even the most basic immunizations. According to the Rumbek diocese, the only people who seem to record such things, the current mortality rate is incredibly high: 150 deaths per 1,000 live births and one in every nine women dies in child birth.

But then there is only one doctor for every 100,000 people in southern Sudan and so for now, diarrhea, malaria, tuberculosis and Kala-azar (black fever) run pretty freely through the population. With the deployment of international peacekeepers the threat of HIV/AIDS increases.

## Useless information
But for the UN the priority problem is digitizing the region, and that is why its snappily named "Sudan Local Governance and Capacity Building through Strategic Participatory Town Planning Communities in Transition Division," prioritized the appointment of a "GIS Training Specialist" for Rumbek. The job description explains that "in order to assist the new Government of Southern Sudan (GOSS)" to respond effectively and in a timely manner to pressing population return and reintegration issues, as well as extend civil authority throughout the New Sudan, there will be a project on the development of Satellite Imagery, digitized town maps, and "Capacity building/technical training" for municipal officials.

Of course, there are other practical projects too, such as the provision of "Scanners for Information Centers," which will offer internet, computer, library, video and TV facilities, and apparently be very useful for ex-pats, NGOs and their visitors, as well as local people, including youth, as well as local authority officials. Internet use, the UN suggests, will include downloading peace agreement documents. People have been known to walk long distances in Africa (not only to get water to cook with) but in order to "seek advice on how to access e-mail and communicate with relatives outside the country."

The twenty-year long civil war, which caused several million deaths is rather hard to encapsulate for a visitor. But the day the dreaded Antonov planes came over (in violation of a humanitarian ceasefire), dropping their bombs on the market and killing a young girl and a pregnant woman, can be recaptured by visiting the market.

## Technical information
Before 2005, there were only about 10 miles (16 kilometers) of paved roads in southern Sudan, an area twice the size of France or California, and no phone lines. The schools and health clinics

had been destroyed by the years of civil war and so, of course, had the farms.

But after Rumbek was designated as the capital of the newly autonomous south, international oil companies and aid officials began to pour in. And they need infrastructure, electricity to run air conditioning, telephones and the Internet. The Sudanese, by contrast, need food, schools, and inoculations against disease. But first things first. "Most countries, even Afghanistan, have at least some infrastructure," one US phone engineer, Richard Herbert complained to reporters. "But southern Sudan—zero."

Soon, he promised, that would be changed. Rumbek's new offices would have a wireless network as advanced as any in high-tech US offices. The good thing about starting from scratch, Herbert adds, is that you can leapfrog old technologies, adding sanctimoniously "There's a lot of energy focused on improving things... Otherwise all the deaths will have been in vain."

And work also goes on apace on Sudan's roads, previously just rough tracks with craters in them large enough to gobble up a phone company executive's SUV whole. The road from Rumbek to neighboring Uganda, for example, a 300-mile (483 kilometer) trip, vital for bringing in supplies of Jerome K. Jerome and maybe some food too, was in such poor condition that the journey used to take nearly a week. So, for example, in the first year following the ceasefire agreement, the UN paid over $1,000 a ton to airlift in a record 192,000 tons (174,000 metric tonnes) of food—that is four times the cost of using trucks. Curiously enough, the UN intended to continue using airlifts as the main method of moving food even after the roads are finished.

Finishing the roads also means clearing at least some of the tens of thousands of land mines that litter Sudan. All the more tricky, as the region has one of the world's largest swamps, which feeds the Nile River. But when the road is finished, it will cut travel time from several weeks to two days, and transform the economics of the region. Which is where Rumbek market comes in.

## Risk factor 

The peace accord concerns the Abyei, the Blue Nile and the Nuba Mountains, but not Darfur, to the west along the Chad border, where fighting continues. At least the oil fields are safe.

## ↳ Side trip: Southern Sudan:
*Rumbek Cathedral (and its crazy Bishop)*

There are several churches in Rumbek as there are plenty of poor African souls available for saving. Most are evangelical Christian churches, funded by strange US sects, but the church we are interested in is the Catholic one, which gives itself the title of "Cathedral" and calls its pastor a "Bishop." Mind you, the diocese is as large as all of Italy, and each of the Bishop's 30 priests watch over a flock of some 350,000 people.

## What to see

Rumbek cathedral is a 65-foot (20 meters) wide, polygonal affair with a zinc roof. As for the Bishop's formal residence, usually a perk of the job, there isn't one. The Bishop sleeps under leafy branch-covered huts, wandering from village to village. After all, as he told reporters: "One in six displaced persons in the world is Sudanese. A displaced person doesn't even have a pot to cook with and must continually move around to flee from war, famine and disease."

In Rumbek, cabbage arrives twice a week from Kenya, but in the 105-125 degree Fahrenheit (38-51 degrees Celsius) heat it doesn't survive long. During the rainy season in Sudan it should be possible to grow something locally, but for some years, the scorching sun has brought only drought. This has been the pattern since 2000.

## Useless information

The present Bishop is Cesare Mazzolari, from Brescia, Italy. Although originally a Combonian missionary, he doesn't try to convert many people. He says that would be like giving them a death sentence. Any that he did convert would be forced to flee, yet "end up being caught and punished, anyway, thousands of kilometers away." As for any Catholics who convert to Islam, they are fire-branded, "literally being stamped on their sides like cows so as to distinguish them from infidels."

When he spoke with fellow countryman Stefano Lorenzetto (of the Milan Daily *Il Giornale*) he was evidently feeling a bit downcast, perhaps because the long war between the Islamic government in the North and the largely Christian South counted so many Catholics among its victims. "The time to be martyred is drawing near," the Bishop asserted in the best tradition of preachers, before adding, "I hope the Lord grants us the grace to face such bloodshed. There is a need for purification. Many Christians will be killed for their faith. Yet a new Christianity will arise from the blood of these martyrs." As he spoke, Stefano relates, the Bishop gazed sadly at a map on the wall of Sudan, his beloved but troubled land, and "his eyes filled with tears."

If this sounds even a bit like the second President Bush following attacks of September 11, the Bishop is actually entirely different. Cesare Mazzolari offers parishioners and visitors alike surprising insights into international affairs and politics. From the vantage point of his perch in Sudan, he sees America waging a furious war of vengeance, which can only lead to hatred. The Bishop says that by contrast his extremely poor "African faithful experience September 11 everyday" in their lives—yet take no revenge. "They suffer injustice and disease without any bitterness. You can only learn from them," he tells Stefano, before now bursting into tears he can no longer hold back.

But in his corrugated iron cathedral, the Bishop offers this insight into modern America: "vengeance belongs to a culture of primitives. The president of the world's most powerful nation scoffed at the planet's highest authorities, the UN and the Pope. This damages trust in authority worldwide. And soldiers who were supposed to carry out such vengeance have gone out of their minds." In sum, he says, "They're doing crazy stuff."

He is most scathing about the supposed new Western interest in human rights.

> Bush cannot boast in front of anybody that he's the world's protector of human rights. I lived in the United States for 26 years. I was even ordained in San Diego, California. I worked among blacks and helped Mexican mineworkers. I know that the rights of the poor and minorities are systematically stepped on in the United States. I always tell my Sudanese acquaintances thinking of heading across the Atlantic in search of prosperity: "Here you experience poverty in terms of food and culture. In America you'll experience the worst misfortune that could ever befall you. There you'll understand what it means to be a slave."

At this, his reporter visitor, Stefano, cannot stay quiet any longer. "I'm sorry" he interrupts, "But it doesn't seem fair to blame this on the United States."

> When their interests are at stake, the Americans are completely ready to dialogue. They write "In God we trust" on their dollar bills. Yet in reality they believe more in the dollar's green than in God himself. Bush has even said he was for introducing the shariah, the Koranic law, all throughout Sudan—as long as there would be peace between the north and the south and they could begin drilling for the sea of oil Sudan floats on.

Stefano scoffs at this old conspiracy theory, perhaps not knowing that by the year 2000, the international oil companies had already divided up the oil riches of Sudan amongst themselves, in the rush following the success of the Greater Nile Petroleum Operating Company in the Heglig and Unity fields. These are 373 miles (600 kilometers) southwest of Khartoum, which puts them, coincidentally of course, not so far from Rumbek, the center of so much otherwise inexplicable media attention.

# 57 No Holiday: **Mogadishu, Somalia**

*A promising experiment in anarchy*

## How to get there
Fly to Mogadishu, and find some armed guards. Do not attempt to drive into the countryside, as this will involve passing through numerous checkpoints, each run by a different militia.

## Background briefing
Somalia is situated on the horn of Africa bordering Ethiopia, Kenya and Djibouti. It is one of the poorest countries in the world, with no known mineral resources and it only exports cattle and (implausibly) bananas—the latter a colonial legacy defying its parched soils. It has the longest coastline of any African country, an asset that critics say it uses mainly for dumping toxic waste. And it is the only country in the world where there is no government. The last one was toppled in 1991.

In fact, its last proper dictator was General Mohammed Barre, who likened his autocratic regime to "scientific socialism." Under him, hospital care, schools and colleges were free. Now the only facilities are privately run. Shops selling mobile phones and Internet cafes also do good business in Mogadishu. Guns of all sizes are also available, up to and including rocket launchers of the kind that brought down the famous US Black Hawk helicopter. Ironically, in view of its fate today, at that time, the country was the most centralized in all Africa. In the 1990s, the US and the UN briefly took an interest in the country and tried to provide "humanitarian aid" by force. Opposition by the warlords led to the "confrontation" between one of the militias and the US Army.

Nowadays, there is a so-called "transitional national government" but it is dominated by Somalia's long-time enemy, Ethiopia, and looks unlikely to be able to "heal the country's divisions" as the UN piously puts it.

## What to see
The first thing to see [ 📷 ] are the "border crossings" at which all vehicles must pay an entry fee, in cash, jewels, or CDs. Whatever the border guards want, really. If it sounds off-putting, we should remember that all customs officials extract money from travelers under threat of imprisonment. Of course, most of the time, the money goes not to the customs officials, but to the government. In Somalia, since there is no government, the money is instead spent directly by the militia on their own needs, usually "khat," a green leaf which, when chewed for hours on end, produces intoxication. And again, better than the Western system (theoretically at least) if you travel with enough armed guards, you can barrel directly through the border controls.

The country is a kaleidoscope of fiefdoms controlled by rival barons, who occasionally fight each other for more territory. Curiously, Somalia does continue to function. It is, in its way, an endorsement of the great economist Adam Smith, who advanced the idea that it is from self-interest, not benevolence (let alone because of the government) that we find bread in the shops and beer in the bars, or rocket launchers in the market and khat in the cafés, as we should say here.

Indeed, even the famous pirates, who hijack ships regularly off the Somali coast, claim to be acting from the best possible motives. They say they are defending coastlines from foreign companies who often over-fish or who come to dump industrial toxic waste into Somalia's territorial waters. Or even to dump tourists.

## ☿ Disinformation point
The European Union is Somalia's main overseas donor, and dispenses huge amounts of euros around the country. The Union warned in a special strategy document that most of the country remained "structurally food insecure whilst social and productive services, formerly provided by state agencies, *have completely collapsed*." But this, it turns out when you arrive, is top quality official disinformation.

## Useful information
So how bad is life in the world's only true anarchist state? According to an upbeat United Nations report, not too bad at all. The level of "extreme" poverty in Somalia today (as opposed to the normal variety) is a mere 43 percent, which is actually quite a bit less than the level of its more conventional neighbors. Since a market economy has replaced a centrally planned economy, far from abjectly collapsing as often predicted, Somalian development has been "market-driven rather than government led." What's happened is rather that, "economic deregulation and privat-ization have accompanied the radical localization of governance." What's all that then? Well, in the "new Somalia" for instance, instead of the government keeping a central land register, you show the world that you own a piece of land by building a house on it and living in it.

Under anarchy, electricity is now available in parts of the country it never reached under central government, at rates assessed by counting the number of light bulbs in the house (35 cents a lightbulb a day). One Somali businessman told *The Economist*: "collapse of Somalia has been good for business. In many ways it is much better off than before. Then, we had state monopolies and bureaucracy and corruption, and all the wealth was in Mogadishu."

Somali public services might generously be called "spartan," but they are little worse than those of their neighbors in the Horn of Africa. They share roughly the same levels of roads and transport infrastructure, and similar access to doctors and hospitals. Educationally, Somalia slumps with its 81 percent illiteracy levels, but then half of its population is nomadic and the whole country has a long-standing and deep distrust of written documents. Even large businesses there rarely keep financial records. And even without any taxes, one third of the primary schools in the country are either free or cost less than $1 a month. At the other end, for example, a decision by one town, Borama, to create a modest university was funded by locals and the income from fees, at $25 a month.

So, far from being the bleak war zone of *Black Hawk Down* fame, parts of the country are flourishing, with skyscrapers sprouting as part of a construction boom. All completely unregulated of course. Or rather, regulated in its own special Somali way.

## Special deals for travelers
Joseph Winter, visiting for the BBC, was suitably impressed to find that in Mogadishu the printing of passports had also been privatized. He noted:

> *For just $80 and in less than 24 hours, I became a Somali citizen, born in Mogadishu.*

*As I had omitted to travel with any passport-sized photos, my supplier kindly left the laminate for that page intact, for me to stick down at home. For a slightly higher fee, I was offered a diplomatic passport, with my choice of posting or ministerial job.*

## Risk factor

The British Foreign Office simply warns travelers NOT TO visit the country due to the "dangerous level of criminal activity and internal insecurity." However, if you still insist on going, it adds implausibly, you should hire armed escorts "at a cost of $4 a day or $7 per 24 hours."

# 58 No Holiday: **Asmara, Eritrea**

*Savor the rich taste of colonial folly from the mountain railway*

## How to get there

Fly to Addis Ababa's fabulous International Airport and get a connecting flight to Asmara (fewer services during wartime).

## What to see

Eritrea's mountain railway is a triumph of self-reliance and national pride. Unlike the grandiose projects of the international banks and aid donors.

The Italians originally built the railway at the end of the 19ᵗʰ century, when they grabbed part of the Horn of Africa, then known as Abyssinia, during the general European push for colonies. They started the railway at the Red Sea and it slowly extended inland to Asmara, about 62 miles (100 kilometers) away, the modernist and surprisingly cosmopolitan capital of Eritrea. This was an expensive and technically difficult exercise, as the line climbs 7,874 feet (2,400 meters) between the two, a fact that railway buffs will find of more interest than the rest of us. It was also mainly mandated by the desire to annoy the French, in neighboring Somalia. It was only finished in 1911 after the building of some 30 tunnels and 35 bridges, which had to be hewn out of rocky mountainsides or constructed over ravines (and these viaducts, unusually for the period, were constructed in stone).

The Italians extended the railway in 1928, eventually arriving at Agordat, and finally equipped it with smart new locomotives in 1936, specially designed for climbing mountains. As the train climbs, the scrubby vegetation changes to pine trees, with large prickly pear cacti clinging to the gorges and cliffs in-between.

In 1975, the Ethiopians tried to close the railway, ordering it to be shut down, the rails ripped up, and all the written records destroyed, but the Eritreans instead loaded the several tons of crucial technical papers into an old shipping container and secretly buried it for 20 years.

During the war, railway sleepers and wagons were often used to construct barricades or bomb shelters. Both desperately poor and justifiably suspicious of outside offers of help, the Eritreans undertook the task of rebuilding their railway entirely without assistance, preferring instead to reclaim all the scattered bits and reassemble them with the aid of long-retired local railway men. The only outside purchases were for new nuts and bolts.

The Eritreans originally took the conventional approach to rebuilding the railway and invited international experts for their advice. An American company wanted $187,000 just to think about it. To actually rebuild the line, one Italian engineering firm quoted $200 million.

So the Eritreans decided to rebuild the railroad themselves, laying in the first year 25 miles (40 kilometers) of line across the sweltering hot coastal plain at a cost of just $1 million. In fact, the budget for the whole railway is only $3 million. Instead, Eritrea's railway is like

everything else in Eritrea, a community effort. Villagers rescued the old rails and steel ties dug up and thrown down the ravines by the Ethiopians. Volunteers working only with sledgehammers and pick-axes, worked in over 100 degrees Fahrenheit (38 degrees Celsius) heat to re-lay the rails.

The railway was reopened (as far as the capital) in 2003 and proudly featured on the fledgling nation's stamps and bank notes. Initially though, only a few special tourist charters and one diesel locomotive used the routes. Commercial freight services await new locomotives.

## Useful information
The passenger cars have wooden seats and as there is no glass in the windows, steam or smoke from the engine fills the carriages whenever it enters a tunnel. There are only hand-operated brakes for slowing the train, operated by a brakeman at the rear who is supposed to listen for whistles from the driver's cab. (When he occasionally misses them, the train speeds up alarmingly.)

Today, the Eritreans retain the Italian taste for olive oil and pasta, and cafés offer cappuccino and espresso from vintage Italian machines.

## Useless information
In 1941, as part of the Battle for Africa during the Second World War, the railway saw a change of hands as the British arrived, chased the Italians north, declared Eritrea a UN protectorate and looted Asmara. Worse still, after the war, the Allies, at the insistence of the United States, imposed a federation on the country with its old enemy and neighbor, Ethiopia (then an American ally). Ethiopia's Great Dictator, Haile Selassie, annexed it a decade later, and as a result, for most of the next forty years, the Eritreans were involved in a brutal war for independence (that would cost over 65,000 lives in due course). The only thing the traveler needs to know about it is that Ethiopia is Stalinist, and used to be backed by both the Soviets and Americans, while Eritrea is Maoist and used to be backed by not much of anyone.

Curiously, Eritrea after independence is now becoming another client state of the US, which has been busy renovating a missile station near the capital, that it built during Haile Selassie's military occupation of the area (and used heavily during the Vietnam War).

But then again, there is oil under the sea off Eritrea. And since from time to time Ethiopia launches attacks on its neighbor, there is a UN force installed—in the capital's hotels and by the swimming pools—so it seems that Africa's newest nation has a long way to go before it can shake off its colonial masters.

## Risk factor
As a legacy of the Ethiopian war, the landscape is still covered with burned out tanks and landmines. Children in the countryside will rush the train not asking for money, but chanting

"pen, pen, pen," for Eritreans are a proud nation who value education above all—except of course, their incredible winding mountain railway.

# 59 Working No Holiday: **Taoudenni, Mali**

*A Working No Holiday in The Salt Mines of Timbuktu*

## How to Get There
Fly to Tombouctou (Timbuktu) and wait a few days until there is a camel train leaving for Taoudenni, which is in the middle of the Sahara desert, and otherwise inaccessible.

## What to see
Traveling by camel is considered the authentic way to see the Sahara Desert. It is also the only way to reach the salt mines. The walk, however, is onerous—that is walking beside the camels, which are carrying goods—some 470 miles (756 kilometers) and you should expect it to take about three weeks. The pace begins gently though, a mere eight hours a day, through land that is relatively lush, where there are tufts of grass which the camels can eat, weeds underfoot, and even the odd boulder to break up the monotony of what is otherwise an extremely flat region. But after the oasis at Araouane, that is some 155 miles (250 kilometers) into the walk, the route reaches the Sahara proper, and the camels are crossing sand, and as the temperature climbs higher, the camel train must press on for a good 12 hours in every 24. However, the pace pays off. Just two weeks later, the sand becomes first pink tinged, and then quite red. This is the sign that you are near the mines.

## Useful information
The area has been mined by the Berabich Arabs for salt, using the same methods since the 16th century. Each year, surprisingly, between 3,000 and 5,000 tons (3,300-5,500 metric tonnes) of salt are extracted this way. There is *no charge* for mining—you can just show up (as above) and start digging. Typically a hole is about the size of a cellar, that is fifteen feet deep. The "white gold" (as the locals call the salt), is extracted in blocks about one foot thick. Each block weights about 310 pounds (141 kilos). But the money is good—if you can get it back as far as Tombouctou intact (the blocks of salt are very fragile), it will be worth about $3. That's a lot of money (by local standards). A skilled miner can manage three blocks a day, and as they work at the mines non-stop for six months at a stretch, they will have made over $500 by the time they get back to town!

## Useless information
Alas, gender equality has not reached Mali, let alone the mines, so women travelers face discrimination. Women miners must both work and eat separately.

## Risk factor
There are no health or other facilities at the mines, but a truck occasionally arrives, which in an emergency can get you back to Tombouctou a bit faster than on (or beside) a camel.

# 60 No Holiday: **Libya**

*The oases of Tagiura and Ain Zara: world's first aerial bombing targets*

## How to get there
Fly to Tripoli (Tarabulus) and take a 2CV into the desert.

## What to see
The Italians in Libya conducted the first true bombing raids in the history of war. The targets were not military or even strategic—but "psych-ops"—psychological warfare. They were the small oases (towns really) of Tagiura and Ain Zara on the North African coast. These were civilian targets chosen as the easiest way to deliver a message to the "Arabs" about the costs of resisting the Italians and their new weapons. Actually, at this stage, there were no bombs designed for planes, so the Italians used small grenades and tossed them out of the side of the bi-planes. Four bombs in total, each weighing 4 pounds (1.8 kilos), were dropped. The official Italian Air Force assessment was that the bombs had had "a wonderful effect on the morale of of the Arabs."

Interestingly, the massive bombardment of the ancient city of Baghdad before the Iraq war at the start of the 21st century was similarly preceded by the US Secretary of Defense saying that the aim was neither military nor economic, but to create "shock and awe" amongst Iraqi civilians.

## Useless information
Italy is home to many great artistic schools and traditions, and one of the most aesthetically noteworthy is that of Futurism. The founder of the movement, one Tommaso Marinetti, followed a long philosophical tradition of glorifying war, conflict and destruction, all seen as part of destroying the old and creating the new. Marinetti said warfare was "hygienic."

For his fellow Italian artists and poets in the movement, one such war in the Horn of Africa in 1911 was especially beautiful, and the new airplanes in particular provided an unmatched opportunity to mix art and practice. They mounted cameras onto their bi-planes and took real pictures of these first bombing runs and raids on African villages and oases. During the Battle of Tripoli on October 26, 1911, Marinetti himself soared into the air to shout encouragement to the Italian troops: "Fix bayonets! Charge!"

## Background briefing
The first recorded bombing from a plane (although there had already been quite a few conducted from balloons) occurred on November 1, 1911 during the Italian-Turkish War over a Turkish camp at Ain Zara in Libya. Italy had been using aircraft to monitor enemy troop movements and search for Turkish artillery positions. One Italian pilot, a Lieutenant Giulio Gavotti, had a creative idea, and took four small grenades from a leather pouch he always carried with him (as one does), screwed in the detonators and tossed each over the side. Alas, no one was injured and little damage was done, but the principle had been established. Curiously though, the aerial bombing raids were at the time seen as barbaric and appalling, "ungentlemanly" even, and there was widespread condemnation of the Italians around the world. The ethical prohibition on bombing civilians remained until World War II, when the British, defeated by Germany at land and sea, found it their sole remaining advantage. Since then, bombing has never looked back.

## Risk factor
Libya continues to experience periodic bombing from the democratic nations.

AZERBAIJAN
TURKMENISTAN
TURKEY
CASPIAN SEA
CYPRUS
SYRIA
63
Golan Heights
LEBANON
MEDITERRANEAN SEA
ISRAEL
62
Erez Crossing
IRAQ
64
Baghdad
IRAN
JORDAN
61
Cairo
KUWAIT
EGYPT
PERSIAN GULF
SAUDI ARABIA
QATAR
GULF
OF OMAN
RED SEA
65
United Arab Emirates
OMAN

# The Middle East

## 61 No Holiday: **Cairo's Al-Azhar Mosque, Egypt**

*An Islamic School for anyone wanting to learn about the Holy War on Infidels*

### How to get there
Fly to Cairo and take a taxi to the heart of the Old Town.

### What to see
There are half a billion Muslims in the world, so a mosque is not in itself anything very special. But recently one or two have acquired a certain political patina, such as the famous Finsbury Park Mosque in London, with its plastic minaret, where the infamous English "Shoe Bomber" originated. The man whose efforts to set fire to his running shoes mid-flight between Paris and Miami left a legacy of futile "shoe checks" at airports afterwards. But then, we must stress, these people do not care about consequences.

But the Holy of Holies (in Islamic Terrorism) is not Finsbury Park, nor even one of the fine ancient mosques of Saudi Arabia or Afghanistan. It is the Mosque of Al-Azhar, in Cairo, a nice enough old building, built in pale sandstone and marble, crowned by five minarets, and home to the Islamic Brotherhood. It was the source of their "first inspiration" to illuminaries such as Abdullah Azzam, and Aymen al Zawahiri, respectively Spiritual Leader to Osama Bin Laden himself and Number Two boss of the al-Qaeda network.

For Muslims and even infidels not terribly well up on Islamic theology, the Mosque is a good place to enroll. After a course in elementary Arabic, and discussion of the philosophy of the Koran, you can join with up to 5,000 other enthusiastic students for a lecture by the Mosque's Director, one

Eid-Abdul-Hamid, on themes such as: "The tyrants have been defeated in Mesopotamia, and the Iraqi resistance is joyfully celebrating the repeated triumphs of Allah the Greatest!"

That at least was the topic of the lecture the day our tour guide visited, carefully written up on a white board behind an earnest, slightly hunched Mr. Hamid. At the end of the lecture, the congregation shout, "Allah is great" and then file placidly out past ranks of Egyptian policemen. The Mosque indeed has been under direct government control ever since 1961.

### Useful information
Tourists, unusually for many such Islamic centers, are permitted to visit the mosque complex and to join lectures. Or at least, this being an Islamic country, the male tourists are. Given the fiery anti-Western nature of the topics, this might seem odd, but then the congregation is already filled with agents of the Egyptian Secret Police, on the look out for extremists, so a few tourists are hardly likely to cause any harm.

### Useless information
The streets outside the Mosque complex are full of little boutiques selling radical pamphlets, with titles like "The Sages of Zion," explaining "How the Zionists destroyed the World Trade Center as Part of Their Plan," or more general accounts of the war on America, and its allies, in which the same "September 11ᵗʰ Conspiracy" disappears to become instead an encouraging first step taken by devout and enlightened jihadists. In fact, the pamphlets range widely. You pays your money and you takes your choice. Which only illustrates that tales of how little freedom of information and debate there is in dictatorships such as the one in Egypt, are not entirely accurate.

Curiously, the Brotherhood is actually the largest political opposition to Egypt's US-backed rulers, with a political program based on making the world happy through Islamic teachings. But the organization is hampered by its being formally banned ever since it was implicated in a plot to assassinate the Prime Minister in the 1950s.

### Risk factor
Egypt has suffered several very nasty attacks on its tourist sites, such as the "Pyramids Massacre" and the Sinai coast bombings—but here at least, so to speak, at the "heart of the storm," you should be safe enough.


# 62 No Holiday: **Erez Crossing, Israel** 👣 **(also known as: part of Palestine)**

*Swim in the most expensive swimming pools in the world*

### How to get there
Fly to Ben Gurion airport and be met by Dodge minivan—it seats eight—and taken to the local shopping center to have lunch at a Burger Ranch. Israel is an exotic outpost of the United States, a blend of ancient stone and orange blossom, and burger bars and drive-in motels with swimming pools. Which is only fitting as it was US weapons, and in the case of the Six Day War, personnel and planes too, that expanded it from the original UN proposed series of cantons. Today the Israelis have increased that to over 80 percent of the whole land of Palestine, and (in some circles) are even beginning to talk about giving a few enclaves back.

One visitor to Israel recalls chatting with a couple, who moved from their apartment in Netanya to live a few miles from the old "Green Line" marking Israel's pre-1967 border with the West Bank, and took them on a short drive to a hill with a commanding view. To the east, was the Arab city of Tul Karem. "Here is Palestine," the husband explained. In the 1948 war his father fought for this hill. Now there were plans to turn it and the surrounding area into a park, complete with an artificial lake. "It will be very nice, and maybe it will help our property values," his wife added with a laugh.

## What to see

The Israelis, like the Americans, are security obsessed—each new house must by law have a security room with a reinforced metal door and rubber seals on the door and window. In the US they're there for repelling nuclear missiles. In Israel, the talk is more likely to be of the Scuds launched by Saddam Hussein during the Gulf War. (And of course only Israel has nuclear weapons...)

And only in Israel would the army organize holidays for tourists. Here is one, organized by the "Friends of the Israeli Defense Forces:"

**SAMPLE ITINERARY**
**Day 1:** Evening Departure from New York City to Tel-Aviv.
**Day 2:** Jerusalem: Arrive at Israel's Ben-Gurion Airport; Kabbalat Shabbat at King David Hotel; Rooftop view of the Old City.
**Day 3:** Jerusalem: Walking/bus tour of the Old City, Western Wall, Jerusalem's early neighborhoods and a light lunch.
**Day 4:** Visit at Central Command: Briefing at Central Command Headquarters; Visit IDF units around Ramallah; Tour at the Ammunition Hill battleground; Tour of Mount Scopus and view of Jerusalem.
**Day 5:** [Busy!] Visit the Northern Command: Visit Chavat Hashomer and meet soldiers from disadvantaged socio-economic backgrounds; Visit Division #36 at the Golan Heights; Lookout from an IDF post onto the Golan Heights; Visit Kfar Giladi including

dinner with Kibbutz members; Briefing on daily life close to the Lebanese border; Night tour to the "Secret Tunnel" [📷 —bring flash].

**Day 6:** Air Force and Navy Day: Visit at Ramat David Air Force Base; Visit the Navy base in Haifa; Night tour of Jaffa and dinner.

**Day 7:** Visit at Southern Command: Flight to Eilat; Visit Armor base; Visit Engineering training school including display of landmine exercises; Farewell dinner party at Timna Park Caves.

This is very tempting. But we want to taste the *real* Israel, and that means a stay at a kibbutz. The kibbutz the political tourist will want to visit will highlight the disparity of life between the displaced Palestinians and the triumphant settlers. There are some 400 rural co-operative settlements, or "kibbutz," in Israel (and surrounding lands) enjoying for a long time a vaguely egalitarian image, despite, with very few exceptions, being based on land either stolen or "confiscated" from the Palestinians.

The idea of kibbutz, and the kibbutz way of life, arose and was formed during what the Israelis refer to as the "heroic" period of settlement, leading towards the creation of the state of Israel. From the 1910s through the 1950s, the kibbutzim fulfilled a central function in this task. The fundamental values of kibbutz are "Co-operation, Responsibility and Mutual Aid within the community" (which for a time gave them a vaguely socialist feel). In all kibbutzim, the principle of common ownership of the means of production was practiced. These are set alongside the less acknowledged third goal: mobilization for national social and security purposes.

## Useful information

In my kibbutz tourist guide, I read:

> You will be able to enjoy the full social life available to Kibbutzniks and volunteers, such as swimming, sport, evening pubs and discos, as well as specially prepared lectures on Israel, folk dancing, arranged outings and tours. And you will experience the exhilaration of country life, healthy food and living, and meeting people from all over the world—all on a shoestring budget. Altogether, this is an experience not to be missed!

P.S. It adds, "only about 15 percent of all kibbutz volunteers are Jewish."

Some kibbutzes, such as Eilat, located at the southernmost tip of the country are blessed, as they say, with everything that "makes a perfect vacation": beautiful mirror-like sea, lively beaches, sea-front bars and restaurants, first-rate hotels, all kinds of water-sports, spectacular underwater world and coral reefs, diving clubs, desert treks, camel tours and even swimming with dolphins.

Others such as Beit Furiq in the parched West Bank, have to make do with swimming pools. Beit Furiq itself, a poverty-stricken Palestinian village, has a timeless history of sheep herding and tending the olive groves that climb up the rocky hillsides towards the imposing Israeli settlements on the heights above. The village's farmers need 50 truckloads of water a day during the summer, when their wells run dry, but these days their water shipments are blocked by Israeli checkpoints. "Yesterday, one truck made it, today none," Atef Hanini, the village mayor told a reporter from *Palestinian Monitor*, as he used some precious spring water to make coffee for rare visitors to the town.

However, Atef adds that the settlements "have swimming pools with enough water to satisfy Beit Furiq for two or three months." A thick Israeli pipeline lifts water to the modern houses of Itamar and Eilon Moreh.

The Kibbutzim are economically very active. To stay there you too must work eight hours a day—or pay for time off. Take Kibbutz Sa'ad, for an example, located in the Northern Negev region, about 20 minutes southwest of Ashkelon. Sa'ad's crops include carrots, potatoes, avocados, almonds, citrus fruit, and dairy and poultry farms. Its industries include Syfan, a kind of plastic shrink film for packaging, and Popli, a brand of popcorn products and pet food as well as a fashion outlet for clothes, handmade jewelry in sterling silver, and even a graphic design studio. (Products like these all enter the despised European Union under special low-tariff arrangements for countries sharing the values of the European Community, for promoting peace, freedom of religion and non-discrimination, things like that.) Tour groups are able to visit the Therapeutic Petting Zoo, as well as the world-renowned cactus garden.

It sounds idyllic. Yet the areas around them have to be "made safe" from the Palestinians. They need always to be watched over by the Israeli Defense Force. An account by Margot Dudkevitch reveals the other side of the Kibbutz life. She reports for a US magazine on a cloudy afternoon at the Erez Crossing at the entrance to the Gaza Strip, where company commander Captain Rafat Halabi is peering through the telescopic site on his gun, amid a burst of gunfire by Palestinians. Rafat takes aim and fires, and misses. Rats! He then turns to calm one of his soldiers, after a bullet hits a sandbag protecting their position.

Two other "armed Palestinians," she reports, are spotted hiding in a nearby field, and the soldiers try to shoot them. However, the battle isn't over until a tank is brought in:

> Once the shooting finally stops, the 24-year-old commander drives to visit another outpost in the fields of Kibbutz Kfar Aza, along the Gaza Strip frontier, where soldiers are keeping a watch on Palestinian police headquarters so that farmers can tend to their crops. Later, Halabi heads back to Erez for a meeting with other commanders to assess the situation.

During the first month of the "Al-Aksa intifada," the soldiers were assigned to guard the Netzarim settlement, site of several heavy battles with Palestinians, and accompanied the convoys traveling to and from the Karni crossing. "The settlers brought us food and welcomed us," one officer recalls appreciatively. "The communities here invite us to use their swimming pools, and every weekend we hold a soccer match. It's good for the soldiers' morale."

"Throughout the day," Dudkevitch continues,

> patrols are sent to check the border fence. The work is dangerous, as the Palestinians often wait for the patrols and detonate bombs as they pass, or lie in nearby fields with their weapons ready, waiting for an opportunity to shoot at the soldiers manning the posts or on patrol. Our mission is to defend and safeguard the communities. But at the same time, we are threatened by Palestinian snipers and bombs.

The previous night, an army bulldozer destroyed the Palestinian position. But the Palestinians have already begun to rebuild it. Now, armed Palestinian policemen guard a tractor clearing the rubble, and the soldiers keep a constant watch. "Sometimes its difficult to sleep because of the shooting," they explain to a sympathetic Dudkevitch.

### Risk factor

Low, especially if you're not Palestinian, in which case the risk factor rises. If you don't share a cranky, antediluvian theory of religious and racial superiority, about God having selected some people over others to live in certain regions of the earth, it can be rather disturbing too.

# 63 No Holiday: **Golan Heights, Syria**

*Enjoy the serenity of the Rubble resort of Quneitra*

## How to get there

Fly to Damascus and hitch a ride in a UN vehicle along the only road between Damascus and the Heights, pausing at the small town of Quneitra some 44 miles (71 kilometers) away. The road then continues to the Heights and various UN "Disengagement Observer Forces" posts.

## What to see

The Golan Heights drop dramatically down from the slopes of Mount Herman to the Yarmuk River in the Jordan Valley. Unlike much of the Middle East, the region is green and fertile, cooled by a gentle breeze that sweeps in from the sea. Once this was a prosperous area, the valleys nearby full of fruit and olive trees. Before the Six Day War, Quneitra itself was a popular holiday resort with cinemas, clubs and villas alongside the mosques and churches. After the Israeli army arrived, it became a military outpost. In 1974, as part of a peace agreement, they

retreated, but carefully destroyed all the buildings as they left, leaving only a wasteland behind. The damage has never been repaired. Today the entire city is a memorial to that day, what the Syrians call the "Museum of Liberation."

As you wander around you can see amongst the dust, the straggly weeds and the rubble, the modest signs of what used to be homes, the cracked minarets of long-abandoned mosques, and the pock-marked walls of the hospital [📷], evidently a particular target for the retreating army.

## Useful information

Israel has occupied the area since 1967. Despite oft-made claims, the area has no military significance, but is certainly useful for control over the neighboring water resources.

## ♡ Disinformation point

As General Matityahu Peled, chief of the logistical command during the 1967 war and one of the 12 members of the Isreali army General Staff, explained in a long article in *Maariv*, the largest circulation Israeli newspaper:

> *Since 1949 no one was in any position to threaten the very existence of Israel. Despite this, we continue to nurture the feeling of inferiority as though we were a weak and insignificant people struggling to preserve our own existence in the face of impending extermination.*

This is still the story put about today, as the new "Security Wall" snakes its way through the Palestinian communities. General Peled clearly explained why: "The thesis according to which Israel was fighting for her very physical survival was nothing but a bluff which was born and bred after the war." Israelis, he added, were never under any threat of destruction "either as individuals or as a nation." Rather, as Mordechai Bentov, a former member of the ruling coalition during the war, wrote: "This whole story about the threat of extermination was totally contrived and then elaborated on afterwards to justify the annexation of new Arab territories."

## Risk factor 

Leave the road and you are likely to be blown up by mines. Point your camera the wrong way, and an Israeli sniper might shoot you.

# 64 No Holiday: **Baghdad, Iraq**

*A visit to Torture Central*

## How to get there

Fly to Baghdad and take a taxi from the airport to the old prison, 16 miles (26 kilometers) due west of the capital.

## What to see

"Torture Central," or Iraq's central prison complex is the size of a small town, covering over 280 acres, surrounded by guard towers and concrete anti-suicide bomber defenses. In Saddam's day, it was divided into different areas for different kinds of prisoners, but each block contained a dining room, prayer room, exercise area and washing facilities. It was officially known as Abu Ghraib, although some referred to it, with good reason, by its nickname.

After the "liberation" of Iraq by the Americans, the prison was used as a concentration camp, which at its peak in early 2004 held more than 7,000 people, almost all held without any formal charge.

This huge, squat ugly prison was briefly in all the world's papers, the backdrop for the reporters breathlessly recounting revelations that hundreds, indeed thousands, of these Iraqi civilians were being tortured there. For some reason that has never been made clear, photographs of all these events were routinely taken, and some of these were passed by a whistle-blower to a general in the US Army, who (even stranger) insisted on investigating them.

The techniques in question included:

- Mock executions, where you are hooded and either "waterboarded" (simulated drowning) or "shot"

- Systematic beatings intended to occasion pain just short of "massive organ failure" (in the words of the next US Attorney General's advice note to the President, although, it seems that, on at least 30 acknowledged occasions, the techniques did in fact cause that, and hence death)

- Electric shocks, including the famous one where you wear a kind of Ku Klux Klan outfit and have to stand on a box

- Cigarette burns (say in the ears)—old fashioned, but doubtless still effective

- Sexual humiliations such as group masturbation, and phosphorescent sticks being inserted into orifices

- And miscellaneous other "college pranks" as one US Senator was pleased to put it, such as making prisoners eat out of toilets.

But as one of the "Baghdad Six" soldiers prosecuted, Staff Sgt. "Chip" Frederick (accused of sitting on top of a detainee, committing an indecent act and assault—not necessarily in that order) told CBS: "We had no support, no training whatsoever. And I kept asking my chain of command for certain things... like rules and regulations."

After the "abuse scandal," (as it was officially termed) the conventional prison blocks, the backdrop to the photos of naked prisoners being arranged in pyramids, or terrified by dogs, were handed over to Iraqi management. But the rest of the complex was retained both as a US military "forward operating" base and "detention facility."

The US president gave a special talk to the Arab world via satellite TV, in which he said that the "abuse" was due to "a few American troops" on the night shift. In May 2004, addressing Marines at the US Army War College in Pennsylvania, George W. Bush announced that the prison would be demolished. A few weeks later, on June 21, a US military judge ruled that the prison was a crime scene and could not be demolished. But the President had the last word. The Judge was unable to prevent the military renaming their detention facility "Camp Redemption."

## Useless information
Prison life in Camp Redemption now includes air-conditioning, pillows, and ice to cool drinking water. Captain Vincent America, a spokesman for the 16th Military Police Brigade, told the usual credulous reporters in Baghdad that nowadays troops receive extra training to remind them that "prisoners should be treated with dignity and respect," because, he added sanctimoniously: "The idea is that when a person is released, we want them to be a productive member of Iraqi society."

Now all detainees (at least those that survive being tortured) receive US $25 and a bus ride back to the place where they were grabbed originally.

## Risk factor
At least at the time of writing, Camp Redemption is probably safer than the rest of Iraq, where alas there is a high risk of being shot on the way to the prison, particularly at Coalition roadblocks (which are, for security reasons, unannounced. You'll know you've hit one when a bullet goes through your windshield), or being blown up either by a suicide bomber or even by a guided missile courtesy of the "Coalition Forces."

# 65 No Holiday: **United Arab Emirates**

*Abu Dhabi, where the Holiday is the Hotel*

## How to get there
Abu Dhabi is the capital of the United Arab Emirates. The hotel is the Emirates Palace.

## What to see
If the Middle East all seems a bit grim, it is not for lack of money. The dictators are all sitting in pots of cash, but seem reluctant to spend it on anything other than armaments. Not so the United Arab Emirates, a tiny creation of the Western powers, which controls a not insignificant part of the region's oil.

The Emirates Palace has many claims to being worth a visit. It is a testament to the inverse relationship of wealth and good taste, with its 1,002 Swarovski Crystal chandeliers (requiring a full time staff of ten people just to keep them clean,) and modern pink marble shopping mall design. The whole resembles a large pink wedding cake, (design courtesy of London firm Wimberly Allison Tong & Goo. And may I say, they really unleashed the Goo in here).

It is perhaps also possible to see as epitomizing the utter futility of the oil wealth flowing smoothly abroad to the rich world (with a bit of froth coating the hands of the local elites).

## Useless information
The hotel has such long corridors (one is a over a half a mile long—that's almost one kilometer!) that the staff needs little golf carts to get around them. Rooms range from around $600 dollars a night to twenty times that, but the best suites (on the top floor) are not available at any price except to visiting royalty. The whole edifice, if nothing else a monument to the social priorities of the Emirates' ruling cliques, cost $3 billion dollars to construct.

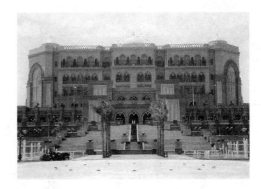

## ↱ Possible side trip
Over in Dubai, more implausible mega hotels have appeared like so many shiny flowers in the dust. One offers "Swiss-style" ski chalets for visitors to indoor ski slopes, adorned with snow and snowmen, while the Burj Tower keeps its final height secret in order to be sure of becoming the highest building in the world. But hotels are all so much the same, after you've fallen asleep in the mini-bar and drunk the Jacuzzi. Perhaps better to tour the Saudi Aramco tower block in Dhahran. This, despite looking like another ludicrous hotel is, it turns out, the headquarters of the world's richest oil company, and one dedicated to keeping down the price of oil (thus helping to avert the need to find ways of sharing out the wealth). It is surrounded, like the Emirates hotel, by a park full of implausibly maintained flowers and, of course, a golf course. And beyond that, the desert.

## Risk factor
Some risk of getting lost in the corridors.

NORTH ATLANTIC OCEAN

FINLAND

RUSSIA

SWEDEN

NORWAY

Trondheim
72

BALTIC SEA

ESTONIA

LATVIA

LITHUANIA

BYELARUS

UKRAINE

MOLDOVA

BLACK SEA

TURKEY

SYRIA

NORTH SEA

DENMARK

POLAND

Oswiecim
67

Copsa Mica
68

ROMANIA

BULGARIA

SERBIA

MACEDONIA

AEGEAN

GREECE

IONIAN SEA

Rosslyn Chapel
74

Gruinard Island
77

Menwith Hill
76

NETHERLANDS

Amsterdam
79

BELGIUM

Berlin
69

GERMANY

CZECH

SLOVAKIA

HUNGARY

AUSTRIA

SLOVENIA

CROATIA

BOSNIA

Mostar
66

MONTENEGRO

ALBANIA

MEDITERRANEAN SEA

Belfast
78

IRELAND

U.K.

London
75

ENGLISH CHANNEL

Luxembourg

80

SWITZERLAND

FRANCE

Languedoc
73

ITALY

CORSICA

SARDINIA

TYRRHENIAN SEA

SICILY

BAY OF BISCAY

Manganeses
de la Polvorosa
70

Catalonia
71

SPAIN

PORTUGAL

# Europe

## 66 No Holiday: **Mostar, Bosnia-Herzegovina**

*The Crescent bridge that divides the communities*

### How to get there
Fly to Sarajevo and take the train to Mostar itself.

### What to see
There are a lot of politically interesting towns in the former Yugoslavia, the region that collapsed into conflict in the 1990s. There's Sarajevo itself, for centuries a center of "multi-faith" harmony, laid siege to for long, cold and hungry months by Serbian militia based in the hills. Before rushing to Mostar, the traveler can pass a few pleasant hours puttering around the marketplace in which a score of people died when it was shelled.

### ♛ Disinformation point
At the time, the Serbian authorities explained that the Muslims themselves had shelled the marketplace in order to discredit the Serbian forces. But the practicalities of the incident, let alone the theoretical aspects, pointed the other way. The whole conflict was based on a vast media barrage of misinformation that is only now beginning to be dispelled.

Or over on the Croatian coast, there's the old sea wall at Dubrovnik, which still sports pockmarks as a legacy of its shelling from the sea by the Serbian navy. This too had some sort of defensive justification by the Serbian government, but I forget now what it was. But perhaps the most obvious symbol of how communities can very quickly come to hate each other is the four hundred year old bridge in Bosnia-Herzegovina.

Mostar Bridge, "a crescent in stone," as one travel writer called it, is a very pretty one, over the steep banks of the Neretva River connecting the two communities of Mostar. It was originally built in 1566 on the Emperor Süleyman's orders to replace a highly alarming chain bridge. As the new one was quite safe, a tradition soon evolved of jumping off it into the fast-rushing river below. (The tradition was revived on the occasion of the re-opening of the bridge.) It is also the practical and symbolic link between the predominantly Muslim community on the left bank, and the mainly Catholic community on the right bank. For centuries it was a very practical symbol of peaceful co-existence between these two religious and culturally distinct communities. And so, because of this, it was deliberately blown up during the Balkan conflict, in this case by Croatian nationalists. It became instead a symbol of how easy it is for politicians to divide communities.

## Background briefing

The Adriatic coast is a very scenic region, full of fine old buildings, bridges and churches. Despite the Balkans' reputation for "ethnic conflict," towns like Mostar and Sarajevo have been peaceful for centuries, and that is the message that their architecture reflects. Cities beset by conflict tend to lose not only their citizens, but their finest buildings too.

When Serbian nationalism, historically the spark for the great bloodletting of what Europeans call "The Great War" of 1914-18, spluttered back into life (after lying dormant under the iron rule of President Tito's communists), a lot of people preferred to "look the other way."

A strange political alliance of the right, such as the British Foreign Minister Douglas Hurd, together with the "Left," who saw in Serbia a socialist beacon, managed to muddy the issues to the extent that Mr. Hurd was allowed to create a strategy of a "level killing field" by imposing an arms embargo on the two sides. That is, no arms to the heavily armed Serbian forces and no arms to the more or less defenseless Croat and Bosnian communities. The policy prevailed over concern at repeated reports, some indeed televised, of civilians being bombed by the Serbian air force and driven from their homes and executed by Serbian soldiers.

Eventually, the Western strategy of leaving the Serbs to finish off their "opponents" fizzled out, as the Serbs, and indeed the Croats and Muslims, even began to fight each other too (which is where Mostar comes in). In a few weeks of its trademark indiscriminate bombing, the US under President Clinton collapsed the Serbian military and the dream of recreating a "Greater Serbia" stretching from Turkey to Hungary to the Adriatic.

In a fine piece of peacemaking and international symbolism, the "Stari Most," or Old Bridge was carefully rebuilt, each stone cut in the traditional way by local craftspeople. As Amir Pasic, the man in charge of restoring the bridge, said rather lamely in 2004: "It's beautiful, it's simple, it's symbolic because crossing the river is something, you know." Alas, the other effects of the bloodletting and racial discrimination are not as easy to correct. Mostar's communities continue to be divided, fearful and bitter.

## Useless information
A lucrative part-privatization of Serbian telecommunications took place at the end of the war in 1997, giving just under half of the company to Italian and Greek investors. It was negotiated with the Serbian President, Mr. Milosevic, by (the now) Lord Hurd in a new job as deputy chairman of one of the biggest UK banks, NatWest Markets. Investigators later discovered that the bank received over £10 million ($17 million) in commissions for its role, an exceptionally high rate of return, as its advertisements for the public might say.

But the privatization was always a little controversial because the billion-dollar windfall came not only after the return of "ethnic cleansing" to Europe, but also after mass demonstrations against the President were taking place in Belgrade. Today, officials in Belgrade also complain that the deal provided Milosevic with cash for the following year's campaign against Kosovo's Albanian population.

Anyway, the contracts came from a now infamous "working breakfast" that the two peacemakers had in the summer of 1996, that is just a year after Mr. Hurd quit as foreign minister and only a few months after the formal end of the Bosnian war. Dame Pauline Neville-Jones joined Lord Hurd in this important mission. She had been the British official on the six nation Contact Group dealing with Yugoslavia and the top British representative at the Dayton peace negotiations.

## Risk factor
Depending which community you come from, only one side of the bridge is safe, years after the end of the war.

# 67 No Holiday: **Oswiecim, Poland**
*Searching for the moral at Europe's heart of darkness*

## How to get there
The small Polish town of Oswiecim is a train ride from Katowice. The Second World War's most notorious death camp, Birkenau, or Auschwitz II, is in the village of Brzezinka, just under two miles away.

## What to see
Now Auschwitz, the most famous of all the Nazi concentration camps, has become a bit of a must-see for political tourists. It must be political because all the politicians go there. In 2005, to

celebrate 60 years of the end of World War II, no less than 30 of them did, including World President Bush and the Russian Tsar, Putin, Prime Minister Blair, and the Emperor of France.

You enter through the famous wrought-iron gates with their promise "Arbeit Macht Frei" (Through Work, Freedom) to a kind of alternative Disney World of horror. Here is the "Book of Deaths" in which names of victims are faithfully recorded alongside, at approximately 5-minute intervals, with fictitious causes. Here are the shower-rooms that never saw any water, only deadly "Zyklon B" delivered to the naked prisoners through the fake shower-heads. (The nakedness saved time later.) Here are the incineration ovens, and here the ponds filled with human ashes...

Everyone agrees it's chilling... sobering. No fun. No Holiday.

## Useful information

But there's not much agreement on just what the lesson is.

Some people seem to think the lesson is: don't vote for anyone with a toothbrush moustache and a swastika armband. If that is the lesson, it has been well learned. Some (more aware) people think that no government should construct gas chambers and extermination ovens to incinerate thousands of people, trucked in cattle wagons from surrounding countries. Again, if that is the lesson, it has been well learned. No government since World War II has even proposed such a program, let alone started to implement one.

But if that is the lesson, it is also rather a limited one. I would like to think the lesson was more general, about our common humanity. About what happens when communities divide along racial or religious lines. And that makes Auschwitz still carry a political lesson.

Yet if the lesson is about our common humanity, then it is one that has evidently not been learned. This may have something to do with the way that we have "simplified" this issue into one that concerns only the Jewish people. In fact, the Holocaust was a multi-dimensional, multi-cultural act of barbarity.

Take Frank Dimant, working for the *Jewish Tribune* (Canada). First of all, he describes the reaction of the first ever Canadian Prime Minister to visit the "Auschwitz Experience:"

> *The emotion that overcame Jean Chrétien and his wife Ilene was evident. He was pale-faced and shaken as he listened to the description of the killing machine and stood in silent reverence as a tour guide described in detail the amount of Jewish bodies that could be burnt on any given day in Auschwitz and Birkenau.*

And this, says Dimant, brings us to the question of what is the lesson for today.

> *Is it sufficient to join us in shedding a tear at Auschwitz? Is it sufficient to believe that a multi-cultural society in Canada is the answer to anti-Semitism domestically and internationally? I believe not! The lesson that must be fully absorbed by Mr. Jean Chrétien as well as by all Canadian Cabinet ministers and specifically the bureaucrats in Foreign Affairs, is that in 1999 there are still elements in the world that are prepared to use the equivalent of Zyklon B gas on the Jewish people. In 1999, there are still states, which tolerate and encourage stereotypic images of Jews, and all the ugly features associated with the caricatures of the Jews, to flourish in their newspapers. And it is incumbent to remember that in 1999, there are elements who still speak of the final destruction of the Jewish people vis-à-vis the State of Israel... We will look to the Security Council and to Canadian Ambassador Fowler's hand as he raises it to*

*cast the vote over and over again on matters relating to the security and safety of the State of Israel. This will be the test of the lesson of Auschwitz.*

Not at all, the Nazis did not build any of the camps solely for Jewish people, they were very inclusive in that sense. Just as they treated men, women and children the same. Auschwitz was originally mainly intended for Poles (which is why it is in Poland) and was only designated in the middle of the war (1941) for the final solution to the "Jewish problem." Jews (and the complicated criteria used to measure "jewishness" was part of the madness) made up the bulk of the victims, but once categorized, the only distinction made between prisoners was the color of badges they wore. Jews had the yellow star, political prisoners wore a red triangle. Gypsies got black triangles, homosexuals pink ones; miscellaneous criminals green ones. Jehovah's Witnesses even had a special color—purple. But they were all worked to death, or exterminated. The mentality of the Nazis cannot be understood if you think of it as simply the Führer's personal antipathy to Jews.

Yet if the lesson of Auschwitz is of man's inhumanity to man, of the consequences once you place individuals into categories and refuse to remember they are also people, then that lesson has not been learned at all.

### Risk factor

In the aftermath of the horrors of the Nazi camps, the world pledged 'never again'. Today, co-opting the holocaust for narrow political purposes, let alone tourist ones, risks (at the least) 'holocaust fatigue' setting in, and at worst, its universal significance being lost.

# 68 No Holiday: **Copsa Mica, Romania**

*Looking at the soot in Europe's most polluted city*

## How to get there

Fly to Bucharest and take a highly polluting Trabant (East German classic) car northeast through the mountains to the town itself. It is worth a look at for itself, a gem of Eastern Europe, where the buildings are grim grey blocks of concrete, the sky is full of grey clouds (more on that later) and the people themselves are grey, grim, and often desperate. [ 📷 ]

## What to see

Romania is one of those former Soviet satellites that are now finding a new identity for themselves. However, in Romania's case, the new identity is not so different from the old one. The country is still desperately poor, riddled with corruption, and retains a police state mentality that has made it a natural ally for the US in its wars on terror.

That said, we are not interested in the secret prisons and holding camps of Romania, nor even the famous orphanages that used to sell babies to would-be mothers in the West. We are content instead to visit instead a rather ordinary town that could be anywhere in the world where industry is the national priority. Which is just about everywhere. Its sole claim to fame is as Europe's most polluted city.

Whether it really deserves that title, is hard to say. However, Copsa Mica's case rests on its two factories, a carbon factory, which (until 1993) used to produce black stuff for tires, and another, a metal smelter, which continues today to belch out lead, cadmium and other notoriously poisonous metals.

When the carbon factory was running at full strength (during the twilight years of Soviet communism) the wheezing machinery released a ton of soot over the already rather grey (in the manner of the Soviets) little town every hour. Famously, the sheep in the surrounding fields were dyed black. And although the last shift was a dozen years ago, and efforts have been made to clean up the town, everywhere the sooty stains are still visible.

## Background briefing

It was under Nicolae Ceausescu (a dictator so reviled that in the aftermath of the Romanian revolution he was executed) that the strategy was devised of situating industry in remote rural communities so as to concentrate pollution in a few small areas, leaving the rest of the country relatively pristine. A bit like the US and European companies that locate their plants in the developing world. The strategy has some advantages, as can be seen when walking through the beautiful Carpathian mountains (where Dracula once roamed) although it was clearly unfortunate for Copsa Mica. It was designated as one of these pollution centers despite being geographically totally unsuitable to the task. But that's the "command economy" for you.

Anyway, in line with the strategy (of small areas of high pollution), the factories had short smokestacks to stop the pollution from spreading over a large area, and local farmers were permitted to sell their toxic produce only to local workers. These people were already being poisoned by the local air and drinking water, and the government paid them a small bonus by way of acknowledgement of the risk.

Additionally, as in much of the West, pollution statistics were state secrets. Yet the reality of both farm animals and people getting peculiar diseases and dropping dead was difficult to hide.

In 1989, the National Salvation Front toppled Ceausescu, introduced a market economy and promised to save the environment too. The carbon factory was shut down in 1993, and the lead and zinc-smelting factory was smartened up. International industrial safety experts from the UN came to put in new filters and emissions monitors. Money was even set aside to ameliorate some of the environmental damage, including some tree planting in the city and district.

Nonetheless, the two factories had helped put Romania on the political map—albeit only as an environmental black spot. And, in fact, Copsa Mica remains extremely polluted. The new Greek management of the metal smelting factory cite economic necessity as justification for continuing to release toxins through the air. The town continues to have the highest infant mortality rate in Europe, as well as many cases of lead poisoning, reduced lung function, and neurobehavioral symptoms among everyone else.

What's more, the city residents are increasingly poor, as the few environmental improvements there have been resulted in the loss of some 4,000 jobs. Even if in the long-term the factories poisoned the people, in the short-term, they fed them. Many now look back at their previous hazardous trades affectionately.

Copsa Mica is, in this way, typical not only of Romania, but of environmental politics in general. The politicians claim to be involved in a delicate balancing act between protecting jobs and protecting the environment (while, naturally, failing to do either). The preferred solution in Romania, as elsewhere, is to continue polluting the environment while advising the "more advanced" nations, that if they want it to stop—they will have to pay.

### Useless information
Romania relies on its Dracula legend for most of its tourists, with sinister looking castles such as those built by the country's most famous son, Vlad the Impaler (he who used to impale his victims on stakes of wood) well-preserved and regularly attracting film crews. Recently it has also become popular as a kind of "vanished America" location for blockbusters like *Cold Mountain*. But my favorite scene comes from a much older and simpler film, indeed a silent one, *Nosferatu, A Symphony of Horror*, featuring Max Schreck in his hideous makeup. This shows a long column of hunched-over citizens staggering down the cobbled main street of an old half-timbered town carrying coffins, just two to a casket, and all in their drab Sunday best. Actually, the town was Bremen, in Germany, and as we've seen, Costa Mica is entirely concrete. But it somehow still conveys both the Romanian spirit and the tragedy.

### Risk factor
Most of the poisons mentioned are cumulative, so a short stay should be okay. But go easy on the local food and the local water. And maybe try not to breathe too much while you're at it.

# 69 No Holiday: **Berlin Art Galleries**

*Behind the Velvet Curtain in search of Socialist Realism*

### How to get there
Twenty years after the pulling down of the Berlin Wall (although, happily, bits of it remain for tourists to speculate over), German museums and art galleries have begun to take a new interest in the ideologically inspired art of the former Soviet Union. No Holidaymakers can track down special exhibitions in many of the big cities, such as Berlin, Bonn and Frankfurt.

## What to see

Paintings, statues and films were needed both to celebrate and to create the pure spirit of the new egalitarian, joyful communism. They started as early as the famous steps scene in Battleship Potemkin, but went on for another eighty or so years peaking, naturally enough, in the 1950s with the period of Stalinist mass compulsory collectivization and purges.

Socialist art, in contrast to Western galleries, with their penchant for nobles on horseback and Renaissance nudes, consists of heroic workers, and paintings of Stalin and Lenin in revolutionary poses. In "Unforgettable Encounter," for instance, painted at the high point of the purges in 1936-7, Stalin is shown graciously smiling and receiving a bouquet of flowers from a Russian female worker. Still exploring the same imagery, the painting "Collective Farm Workers Greeting a Tank" (by Katerina Sernova) portrays an everyday scene from the farm, as a group of men, women and a child wave their caps at a tank and bedeck it with flowers. Such works are obviously of merit, but so too are ones with coded messages, such as the otherwise uninspiring representation of a suitably concerned looking Stalin "at Gorky's sick bed" (by Vassili Yefanov). This is noteworthy because Gorky, a celebrated writer, had been assassinated on Stalin's orders.

## Useless information

In the period immediately following the 1917 October Revolution, under Lenin, many artists enthusiastically rushed to place their skills at the service of the State, which responded by making special provision for them even in the bleak economic conditions of the times. Works by Tatlin, Malevich and Rodchenko date from this optimistic period. An early sketch by Isaac Brodsky shows Lenin at work in the revolutionary HQ, scribbling on papers on his lap, while next to him there is a table covered in newspapers. The piece later became Lenin's widow's favorite image when he turned it into a full-scale paining.

Alas, soon after Lenin's death (in 1924) the approach became more "dirigiste," and artists were now policed to ensure their works carried the appropriate political message. Even Brodsky's painting of Lenin was singled out for revolutionary criticism, although it was not actually added to a new art collection of "forbidden art."

Trotsky himself wrote a book on *Art and Politics in Our Epoch* shortly before Stalin had him killed with the ice pick, which explains:

> The style of present-day official Soviet Painting is called "socialist realism"... It is impossible to read Soviet verse and prose without physical disgust, mixed with horror, or to look at reproductions of paintings and sculpture in which functionaries armed with pens, brushes and scissors, under the supervision of functionaries armed with Mausers, glorify the "great" and "brilliant" leaders... The art of the Stalinist period will remain as the frankest expression of the profound decline of the proletarian revolution.

## Risk factor 

Evidently some risk of physical disgust, mixed with horror.

was forbidden and replaced by a new procedure where the goat had to be let down hanging on ropes. But by 1996 the goats were being thrown again. The mayor defended his decision by saying that "a fiesta without throwing a goat is like Christmas without a Christmas tree."

### Additional information
If the goat (by some miracle) survives, it is drowned in the town fountain.

### Risk factor
Statistically speaking, there is a surprisingly high risk of being killed by falling animals. But whether joining in the Spanish fiestas increases that risk, the research does not say.

# 71 No Holiday: **Animal Cruelty Outings II: Catalonia, Spain**

*Finding spiritual intensity in bullfighting*

### How to get there
Fly direct to the Costa Brava to join what's left of Catalonia's organized bullfighting, and savor what the American author, Ernest Hemingway, called its "spiritual intensity."

### What to see
Bullfighting is widespread in both Spain and Portugal. Estimates of how many bullfights occur annually vary, but it seems to be in the tens of thousands. But if the Spanish have chosen the ritual to define themselves, today it is tourists who prevent the ritual from becoming history.

Many of them will be clutching copies of *Death in the Afternoon*. In this classic account by Ernest Hemingway, the American turns bullfighting into a richly choreographed ballet led by a matador, playing out a role, ranging from that of coward to glory seeker. (James Joyce also describes bullfights in his novel *Ulysses*.)

But bullfighting is becoming controversial—even within Spain. Barcelona's mayor received a petition of 250,000 signatures asking the city to ban the practice, and rather to everyone's surprise, it did. So should tourists hesitate to support the tradition? As one travel writer says, "I sit happily on the fence. A bullfight is an exciting event to see and if you want to see it I say go buy a ticket! If you think the event is cruel and horrible then I say stay away, but don't look for me to make a decision or opinion on it here."

But there are many supporters still prepared to defend it left. One such, the Catalan Bullfighting Federation's spokesman, German Jimenez, for example, told a reporter: "Bullfighting is an art form and a vital part of our history and culture." A ban would involve caving in to the "ignorant" as well as pandering to excessively delicate modern sensibilities about animal welfare.

A typical Spanish bullfight lasts all afternoon and is somewhat of a play in three Acts. Or maybe a pantomime, for the crowd is encouraged to show its approval or impatience. As the animals writhe and bleed the tourists shout "Olé!" or "Torero!" to mean they like what they see—or whistle or slow handclap to show impatience. After a particularly exciting fight, the crowd will wave handkerchiefs to ask that the matador be awarded the coveted bull's tail (or ear) as a trophy.

Anyway, what will the day-tripper get to see? During Act I the matador sizes up the bull and with help from his assistants, the banderilleros, starts to wear him down. This is where he twirls the famous cape to attract the bull, and then directs the animal past his body, as close as his bravery allows. After a few such thrills, the picadors enter, mounted on horseback, and usually some others too, and jab swords into the muscle at the back of the bull's neck.

These horses are also important. They are what Hemingway calls the "comic characters." As horses don't like fighting bulls, they have to be drugged and blindfolded to get them into the ring, and as they are often injured during the fights, only old tired ones are used. Hemingway writes:

> In the tragedy of the bullfight, the horse is the comic character... I have seen these, call them disemboweling, that is the worst word. When due to their timing, they were very funny. This is the sort of thing you should not admit, but it is because such things have not been admitted that the bullfight has never been explained.

In Act II, the bull is alternately enraged and weakened. The banderilleros leap around the bull, plunging brightly colored, barbed sticks into the bull's neck muscles, weakening the thrust of his horns.

At this point, the matador will bow to the crowd and ask permission to kill the bull. Then, after a bit more cape-work, the matador thrusts his sword between the animal's shoulder blades—usually taking several thrusts.

Typically, the bull is still alive, (and fully conscious) as his ears and tail are cut off.

## Useful information
Bullfighting "in the ring," like the ancient gladiatorial contests of Rome, where the "ferocious lions" were frequently too sick to stand up, is a spectacle relying on a lot of behind the scenes preparation.

In order to get the animals reliably frenzied, they may need to be subjected to electric shock prods and poked with sharp sticks before being released in front of the crowds. This is particularly necessary as the bull may have had several weeks of being beaten before the fight. Blows may be administered to the kidneys and heavy weights hung around the animal's neck for several weeks before. As well as being kept in darkness prior to being released into the ring, petroleum jelly may be rubbed in their eyes to ensure that they are only barely able to see their tormentors. Some bulls have their horns "shaved" to ensure their thrusts miss.

## Risk factor

In 200 years of bullfighting in Sevilla, only one matador has ever been killed, although from time to time bulls have plunged into the crowds. So you are probably better advised to see bull fighting from the relative security of standing in the ring with a cape.


# 72 No Holiday:
# Animal Cruelty Outings III: Trondheim, Norway

*A safari in the European Union's wild northern neighbor*

### How to get there
Travel, preferably by whaling trawler, to Trondheim, or any one of Norway's great fishing ports.

### What to see
Norwegians guard their local traditions fiercely: they all center around killing endangered marine species such as whales and seals with maybe the odd polar bear. But in recent years, apparently as a result of the rest of Europe trying to increase their numbers, the need to kill seals has driven the Norwegian government to offer special quotas to businesses, in a bid to encourage more people to experience the thrill killing of the furry mammals with the long whiskers.

Nor are the opportunities being restricted only to Norwegians. Companies such as NorSafari offer a characteristically Norwegian day out in which holidaymakers get to use a little boat, and dress up in military fatigues. On a good day, they can shoot a seal, chop its head off ("training in butchering and preserving the carcasses") and pose for trophy photographs. [  ] For quite a few kroner more tourists are tempted to make it a four-day hunt with at least two kills guaranteed. That is, of course, kills of seals, not fellow amateur hunters, let alone any stray animal rights campaigners who may appear from time to time over the frozen floes.

### Useful information
Fishermen blame seals for eating up all the fish in the North Sea, unlike the giant Norwegian factory trawlers, which are in an otherwise perfect and sustainable ecological relationship with the sea. Killing seals is needed, says the Norwegian Directorate of Fisheries, to (a) reduce the seal stock, and (b) to meet government quotas on killing seals, which provides (philosophers will note), altogether three ways of saying the same thing, and so no explanation at all.

### Useless information
Det er meget gode fiskemuligheter i området. Hvis man ønsker er det mulig å ta med familien, ta en ekstra dag til fisking å ta med fisken hjem!

### Risk factor
Seals are, as noted earlier, gentle furry creatures with long whiskers and, while hunting them

must of course be very exciting, they are still only really dangerous to fish. Amateur seal hunters clutching harpoons and other automatic weapons are, on the other hand, dangerous and should be avoided at all costs.

Additionally, there is a risk acknowledged by some Norwegian ministers that this particular aspect of Norwegian culture will actually drive tourists away.

# 73 No Holiday: **The lovely Languedoc, France**

*The Da Vinci Trail*

### How to get there
Whatever you do, don't use a specialist literary tour travel company.

### What to see
Fifty million or so copies later, Dan Brown's book, *The Da Vinci Code* is now not only a publishing phenomenon, but a tourist one. There are $3,000 transatlantic tours offering strolls in Paris and forays in Scotland, not to forget the Vatican itself.

The book itself is a cunningly paced adventure or chase thriller aimed particularly at women, who buy most fiction. It was launched onto an unsuspecting world in 2003, backed by an advertising campaign that included a $500,000 TV commercial.

### Useful religious information
The best summary of the politics of *The Da Vinci Code* comes from Opus Dei, a formerly obscure sect of the Catholic Church. This says that the novel has misstated the Church's poison, sorry *position*, in four main areas. These are: man and woman, the Bible, Jesus Christ, and lastly, the Church itself. "We hope that this book will spur people to look deeper into what the Catholic Church actually teaches on these important themes," Opus Dei notes sanctimoniously, if implausibly, before adding (now well into the realms of make-believe) "We offer the following bibliography for those who are interested in further study." Others in the Church have taken a more pragmatic line and added the book to the banned list.

Opus Dei is concerned that, for example, in *The Da Vinci Code*, "the Church is incorrectly said to teach that sexuality is bad in itself, and that marriage is bad, when in fact marriage is considered by Catholics to be one of the seven holy sacraments." (So only sex is bad, then.) And, as for the Bible, *The Da Vinci Code* says that in order to consolidate its power and its chauvinistic view of Christianity, the Church suppressed other gospels, which, prior to their unjust suppression, had a following equal to that of the canonical four. "In fact," continues Opus Dei, "the familiar four Gospels of Matthew, Mark, Luke and John are in the Bible because there was unanimous agreement among the early Christians that they presented the true teachings Jesus had left his Apostles. The Church did not include the later Gnostic 'gospels' in the canon of Scripture because they contained ideas contrary to the Christian faith." So that's clear. Most intriguingly of all, *The Da Vinci Code* portrays the divinity of Jesus Christ as a politically motivated 4th century invention. It is said that prior to this, he was considered to be a great moral teacher and political leader, but not divine. And of course, the book is wrong to say the Church reinvented Jesus as a God rather than as a human, as "the Church actually teaches Christ as both."

"Underlying the above inaccuracies," continues Opus Dei helpfully, "is *The Da Vinci Code*'s presupposition that the hierarchy and Magisterium of the Church are not established by Christ and guided by the Holy Spirit, but rather are organs of political power, created and exercised by men so as to satisfy greed and ambition." Hear, hear to that! So that makes the Da Vinci Trail quite a useful political journey too.

## Useless writing
The book itself opens with a mysterious murder at the Louvre, and becomes an exciting race between handsome Harvard symbologist, Robert Langdon, and Sophie, his attractive French cryptographer, against the sinister aforementioned fundamentalist sect, Opus Dei, to stop it destroying evidence of a 2,000-year-old cover up of the "fact" that Jesus was an ordinary guy, and Mary Magdalene was his missus.

## Useless information
So-called "literary tours" are quite the thing nowadays. Very expensive and completely pointless, they seem to offer an educational aspect to the otherwise rather dull cycle of self-indulgence. The Da Vinci Canal Cruise, for example, offers "a fully-equipped restored canal barge, suitable for up to six passengers at $4,500 per person." Enjoy cabins with en-suite baths and on-board bicycles while the "gourmet kitchens turn out exquisite local specialties." Turn out? Surely not. "Create," at least.

## Risk factor
Considerable risk of being ripped off and fed a lot of crap.

# 74 No Holiday: **Rosslyn Chapel, Scotland** 🐴
*The Da Vinci Trail too*

## How to get there
Fly to Scotland, which (for US visitors) is near London, and head to Roslin, Midlothian, which (for everyone) is on a "remote hillside" about seven miles (11 kilometers) from Edinburgh.

## ☐ Disinformation point
Actually, seven miles (11 kilometers) from Edinburgh isn't really remote, but it sounds good in the marketing materials.

## What to see
Rosslyn is a working church, or at least as much as any church is nowadays, officially Episcopal, although originally Catholic. It is interesting to visitors because there are lots of mysterious stone carvings, notably the one hundred and three "Green Men," that is human faces with leaves and things sprouting from their noses and mouths.

## Useful religious information
William St. Clair founded the church, designed in the shape of a large cross, in 1446, a Prince of Orkney reputed to have been a grandmaster of the Knights Templar. It was in this lofty capacity that he was supposed to have placed and hidden many religious relics taken from Jerusalem.

## Useful information
It costs good money to go inside Rosslyn Chapel, although children get in for free. It is open Monday to Saturday, 10 am to 5 pm and on Sunday afternoons, the morning of course being devoted to worshipping Dan Brown for saving the Church Restoration Fund.

## Risk factor
Visitors have complained that the Chapel is *so* cold they can see their breath freeze. *But that's not the Chapel, that's Scotland.*

SCOTLAND

NORTH SEA

NORTH
CHANNEL

NORTHERN
IRELAND

ISLE OF MAN

76
Menwith Hill

IRISH SEA

IRELAND

ENGLAND

WALES

75
London

STRAIT OF DOVER

ENGLISH CHANNEL

* England has its own map because since World War II it has been part of the United States, or at least the
"Atlantic Alliance," and so is not strictly speaking still in Europe. Sometimes Wales and Scotland—even
Ireland—are considered part of England—to their citizens' annoyance—but of course they are not here.

# England*

## 75 No Holiday: **London, England**

*In search of the Ethiopian Emperor's treasures (and hair)*

### How to get there

After the quest for Da Vinci's secrets, whilst in Edinburgh, pop into the historic university which boasts a good selection of ancient manuscripts grabbed from countries around the world which it guards carefully. Whether they give any useful clues as to the location of the "real stuff" I cannot say, but certainly Edinburgh's Episcopal Church, until very recently, had a piece of the Ethiopian box where Moses was said to have kept the Ten Commandments—or a "tabot," as it is known in the trade. Alas for us, the Reverend McLuckie (no less) decided to return it in 2004. So the quest leads to Waverley Station and a train to Kings Cross London.

### What to see

It might seem odd that Ethiopia's treasures should be found in London, but it should not. After all, the British Museum is home to the collected booty of one of the world's largest empires. Still there are the famous Elgin Marbles, the Benin Bronzes, *etc. etc.*

And perhaps one of the most curious stories is that of the raid over 130 years ago by British troops on the unfortunate Emperor of Ethiopia. He had offended English public opinion by taking some British soldiers hostage whilst demanding a reply to his letter to the Queen of England. "Your Queen can give you orders to visit my enemies, and then to return to Massowah, but she cannot return a civil answer to my letter to her. You shall not leave till that answer comes," the King had threatened the British discontentedly. When it came, the reply was not a letter, but "the battle of Magdala," in which most of the King's army was massacred and the British troops went on a looting rampage. The King himself only avoided being captured by shooting himself with a silver pistol (ironically enough, a present from Queen Victoria). The thing about all this was that later several thousands of the best "objets trouvés" were auctioned to raise "prize money" for the troops. These in large part duly made their way back to Britain where they ended up in various venerable national collections.

So London's Ethiopian treasures include:

• Eleven wooden tabots, ornately carved tablets supposed to represent the original box in which the Ten Commandments were housed, are in the British Museum. These are now in the basement in a locked room no one is allowed to enter.

• About fifty objects including a gold crown and gold chalice, a shield and silver cross are now in the Victoria and Albert Museum. There is also the dress of the favorite wife of the King, who died one month after being "grossly insulted" by British soldiers, as Clements Markham, who was present at the time tactfully put it in his history of the expedition. None of these are currently on display, but you can ask to be allowed a peek.

• A silver coated crown that was once at the Victoria and Albert Museum was returned to the Ethiopians in 1924. The British government at this time wanted to give the Empress of Abyssinia an honor, but as honors were not then given to women, decided to offer the crown instead. The museum's expert wrote to the government recommending the crown saying "It is a crude barbaric object and I cannot imagine that, except as a curiosity, it is of the slightest value." So that made it a very suitable gift.

• Around 350 ancient manuscripts dating from the Battle of Magdala. These are held by the British Library, now next to Kings Cross Station conveniently enough, and are at least said to be "freely available" for study.

• Other bits and pieces, including a number of illuminated manuscripts are in the Royal Collection, at Windsor Castle, and are not generally available to the public to see.

• Lastly, the tufts of the Emperor's hair are kept at the National Army Museum in Chelsea.

## Background briefing
In 2005 the Ethiopians at least celebrated the return of a final section of a 200-year-old granite obelisk from Rome, but, the English might say, it's easy for the Italians to return things, they have lots of their own art. In England, the government rightly fears that once you start returning things to their rightful owner, you may soon have very little left. So, ever since the demands for the return of the 11 tabots in the British Museum, they have been moved out of the "ethnography store" at Hackney to a more glamorous location in the basement of the main British Museum building. The *Art Newspaper* retells what happened next. The tabots were carried

*by a senior member of the Ethiopian Church in Britain and were covered during the transportation. Once inside the special room and alone, the priest placed the tabots, wrapped in a cloth, on a shield covered with conservation-quality [no less] purple velvet. No museum staff, not even curators or conservators, is permitted to enter the locked room.*

As the paper notes, "it is of course somewhat pointless for a museum to hold objects that can never be seen by scholars, let alone by the general public." "Delicate discussions," it says, are underway to resolve the apparent paradox and find a long-term solution, probably involving renewable loans of the items to the Ethiopian Church, but even then, only the one in London.

## Useless information
How did the tufts of hair get there? King Theodore, as has been noted, shot himself rather than surrender to the British. The British love fox hunting, and it is tradition to take the tail of the fox after its kill. Here, deprived of the kill but finding the body of the king, according to Clements Markham, "they gave three cheers over it as if it had been a dead fox and began to pull and tear the clothes to pieces until it was nearly naked." They then pulled out his hair in tufts as souvenirs. After a quick loot round, they loaded up no less than 15 elephants and 200 mules and left the palace.

The British Prime Minister, perhaps reflecting the Queen's disquiet, told Parliament that he "deeply regretted" that the articles were ever brought from Abyssinia, and could not "conceive" why they had been. The official record states that he "deeply lamented, for the sake of the country and for the sake of all concerned, that those articles, to us insignificant, though probably to the Abyssinians sacred and imposing symbols, [the tabots] or at least hallowed by association [the king's tufty hairs] were thought fit to be brought away by the British army."

Nonetheless, few of them were returned.

## Risk factor
There is a risk of catastrophe if the holy tabots are seen by non-believers. Nowadays this is less likely to happen, but poor attention to this rule earlier could well explain the various disasters of the 20th Century.

# 76 No Holiday: **Menwith Hill, England**

*In the heart of the Yorkshire Moors—the world's biggest spying operation*

## How to get there
Return to Euston station for a train up to Manchester and from there, take the TransPennine Express to Leeds and connect onward to Harrogate. From here, bicycle covertly into the moors on the Skipton road and past the top-secret listening station. [  ]

## What to see
RAF Menwith Hill looms out of the mist on the North Yorkshire moors as a series of huge polygonal domes, incongruous among the pink heather, dry stone walls and flocks of sheep.

From a distance they seem like giant golf balls, carelessly struck, ending up in the heather, far from the green. Incongruous, yes, but not careless. For the golf balls are the latest hi-tech protection covers for hiding and protecting satellite dishes and radio masts. [  ] Well worth photographing, particularly in the summer when the heather is in bloom, albeit not from the road, as you may be arrested.

The site covers over 500 acres, and is surrounded by a barbed wire security fence equipped with watchtowers, US style, but patrolled by the UK's Ministry of Defense doggies. By night, a glow from the ever-burning lights of its operation rooms and high-tech listening equipment gives the base a more sinister ambience.

## Useful information

Menwith Hill is the biggest spy station in the world. Inside, over a thousand (mostly bearded) secret agents sort through endless millions of intercepted phone calls, faxes and, nowadays, emails. (Aided these days, of course, by powerful computers.) It searches tirelessly for business, government and occasionally (or so at least the papers tell us) terrorist secrets.

There is an operation center and residential area of houses and shops, including a chapel and a sports center. If you were allowed in, which you will not be, it might make quite a good holiday camp, in the highly marshaled spirit of Butlins, albeit with "red berets" on the military police instead of the famous "red coats."

Notwithstanding that, by the end of the 1990s, the number of staff there had risen to nearly 1,500 American engineers, physicists, mathematicians, linguists and computer experts, alongside several hundred UK staff from the Ministry of Defense—mainly cleaners, groundskeepers and tea-makers and stuff like that. In fact, "RAF Menwith Hill" is home to more people than the whole of MI5, Britain's secret intelligence agency.

## ♿ Disinformation point

That name "RAF Menwith Hill," after the original World War II airbase, is misleading—it is not a British airbase. The government leases it directly to the US National Security Agency who call it "Field Station F83."

## Useless information

Although apparently situated in the middle of nowhere, that is to say eight miles west of Harrogate, the bugging center is actually strategically situated neatly at the heart of the UK telecommunications network, not least because the UK government obligingly constructed this to US specifications in the 1950s and '60s. Additionally, the UK itself has a special role in much of the rest of Europe's transatlantic communications.

"Field Station F83" was officially opened in 1960, almost unnoticed, but lost some of its anonymity in the mid-1970s when the US Congress investigated its activities, and found that it was intercepting millions of transatlantic phone calls, flaunting the US citizens' right to privacy. Congress, however, was reassured that the Constitution was being scrupulously followed and US citizens were never listened to. Except maybe by accident.

In 2001 the European Parliament, following a report from its own secretive organization based in Luxembourg, "STOA," sent a delegation to Big Brother to find out whether the Americans had used intercepted information to derail European business. Boeing and McDonnell Douglas were suspected of having beaten France to a $6 billion contract to supply Airbus jets to Saudi Arabia, using intercepts of faxes and phone calls. The French also complained that a French electronics company, Thomson-CSF, had lost a billion dollar project to supply Brazil with a radar system after someone intercepted and passed details of the negotiations to an American firm, Raytheon. Alas, the delegation went home empty-handed. The NSA said that what it got up to in Yorkshire was simply too secret to be discussed with them. And, after all, conversations can be overheard!

Some think that if the veil was lifted too far, the UK government might find itself in breach of commitments under the European Convention on Human Rights, which is superior to national law, even if a special section of its own "Interception of Communications Act" (1985, 2000) allows bugging to intercept any general type of international messages to or from Britain if this is "in the interests of national security" or "for the purpose of safeguarding the economic well-being of the United Kingdom."

Funnily enough, the British Government itself is one of the main targets of the US monitoring. The whisper is that during the Suez crisis the US successfully pre-empted the British and French plans using information thus overheard. Certainly the "Fink Report," the one and only Congressional investigation into FSF83 in 1975, notes that the "NSA monitors the traffic of specific countries including Great Britain, our closest ally. There was a whole bank of machines [and] a whole team of men whose only job was to read and process intercepted British communications." Actually, the report was supposed to be secret too, but parts were released accidentally in 1978 as part of another inquiry.

### Risk factor
Any who wander too close or linger too long will be brusquely challenged by MoD Police demanding to know the nature of their interest. Or shot.

# 77 No Holiday: **Gruinard, Scotland**

*Go walking through the heather on Scotland's own Anthrax Island*

### How to get there
From Edinburgh take a train to Ullapool and rent a small fishing boat. The island of Gruinard is just off the Scottish mainland, in Gruinard Bay, half way between Ullapool and Gairloch in the Scottish Highlands.

### What to see
Gruinard is an otherwise rather ordinary bit of Scotland, covered in heather and normally rather boggy underfoot. But it is also the site of the world's most ambitious biological weapons test.

British scientists demonstrated the killing power of anthrax on this remote (well, to London) Scottish island during World War II to wipe out a flock of sheep. A film was made of the test and it shows the sheep, obedient in the manner of sheep everywhere, being taken to the island, secured in wooden frames, and left there while bombs scattered spores of anthrax. The sheep started dying three days later.

This left the island so contaminated that it was officially out-of-bounds for the next 50 years. The final government report on the Gruinard Island tests, classified until 1997, suggested optimistically that anthrax could be used to render cities uninhabitable "for generations."

Anthrax has always been one of most admired agents of biological warfare with governments—and possibly one of the most feared. The bacterium occurs naturally, in low levels, in some animals. It was not uncommon for farm workers to become infected with anthrax through skin contact—it was called "woolsorter's disease" at one point—when a boil would appear which would eventually form a black center, and it can be spread through skin contact and ingestion, but it is only when it is airborne and can be inhaled by humans in the form of spores that it is deadly. Then it is fatal in a good 95 percent of cases, even with medical treatment. Experts on biological weapons have calculated that a mere 220 pounds (100 kilos) of anthrax sprayed on a major city could kill more than three million people.

In 1986 an English company was paid half a million British pounds ($890,000) to decontaminate the 520-acre island by soaking the ground in 309 tons (280 metric tonnes) of formaldehyde diluted in 2,205 tons (2,000 metric tonnes) of seawater. Topsoil was also removed in sealed containers. To prove that the clean-up was successful, a flock of sheep is allowed to graze the island at the behest of an independent watchdog set up by the Ministry of Defense.

On April 24, 1990, the then junior Defense Minister, Michael Neubert, made the half-mile journey from the mainland to declare Gruinard safe by removing its red warning sign. But the *Glasgow Herald* newspaper found an archaeologist, fresh from excavation of a medieval hospital near Edinburgh, to say that his team had encountered buried anthrax spores, which had survived for hundreds of years. Dr. Brian Moffat told the paper: "I would not go walking on Gruinard... It is a very resilient and deadly bacterium."

## Background briefing
The British are world experts in biological warfare. As long ago as the 18th century, British officers, such as Captain Ecuyer, under the guidance of General Sir Jeffrey Amherst were distributing smallpox infected blankets (Variola major) to the North American Indians. The colonization of Australia also included the systematic infection of its native peoples by the British authorities with smallpox by forced incarceration of (healthy) Aboriginals on "quarantine islands."

But the largest use of biological weapons that has ever occurred took place during World War II, when the infamous Japanese Army Unit 731 based in occupied Manchuria killed thousands of prisoners and villagers. The unit conducted cruel biological warfare experiments on prisoners of war and large-scale biological weapons attacks on Chinese villages with bombs and devices laced with plague and other diseases. In 1941 the Japanese attacked the city of Changteh with cholera killing 10,000 civilians. Disappointingly, even for the Japanese war-planners, some 1,700 of their soldiers also died.

It was at this time that the tests with anthrax bombs were carried out on the island of Gruinard. Impressed by this, the United States built a biological bomb production plant in 1944 capable of producing half a million four pound anthrax bomblets every month. The UK also produced millions of cattle cakes (feed) contaminated with anthrax, designed to be dropped from airplanes over Germany in order to kill livestock and cripple the country's food supply.

## Useful information
After visiting the island, if you experience any of the following symptoms: mild fever, malaise, fatigue, coughing and, occasionally, a feeling of pressure on the chest, you may have inhaled an anthrax spore. Death usually then takes around seven days and will be as a result of symptoms like internal bleeding, blood poisoning or even meningitis. Seek medical advice.

## Risk factor
Antibiotics can treat anthrax if caught early.

# 78 No Holiday: **Belfast, Ireland**

*Painting murals on the Shankhill Road*

## How to get there
Take a train from London to Liverpool, take the ferry across to Belfast docks and get a taxi to the City Center.

## What to see
During the Troubles, so many taxis were hijacked, and so many taxi drivers were shot, that most of them gave up the job. But nowadays the Troubles are a tourist pull, and there are so many requests from visitors to be taken around the Falls Road and Shankhill Road that taxi firms offer special "Mural tours:"

> Experience Belfast's dark side in the form of the murals at the (Catholic) Falls Road and (Protestant) Shankhill Road. Historical scenes, religious symbols and party slogans are emblazoned on almost every street corner of this infamous district.

As one such driver, Michael Johnston, explained to a visiting reporter from the *Irish American Post*:

> Most people do want to see the areas they've seen on the television, and they want to know more about what's gone on, you know? You can ask anything you want to ask. Most people are a wee bit shy, but they want to know, so just ask. And feel safe.

The tours start with Lanark Way—known as Murder Mile, at the end, and passes through the iron gates of the optimistically named Peace Wall, built to separate the two sides in an attempt to reduce the violence. It is made of concrete and steel, topped with barbed wire, and stained by gas bombs, which have blackened the window frames of the houses on either side.

On the one side is the Falls Road, the Catholic area and a Republican stronghold; on the other, the heart of Belfast's blue-collar loyalists, the Shankhill Road. House size murals of demonic British soldiers covered the walls of the former, while black-hooded men holding automatic weapons survey the Shankhill coldly. Union Jacks and the Red Hand flags (symbols of the Protestant paramilitaries) adorn every spare inch or wall. Even the curbstones are painted red, white and blue, in a warning to Irish intruders.

Some have noticed that while the Republican murals are generally commemorative, such as the

benignly smiling one of Bobby Sands, the young hunger striker sent by Mrs. Thatcher to an early grave, the loyalist images are invariably violent, featuring tanks and guns, tombstones and grim reapers in hoods. Even a mural depicting Cromwell, who oversaw a near genocide of the Irish people, is fashioned around some strange sort of battlefield skewering.

"The murals really are impressive and worth seeing, it's just a shame that there is so much extra baggage attached to them," observed one visitor enthusiastically.

A rabbi taking the Mural tour was offended to see that some of the Murals compare the struggle of the Palestinians for their land with the struggle of the Irish against the "Protestant settlers," transplanted there from England and Scotland by King James I in the 17th century.

Right beside an Irish Republican Tricolor, is a mural depicting Palestinians behind barbed wire fences while Israeli soldiers point rifles at them, together with the message: "Palestine: The World's Largest Concentration Camp." And conversely, traveling through Unionist towns and villages one may well see Israeli flags flying proudly.

There are other sights as well as the murals, such as the place where two soldiers were dragged from their vehicle and impaled on the metal stakes of a wrought-iron gate, or a church in which the pastor was murdered. There's the Sinn Fein headquarters, a rather ordinary looking house, with a mural around the corner which says, "Everyone Republican or otherwise, has their own particular role to play. Our revenge will be the laughter of our children." Then there's the Royal Victoria Hospital, specialists for fixing elbows and kneecaps, and with a pretty good burn unit too.

## Useful information
Disliking each other is a way of life for Protestants and Catholics in Northern Ireland. Since 1969, more than 3,000 people have been killed in sectarian violence. Nowadays that has subsided as the British and Irish governments perform a slow "peace dance" towards an eventual compromise solution over the "Six Counties." But if the killing is over, the bitterness and hatred remains.

Today Belfast City Center is like many other British cities, with its Victorian architecture, like the City Hall and the leaning Albert Clock. And it's also like the other cities in the sense that there are surveillance cameras everywhere (and often helicopters hovering too), broken glass is all over the streets, burned out cars are left in the middle of intersections, and burned out buildings and boarded-up windows. The only difference is that here, security is carried out by tanks, and soldiers with machine guns.

## Risk factor
Don't get out of the taxi, this is still considered the most dangerous street in Western Europe, and the murals really aren't much better close up.

## ↱ Side trip
Rossport, Ireland, Ogoniland, Nigeria, and an unusual twinning arrangement

## How to get there
Wild and elusive, green and wet, Rossport emerges out of the sea mist in Broadhaven Bay, County Mayo, alongside a bumpy bog landscape populated only by sheep and occasional gas pipeline engineers.

## What to see
You may catch site of several rare bird species, such as the Little Egret or the Hen Harrier. Then again, here and there the visitor may catch site of mysterious signs referring to a twinning arrangement with Ogoniland, or hear snatches of what (at least according to the local papers) is the new song in the bars:

> Davitt, Pearse and Tone
> fought to free our land
> But Fahey, Burke and Ahern
> gave it back with the other hand.
>
> We're not like dogs on leads
> We shall not be led
> They'll have to do like in Nigeria
> Hang us or shoot us dead.

## Background briefing
In fact, there's not much to see. No problem for a No Holiday. One of the things you used not to see were the five local County Mayo men, sentenced to indefinite terms in jail—for obstructing Shell Oil in its efforts to construct a high-pressure pipeline across the famous bog to a new refinery inland. The signs offering an unofficial twinning arrangement between Rossport and Ogoniland, Nigeria are a nod to the experience of their African fellow Shell-watchers in the Niger Delta, where an estimated 6,000 locals have died since Shell came to extract the mineral wealth

that lies off the coast there. It is also a salute to Ken Saro-Wiwa, author and spokesperson for the "Movement for the Survival of the Ogoni people," who wrote that Shell's activities had destroyed wildlife, and plant life, poisoned the atmosphere and therefore also the inhabitants of the surrounding areas. "Whenever it rains in Ogoni, all we have is acid rain which further poisons water courses, streams, creeks and agricultural land." In 1995 though, along with eight colleagues, Ken was hanged by the Nigerian government. In his final address to the court he declared defiantly: "I and my colleagues are not the only ones on trial. Shell is here on trial and... the crime of the company's dirty wars against the Ogoni people will also be punished."

Back at the Irish High Court, Justice McMenamin told the five that he "reluctantly" had no option but commit them to prison *indefinitely* for contempt. (Perhaps the reluctance was because he would have preferred to have them hanged.) And if Shell's investments in Nigeria are flourishing, back in Rossport, the game is not going entirely its way. Where once an invading French army perished, sinking into the Irish bog several centuries ago, now several sections of pipe and items of earth-moving machinery, lie at the bottom, like the soldiers before them, sunk without trace.

## Useless information

There are a lot of controversial oil projects and pipelines. It seems that international oil companies run a quarter of Africa, whilst huge swathes of Central Asia and the Middle East jump only to their call. Global oil production is said to be now in its last bloom, running sharply down over the next fifty or so years, and competition for the last few profitable fields grows more and more intense. Take Azerbaijan and Kazakhstan, for example, bordering the Caspian Sea. These two oil republics, run by US-friendly dictators, together hold oil reserves three times as great as those of the entire United States. A pipeline planned by the British transnational "British Petroleum" would take this oil through Georgia and Turkey to the Mediterranean. A special arrangement with the Turkish government gives the consortium building this pipeline the power to ignore all "environmental, social human rights" and other laws, an arrangement that certainly simplifies things. Then there is Russia with its huge oil and gas resources, busy constructing a pipeline under the Baltic Sea to supply Germany and Britain, and in the other direction, starting from the pristine Siberian wilderness of Perevoznaya, home to black-spotted leopards, 2,500 miles (4,023 kilometers) to Japan and China. Not to forget the pipelines and flares across Nigeria where the derricks nodding in the tropical delta are slowly poisoning the Nigerian people.

## Useful information

Responding to criticism of Shell's pipelines in Nigeria, one Richard Tookey said in 1992 that: "You suggest that the pipelines should be buried as a means of preventing pollution. Much of the area SPDC (Shell Petroleum Development Corporation) is operating in is swamp, so burying pipelines could, in fact, exacerbate the risk of fractures and spillages." But evidently what is true for swamps is not true for bogs.

## Risk factor ▧

Some risk of sinking into the bog.

## Twinning arrangements

It seems everywhere is officially twinned with somewhere else, someone's hopeful initiative to bring the world a little bit closer together in suitably apolitical friendship. Some towns are twinned roughly by size, but some are unlucky, like my local town, Alençon, which is twinned with Gravesend in the UK. For French speakers, and as Alençon is in France this may be relevant, "grave" means "serious" and it probably seems a good thing to put on their proud county town's signs. But to Londoners, the dismal suburb of Gravesend is indeed a place best avoided until you die.

# 79 No Holiday: **Amsterdam, Holland**

*A street retreat in Holland's alternative capital*

## How to get there
Fly to Schiphol Airport and take the connecting train to Amsterdam Central Station. DO NOT RENT A BICYCLE. You are here to beg.

## What to see
Since their arrival in the early 1990s, organized begging experiences, or "Street Retreats" have been held in many cities around the world including neighboring Brussels, Paris, Cologne and Düsseldorf in Germany and lots in the United States. There has even been a special "Auschwitz retreat," although quite how much money was raised there, I don't know.

And money is what it is all about. To start with, says the organizer, the "raising of the registration fee, by begging," is the beginning of the participation in the street retreats. "It raises the participant's consciousness and that of others towards living on the streets, begging for sustenance and the work of the inner-city. It is an initiation into the life of a street dweller."

Curiously, the retreats seem to take place more in the small minority of rich countries that do have some sort of social security and safety nets, rather than in the great majority of the world's cities where begging is never a lifestyle experiment but always a desperate last resort.

### RULES
**1.** Do not shave, and do not wash your hair for at least one week prior to the retreat. "This will also start your street experience prior to leaving home," the organizers promise, albeit not if you normally don't wash your hair.
**2.** Wear old clothes, "as many layers as you feel appropriate." But don't bring a change of clothes, of course.
**3.** Do not bring any books, or bedding, or "conveniences," etc. Do not bring any money, not even, perhaps, to embarrass passers-by by throwing it at them.
**4.** Finally, do bring an empty plastic bag. This will be useful for collecting food, "et cetera," (jewelry, bank notes, cash?) in.

## Useless information
Upcoming street retreats and other "bearing witness" events are listed on what is called the "House of One People Bearing Witness" website.

## Risk factor
Street retreats are not all fun however. Prior to starting, there is an orientation for all those wishing to participate. There are handouts called "Street Sheets" that list soup kitchens, shelters, and so on. Retreatants are divided up into their street cohorts and assigned a facilitator. Retreatants and facilitators discuss what to expect, but as the organizers say, at the end of the day, "the unexpected is the main teacher on the street."

# 80 No Holiday: **Luxembourg**

*The forgotten Parliament of the European Union*

### How to get there
Travel to Luxembourg on the train from Brussels, the true heart of the European Union. The Parliament is on the outskirts, distinguishable by its array of 25 or so flags, all of which have to be taken down and rotated each day, to avoid giving precedence to any one country.

### What to see
The Parliament is on the edge of the ancient walled citadel of Luxembourg, a country so small that it seems not to need a separate name for its main town. Visitors to the still active administration building can see the mothballed auditorium with its smoothly upholstered seats, each with its own microphone and voting button, and headphones connected to the booths for translators. All are sadly now mothballed and unused. But then, the European Union already has two other Parliaments.

### Background briefing
Everyone knows that the European Union wastes lots of money. Naturally then it has not one, but three separate Parliaments, each with its own huge back-up bureaucracy. What is less well appreciated is that the Europeans see this as "job creation" and the buildings as national monuments. The Anglo-Saxons seem to think this is bad, but as any convinced European could tell them, money spent like this creates more money.

### Useless information
Curiously enough, under the European Union's constitution, those debates in the Parliament have no significance at all anyway. Even if there is an effort to give the Parliament a rubberstamp role recently, the arrangement is that all the decisions (with the possible exception of the single vote every few years over whether to accept the new make-up of the European Commission) are made elsewhere. Quite unlike other parliaments, of course!

### Risk factor
No one has ever tried to blow up this Parliament, and there do not seem to be many protests outside it either. It is the Perfect Parliament.

# Epilogue

# No Holiday: **Normandy, France**

*The garden of Chateau Sassy*

### How to get there
Take the train from Luxembourg to Paris and then on to Argentan. From there bike south to Saint Christophe-le-Jajolet with its 18<sup>th</sup> century Chateau and formal gardens, celebrating what the French like to call the "total domination of man over nature."

### What to see
From the grand terrace overlooking the formal gardens, a drop of about 100 feet, the gardens of the aptly named Chateau Sassy seem to be a collection of swirls and whorls, with triangular hedges dotted about. Most curiously, the effect is inescapably one of looking down on a plastic model. If most people try to make plastic flowers look like real ones, the French, conversely, like to make real plants look like plastic. There are only three colors in the whole garden, the light green of the "buis," or little bushes, the dark green of the big bushes, trained into improbable geometric shapes, and the pink of the gravel. (The French call it charmingly, a sprinkle of "sable rose.") It's an extremely impressive sight, and a tribute to Etienne d'Audiffret, the nephew of Chancellor Pasquier, who decided to ask the famous gardener, Achille Duchene, to convert the old "potager" (or vegetable garden) into something more formal, or useless. In fact the gardens are second only to their more famous cousin at Versailles in exactness of ornamentation.

The gardens (unlike the Chateau) are open free to the public to inspect, a tribute to the French spirit of community. Alas, they also reflect all too well a view of the natural world, which has made all holiday trips very tame. Not risky at all! (Hence, white-water rafting, bungee swallowing, etc.)

### Useful information
French gardeners, no less than their compatriots, have no time for nature. They see wild land as at best useless, or more often, as a threat. Emblematic of this, is that driveway embankments, flower displays, private house gardens, are all swathed in plastic sheeting to prevent weeds growing. Officially the plastic is only temporary, but since no one has the intention of digging it out again, it is certainly there for the next thirty years.

Plastic hedges are also popular, [ 📷 ] for those who tire of the weekly electric pruning of the other kind. Elsewhere, the country's lakes and rivers, not to mention its beautiful wild Atlantic coast, are subject to numerous laws prohibiting swimming. (Except in August, in tiny little cordoned off squares—no more than a few feet deep—under the watchful eye of "Master Lifesavers.")

And although France is large and still full of undeveloped areas, the "right to go hunting," enshrined in the glorious revolution of 17-something, means that walking on the hills or in the woods is simply too dangerous. In this way, France also offers No Holidaymakers some of the last truly risky outings, and a reminder that it is not places that are dangerous, but people.

### Useless information
The little bushes are also known as "cemetery bushes," on account of their use to surround burial plots. The big bushes are made of yew, which is traditionally the main tree in Christian graveyards because its long roots are supposed to keep the spirits from rising up out of the earth.

### Risk factor 
As all dangerous elements have been removed, the gardens are at least as safe as the house. That said, there is an unfenced moat with goldfish in it, which a visitor could potentially fall in.

# Further
# Information

# Central Eurasia

**1** No Holiday: **Chernobyl, Ukraine**
• Chivers, C.J. "Pripyat Journal; New Sight in Chernobyl's Dead Zone: Tourists." For the *New York Times*.
Available online:
[http://query.nytimes.com/gst/fullpage.html?sec=travel&res=9902EEDD163BF936A25755C0A9639C8B63]
June 15, 2005.
• Savchenko, V. K. *The Ecology of the Chernobyl Catastrophe Scientific Outlines of an International Programme of Collaborative Research.* Man and the Biosphere Series. Volume 16. UNESCO, Paris, and Parthenon Publishing, Carnforth.
• Children's Chernobyl Project International: [http://www.historicwrc.org].

**2** No Holiday: **The Aral Sea, Uzbekistan**
• "Changing the world: Documentation of large-scale human-induced earth-surface change in images from satellites, the Space Shuttle program, and the International Space Station." Available online [http://www.gly.uga.edu/railsback/CTW.html].

**3** No Holiday: **Sempalatinsk, Kazakhstan**
• Chivers, C.J. "It Was Once Ground Zero. Now Little But Danger Is Left" For the *New York Times*.
March 3, 2005. Available online [http://www.nytimes.com/2005/03/03/international/asia/03bomb.html])

**4, 5** No Holiday: **Tora Bora, Afghanistan And Camp Salerno, Afghanistan**
• Levy, Adrian and Cathy Scott-Clark. "One Huge US Jail." For *The Guardian*. Available online [http://www.guardian.co.uk/afghanistan/story/0,1284,1440836,00.html] March 19, 2005.
• Borger, Julian. "Report Implicates Top Brass In Bagram Scandal." For *The Guardian*, May 21, 2005.

**6** No Holiday: **Mount Everest, Nepal**
• Joe Simpson. *Dark Shadows Falling*. Vintage, 1998.
• World Surface travel website [www.Worldsurface.com].

**7** No Holiday: **Bhutan**
• US Department of State, Country Human Rights Reports for 1999, Human Rights Council of Bhutan, (Kathmandu) position paper, November 2003.

# India

**8** No Holiday: **The Great Hedge Of India**
• Moxham, Roy. *The Great Hedge Of India*. Constable and Robinson, 2001.

**9** Working No Holiday: **Makrana**
• Das, Snehasis. "Miner's Plight In Marble Land: Makrana." Available online from South Asia One World site: [http://southasia.oneworld.net/article/view/107467/1/1897] March 11, 2005.

**10** No Holiday: **Bhopal Poison Factory**
• Sinha, Indra. "Bhopal: Holding Corporate Terrorists Accountable." Available online [http://www.alternet.org/story/15845/] May 6, 2003.

**11** No Holiday: **Kerala, the rice bowl of India**
• Krishnakumar, R. "Growing Resistance Against Coke And Pepsi." Available online from India Resource Center; [www.indiaresource.org/campaigns/coke/2003/growingresistance.html] June 7, 2003.

- Vandana, Shiva. "India: Soft Drinks, Hard Cases" in *Le Monde Diplomatique*, March 2005.

**12** No Holiday: **The Towers Of Silence**
- Sharan, Abhishek. The National Network, Monday, July 16, 2001, see indianexpress.com.


# The Far East

**13** No Holiday: **Phnom Penh, Cambodia**
- Falise, Thierry. "Angkor, Le Temple Du Pillage." For *Le Figaro*, December 31, 2004.
- Pilger, John. *Tell Me No Lies*. Vintage, 2005.

**14** No Holiday: **Myanmar, Also Known As Burma**
- Martin, Steven. "Orwell's Burma." For *Time Asia*. Available online
[http://www.time.com/time/asia/traveler/021017/orwell.html], Fall 2002.

**15** Working No Holiday: **Plet Me, Vietnam**
- Human Rights Watch "Landmine Monitor." Available online [http://www.icbl.org/lm/2003/vietnam.html].

**16** No Holiday: **The Mao Trail, Shaoshan**
- Hill, Ben. "The Cult Of The Leader Mao's Hometown." For *Escape From America Magazine*. Volume 5, Issue Number 10, October 2003. Available online from Escape Artist's site:
[http://www.escapeartist.com/efam/51/Mao_China.html].

**17** No Holiday: **The Mao Trail, Tiananmen Square**
- Watts, Jonathan. "Satellite Data Reveals Beijing As Air Pollution Capital Of World." For *The Guardian*. Available online [www.guardian.co.uk/china/story/0,7369,1605146,00.html] October 31, 2005.

**18** No Holiday: **Shantou, China**
- Yanchi, Quan. *Mao Zedong: Man, Not God*. Foreign Languages Press, 2002.

**19** No Holiday: **Beijing, China**
- Zi, Chuan. "A Walk in the Dashanzi." *China And The World Cultural Exchange*. Vol. 74 No. 6.

**20** No Holiday: **North Korea, The Demilitarized Zone**
- Fisher, Scott. "Journey Into Kimland." For One Stop Korea. Available online [http://1stopkorea.com].
- Cannon, Jon. "In North Korea" For *London Review of Books*, Vol. 22 No. 15, August 10, 2000. Available online [http://www.lrb.co.uk/v22/n15/cann01_.html].

**21** No Holiday: **Tokyo, Japan**
- Onishi, Norimitsu. "Tokyo Shrine Rubs Feelings Raw In Asia." For *International Herald Tribune, Asia-Pacific*. Available online [http://iht.com/articles/2005/06/22/news/japan.php] June 23, 2005.


# USA

**22, 23** No Holiday: **Los Alamos National Laboratory, New Mexico; Journey to Death**
- The Los Alamos Education Group, P. O. Box 386, Los Alamos, NM 87544, USA try to give a different picture than the "official" museum's.

**24, 25, 26** Travel and the American Mind: **William Bartram's Alligators; Fields of Strawberries and the black drink of the Cherokee; The Magic of Magnolia Mountain**
• Bartram, William and Francis Harper. *The Travels Of William Bartram: Naturalist's Edition*. University of Georgia Press, 1998.

**26 Fort Payne And Day 1 Of "The Trail Where They Cried" And The Side Trips**
• The Text Of The Indians Removal Act is reproduced at [http://www.civics-online.org].
• National Park Service "Trail Of Tears." Available online [http://www.nps.gov/trte/].

**28** No Holiday: **Fort Benning, Georgia**
• Fort Benning features in the Public Broadcasting debate "NewsHour with Jim Lehrer," on the occasion of the House- Senate Conference Committee discussion of School of the Americas funding, September 21, 1999 between US Rep. Joseph Moakley (D-Mass) and Army Secretary Louis Caldera.
• Quigley, Fran. "Standing up to the School of the Americas." For *Counter Punch*, available online [http://www.counterpunch.org/quigley01142003.html] January 14, 2003.

**29** No Holiday: **NSA Headquarters, Fort Meade, Maryland**
• NSA's official site: [www.nsa.gov].

**30** No Holiday: **Washington, D.C.**
• Watson, Ronald. "Where Deep Throat Downed Nixon." For *The Times* (London). Available online [http://www.timesonline.co.uk/article/0,,11069-1677552,00.html] July 2, 2005.

**31** No Holiday: **Bronx Zoo, New York**
• Bergman, Jerry. "Ota Benga: The Story Of The Pygmy On Display In A Zoo." Available online [www.rae.org/otabenga.html] November 25, 1997.
• White Rock Cemetery website [www.historicwrc.org].

# Central America

**32** No Holiday: **Guantánamo Bay, Cuba**
• Reuters. "Military Extends Guantánamo Abuse Probe." February 2, 2005.

**33** No Holiday: **El Salvador**
• Danner, Mark. "The Truth Of El Mozote." For *The New Yorker*, December 6, 1993. Available online [http://www.markdanner.com/newyorker/120693_The_Massacre.htm].
• United Nations Report of the Commission for Truth. "From Madness To Hope: The 12-Year War In El Salvador: Report Of The Commission On The Truth For El Salvador" pages 114-119, March 15, 1993. Available online [http://www.usip.org/library/tc/doc/reports/el_salvador/tc_es_03151993_toc.html].

**34** No Holiday: **Panama**
• Pugliese, David. "Panama: Bombs On The Beach." For *Bulletin of Atomic Scientists*, July 2002.
• Lindsay-Poland, John. "Pressured in Panama, Bush Leaves Door Open for Explosives Cleanup." For Fellowship of Reconciliation Task Force on Latin America and the Caribbean, Available online [http://www.forusa.org/programs/panama/default.html] December, 2005.

# South America

**35** No Holiday: **The Favelas Of Rio de Janeiro, Brazil**
• www.favelatour.com.
• O'Dea, Wendy. "Building Brazil: Brick by Brick" For *Road & Travel Magazine*. Available online [http://www.roadandtravel.com/travel%20directory/Brazil/riofavelatours.htm].
• Wright, Jo. "Rio slums blighted by gun crime." For *BBC News*. Available online [http://news.bbc.co.uk/2/hi/americas/4338652.stm] October 21, 2005.

**36, 37** No Holiday: **Bolivia; Valle Grande, Bolivia**
• Guevara, Ernesto Che, Cintio Vitier, Aleida Guevara. *The Motorcycle Diaries: Notes On A Latin American Journey*. Ocean Press, 2003.


# Oceania

**38** No Holiday: **South Surin Island, Thailand**
• Goodnough, Abby. "How A Tribe Of Thai Animists Listened To The Sea And Survived." For the *International Herald Tribune*. Available online [http://www.iht.com/articles/2005/01/23/news/thai.php] January 24, 2005.

**39** No Holiday: **Manila, Philippines**
• BBC News. "Homage to Imelda's Shoes." Available online [http://news.bbc.co.uk/1/hi/world/asia-pacific/1173911.stm] February 16, 2001.

**40** No Holiday: **Bikini Atoll, Marshall Islands**
• "Nuclear Testing." From Wikipedia, The Free Encyclopedia [http://en.wikipedia.org/wiki/Nuclear_testing].


# Australasia

**41** No Holiday: **Outback Art At Carisbrooke Cattle Station**
• Horrigan, Ken and Kristal Buckley. "Heritage At Risk 2002-2003 Report." For the Australia ICOMOS Executive Committee. Available online [http://www.international.icomos.org/risk/2002/australia2002.htm].
• Aboriginal art see [www.Aboriginalartonline.com.au].

**42** No Holiday: **Murdering Creek, Australia**
• Windolf, John. *An Evaluation Of Knowledge Of The Massacre Of Murries At Murdering Creek, Sunshine Coast*. Maroochy Libraries Heritage Unit, 2000.
• Adams, R.J.L. *Noosa and Gubbi Gubbi: The Land, The People, The Conflict*. Pages 128, 129. Ultreya Publications, 2000.

**43** No Holiday: **Auckland, Aoteroa**
• Robie, David. *Eyes of Fire: The Last Voyage Of The Rainbow Warrior*. New Society Publications, 1987.

# Africa

**44** No Holiday: **Madagascar**
• Camus, Albert. "Combat on May 10, 1947." For *Le Monde Diplomatique*, English Edition, March 1997.

**45** No Holiday: **Manzini, Swaziland**
-Fottorino, Éric. "Roi Et Carrosses." For *Le Monde*, February 15, 2005.

**46** No Holiday: **Molapo, Botswana**
• Meldrum, Andrew. "San Fight To Keep Their Kalahari Hunting Grounds." For *Guardian Weekly*. Available online [http://www.guardian.co.uk/guardianweekly/story/0,12674,1171346,00.html] March 18-24, 2004.
• Simpson, John. "Bushmen Fight For Homeland." For BBC. Available online [http://news.bbc.co.uk/2/hi/africa/4480883.stm] May 2, 2005.

**47** No Holiday: **Angola**
•Senzangakhona, Makhanda, Edwin Mabitse, Uriel Abrahamse and George Molebatsi. "Umkhonto We Sizwe: Within Living Memories." Available online [www.anc.org.za/ancdocs/pubs/umrabulo/umrabulo15/mk.html].

**48, 49** No Holiday: **Morogoro, Tanzania: African White Elephants (Not endangered); Lake Turkana, Kenya: African White Elephants (Not endangered)**
• Clayton, Jonathan and Richard Beeston. "Twenty years on, why are things so bad in Ethiopia?" For *The Times* (London). Available online [http://www.timesonline.co.uk/article/0,,3-1677418,00.html] July 2, 2005.

**50** No Holiday: **Addis Ababa, Ethiopia: African White Elephants (Not endangered)**
• "Addis Ababa Bole International Airport…African's New Super Hub." For Selamta magazine published by Camerapix Publishers International, Nairobi. Available online from [http://www.ethiopia.ottawa.on.ca/airport.htm].
• Haile-Mariam, Teketel. "The Fallacy of Foreign Aid as Engine of Economic Development" For *Addis Tribune*. Available online [http://www.globalpolicy.org/socecon/ffd/2002/1004fallacy.htm] October 4, 2002.

**51** No Holiday: **Ugoli, Nigeria: African White Elephants (Not endangered)**
• Antony Barnett. "UK arms sales to Africa reach £1 billion mark."
For *The Observer*. Available online [http://observer.guardian.co.uk/politics/story/0,6903,1504698,00.html] June 12, 2005.

**52, 53, 54** No Holiday: **Rwanda Genocide Outings: The Hotel of a Thousand Hills; A tour round Kigali; Kigali College**
• Courtemanche, Gil and Patricia Claxton (trans.). *A Sunday at the Pool in Kigali*. Knopf, 2003.
• Organization of Africa Unity. "Rwanda: The Preventable Genocide." Available online [http://www.visiontv.ca/RememberRwanda/Report.pdf] July, 2000.

**55, 56** No Holiday: **Southern Sudan: The Rumbek Bookshop; Southern Sudan Rumbek Business Center: Market And UN Office; Side Trip: Rumbek Cathedral (And Its Crazy Bishop)**
• "Southern Sudan's Only Bookshop: A River Runs Through It." For *The Economist*. Available online [http://www.economist.com/printedition/displayStory.cfm?Story_ID=2388854&no_na_tran=1] January 29, 2004.
• Magister, Sandro. "Enemy Islam: An Interview With The Bishop Of Rumbek, Sudan." Available online [http://www.hvk.org/articles/0604/77.html] June 10, 2004.
• Lorenzetto, Stefano. "A Clash of Civilizations? This Is Just The Beginning." Interview with Bishop Cesare Mazzolari (published originally in *Il Giornale*, May 23 2004). Available online

[http://www.chiesa.espressonline.it/dettaglio.jsp?id=7044&eng=y].

**57** No Holiday: **Mogadishu**
• Somali Net. "Somalia: Pirates Almost Capture American Luxury Cruise Ship." Available online
[http://somalinet.com/news/world/Somalia/1157] November 5, 2005.

**58** No Holiday: **Asmara, Eritrea**
• Phillips, Don. "High In The Mountains, A Symbol Of Eritrea's Rebirth." For *International Herald Tribune*.
Available online [http://www.iht.com/articles/2005/02/14/features/eritrea.php] February 15, 2005.

**59** Working No Holiday: **Taoudeni, Mali**
• "Mali: Ancient Crossroads of Africa" Available online
[http://mali.pwnet.org/geography/geography_resources.htm].

**60** No Holiday: **Libya**
• Lindqvist, Sven and Linda Haverty Rugg (translator). *A History of Bombing*. W.W. Norton, 2003.

# The Middle East

**61** No Holiday: **Al-Azhar Mosque, Cairo, Egypt**
• "La contagion de la haine" For *Le Figaro Magazine*, July 30, 2005.

**62** No Holiday: **Erez Crossing (also known as: part of Palestine), Israel**
• Sifry, Micah L. "Israel Diary." For *The Nation*. Available online
[http://www.thenation.com/doc/19990524/sifry] May 6, 1999.
• Friends of the Israel Defense Forces "Mission To Israel, Guided Tour For June 2003."
• Dudkevitch, Margot. "The sword battalion in Gaza." December 4, 2000.

**63** No Holiday: **Golan Heights, Syria**
• Shankar, Sadhna. "Shouting For Marriage And The Hope For Peace." For *The International Herald Tribune*. November 6, 2004.

**64** No Holiday: **Baghdad, Iraq**
• See IRIN (The Integrated Regional Information Networks). Available online [http://www.irinnews.org/].
• Greenberg, Karen (ed.). *The Torture Papers: The Road To Abu Ghraib*. Cambridge University Press, 2005.

**65** No Holiday: **United Arab Emirates**
• Pohl, Otto. *Cahier Du Monde,* March 26, 2005.

# Europe

**66** No Holiday: **Mostar, Bosnia-Herzegovina**
• http://www.2camels.com/festival238.php3
• "Mostar Online" Available [http://www.geocities.com/Heartland/1935/introduction.html].

**67** No Holiday: **Oswiecim, Poland**
• Dimant, Frank. "Chretien, Auschwitz And The Security Council." For the *Jewish Tribune*. Available online
[http://www.bnaibrith.ca/tribune/jt-archives/1999/jtar-990211.shtml] February 11, 1999.

• An interesting essay on Zionism is in *The Essentials of Philosophy and Ethics* (Hodder Arnold, 2006), edited by the author on his day job.

## 68 No Holiday: **Copsa Mica**
• Udelhofen, Eric. "The People and Pollution of Copsa Mica, Romania." Available online [http://www.fragilecologies.com/july22_05.html] July 22, 2005.

## 69 No Holiday: **Berlin, Germany**
• Arens, Marianne and Sybille Fuchs. "More of the 'big lie' that Socialist Realism emerged from Soviet revolutionary art." Available online [http://www.wsws.org/articles/2004/jan2004/schi-j17.shtml] January 17, 2004.

## 70, 71 No Holiday: **Animal Cruelty Outings: Manganeses de la Polorosa, Spain; Catalonia, Spain**
• Best, Steven. "Barbarism In The Afternoon: Bullfighting, Violence, And The Crisis In Human Identity." Available online [http://www.iwab.org/ArticlesEng.html].
• [http://www.exploreseville.com/books/books-toro-flamenco.htm]
• Spielvogel, Jeff. "Books, Flamencos and Toros." Available online [http://www.exploreseville.com/books/books-toro-flamenco.htm].

## 72 No Holiday: **Animal Cruelty Outings: Trondheim, Norway**
• Nor Safari site. Available online [http://www.norsafari.com/].

## 73, 74 No Holiday: **The Lovely Languedoc: The Da Vinci Trail; Rosslyn Chapel, Scotland: The Da Vinci Trail Too**
• Brown, Dan. *The Da Vinci Code*. Doubleday, 2003.

## 75 No Holiday: **London, England**
• "Abyssinia." Available online [http://www.britishempire.co.uk/forces/armycampaigns/africancampaigns/campabyssinia.htm].

## 76 No Holiday: **Menwith Hill, England**
• Further reading, see Duncan Campbell's website with report. Available online [http://duncan.gn.apc.org/stoa.htm].

## 77 No Holiday: **Gruinard, Scotland**
• Cobb, Allan. *Biological And Chemical Weapons: The Debate Over Modern Warfare*. Rosen Publishing Group, 2000.

## 78 No Holiday: **Belfast, Ireland**
• Neylon, Tina. *The Hunter Travel Guides Adventure Guide To Ireland*. Hunter, 2004.

## 79 No Holiday: **Amsterdam, Holland**
• Available online [http://www.houseofonepeople.org/]

## 80 No Holiday: **Luxembourg**
• European Parliament website [http://www.europarl.eu.int].

# Photo Credits

# About The Author

Martin Cohen's popular and accessible introductions to philosophy have been translated into many foreign languages, except the language of Voltaire, near whose Château he now lives and writes. (But in a cowshed, not in a Château.) He has a PhD in Philosophy of Education from Exeter University, and has written for *The Guardian*, *Times Higher Education Supplement*, and *The Independent*. Martin is the author of several books including *101 Philosophy Problems*, which has been translated in many exotic locations from Iran and Brazil to China and Korea.